Contents Table

~ Welcome & What You'll Learn

Section I: Getting Started with WordPress

- Chapter 1: What is WordPress and Why Choose It?
- Chapter 2: Choosing a Domain Name and Web Hosting
- Chapter 3: Installing WordPress: Step-by-Step Guide
- Chapter 4: The WordPress Dashboard: Your Command Center
- Chapter 5: Themes: The Foundation of Your Website's Design
- Chapter 6: Plugins: Enhancing Your Website's Functionality
- Chapter 7: Core Settings and Configurations

Section II: Mastering Elementor Page Builder

- Chapter 8: Introduction to Elementor: The Power of Drag-and-Drop
- Chapter 9: The Elementor Interface: A Tour of the Essentials
- Chapter 10: Templates and Blocks: Building with Pre-Designed Elements
- Chapter 11: Widgets: The Building Blocks of Your Pages
- Chapter 12: Styling: Colors, Fonts, and Making It Your Own
- Chapter 13: Sections and Columns: Organizing Your Content
- Chapter 14: Responsive Design: Optimizing for All Devices

Section III: Creating Essential Website Pages

- Chapter 15: Designing Your Homepage: First Impressions Matter
- Chapter 16: Building an About Us Page: Tell Your Story
- Chapter 17: Crafting a Services/Products Page: Showcase Your Offerings
- Chapter 18: Setting Up a Blog: Share Your Expertise
- Chapter 19: Creating a Contact Page: Make It Easy to Reach You

Section IV: Advanced Elementor Techniques

- Chapter 20: Dynamic Content: Personalization and Automation
- Chapter 21: Popups: Engaging Visitors with Targeted Messages
- Chapter 22: Theme Builder: Customize Every Aspect of Your Site
- Chapter 23: WooCommerce Integration: Building an Online Store (Optional)
- Chapter 24: SEO Basics for Elementor: Get Found on Google

Section V: Tips, Troubleshooting, and Maintenance

- Chapter 25: Common WordPress Errors and How to Fix Them
- Chapter 26: Speeding Up Your Website: Optimization Tips
- Chapter 27: Security Essentials: Protecting Your Site
- Chapter 28: Regular Maintenance Tasks: Keep Your Site Healthy

Appendices

- Appendix A: Elementor Shortcuts and Tips
- Appendix B: Resources for Further Learning

~ Conclusion

Welcome & What You'll Learn

Welcome to "WordPress Made Easy: Build Your Dream Website with Elementor"! Whether you're a budding entrepreneur, a small business owner, a blogger, or simply someone with a message to share, having a website is essential in today's digital world. And with WordPress and Elementor, building that website has never been easier.

Why WordPress and Elementor?

WordPress is the world's most popular content management system (CMS), powering over 40% of all websites on the internet. Its user-friendly interface, vast library of themes and plugins, and flexible customization options make it the perfect platform for beginners and experienced users alike.

Elementor, on the other hand, is a revolutionary drag-and-drop page builder that empowers you to create stunning, professional-looking websites without writing a single line of code. Its intuitive interface, rich selection of widgets and templates, and seamless integration with WordPress make it the ideal tool for unleashing your creativity.

What You'll Learn

This comprehensive tutorial will guide you through every step of building your dream website using WordPress and Elementor.

- **In Section I: Getting Started with WordPress**, you'll learn the fundamentals of WordPress, from choosing a domain name and web hosting to installing WordPress and configuring its core settings. You'll also discover how to select the perfect theme and plugins to enhance your website's functionality and design.
- **Section II: Mastering Elementor Page Builder** will take you on a deep dive into Elementor. You'll learn how to use its drag-and-drop interface, leverage its vast library of templates and widgets, and customize every aspect of your pages to match your vision.
- **Section III: Creating Essential Website Pages** will guide you through building the essential pages of your website, including your homepage, About Us page, services or products page, blog, and contact page.
- **Section IV: Advanced Elementor Techniques** will introduce you to more advanced Elementor features, such as dynamic content, popups, and the Theme Builder, allowing you to create truly personalized and engaging websites. If you're interested in building an online store, you'll also have the option to explore WooCommerce integration.
- **Finally, in Section V: Tips, Troubleshooting, and Maintenance**, you'll learn how to troubleshoot common WordPress errors, optimize your website's speed, ensure its security, and perform regular maintenance tasks to keep it running smoothly.

By the end of this book, you'll have the skills and confidence to build a stunning, professional website that showcases your brand, engages your audience, and achieves your goals.

Are you ready to embark on this exciting journey? Let's dive in and start building!

Section I:
Getting Started with WordPress

What is WordPress and Why Choose It?

Outline

- What is WordPress?
- Understanding Content Management Systems (CMS)
- Benefits of Using WordPress
- Why WordPress is the Top Choice
- Chapter Summary

What is WordPress?

WordPress is a free and open-source content management system (CMS) that empowers millions of users worldwide to create and manage websites with ease. While its roots lie in blogging, WordPress has blossomed into a versatile platform capable of building a diverse range of websites, including:

- **Blogs:** The original purpose of WordPress, allowing individuals and businesses to share their thoughts, ideas, and expertise.
- **Business Websites:** Showcasing products, services, and company information to potential customers.
- **eCommerce Stores:** Setting up online shops to sell products or services using plugins like WooCommerce.
- **Portfolios:** Displaying creative works, such as photography, artwork, or design projects.
- **News Websites:** Publishing articles, stories, and updates for a wide audience.
- **Membership Sites:** Creating exclusive content and communities for paying members.
- **Educational Websites:** Sharing courses, tutorials, and resources for online learning.
- **And much more:** The possibilities are virtually limitless, thanks to the flexibility and extensive customization options offered by WordPress.

What sets WordPress apart is its user-friendly interface, even for those without technical expertise. It provides an intuitive dashboard where you can easily add, edit, and publish content, manage media files, customize the appearance of your website, and install plugins to extend its functionality. This simplicity, combined with its powerful capabilities, has made WordPress the most popular CMS on the internet, powering over 40% of all websites worldwide.

Understanding Content Management Systems (CMS)

A Content Management System (CMS) is a software application that simplifies the process of creating, managing, and modifying the content of a website. Think of it as a user-friendly toolbox that allows you to build and maintain your website without needing to write code or understand complex web development techniques.

How does a CMS work?

A CMS typically separates the content of your website (text, images, videos) from its design (layout, colors, fonts) and functionality (features, plugins). This separation makes it much easier for non-technical users to update and manage their websites. Here's how it works:

1. **Content Creation:** You use a simple editor (similar to a word processor) to write and format your content.
2. **Design:** The CMS applies a pre-designed template (theme) to your content, giving your website a visually appealing look.
3. **Functionality:** Plugins add extra features and functionality to your website, such as contact forms, social media integration, or e-commerce capabilities.

Benefits of using a CMS

- **Ease of Use:** You don't need to be a web developer to create and manage a website.
- **Flexibility:** You can easily change the design or add new features without affecting your content.
- **Collaboration:** Multiple users can work on the website simultaneously.
- **SEO-Friendly:** Most CMS platforms have built-in features to help your website rank higher in search engines.
- **Security:** Regular updates and security patches help protect your website from vulnerabilities.

Popular CMS Platforms

While WordPress is the most widely used CMS, there are other popular options available:

- **Joomla:** Known for its flexibility and advanced user management features, often used for larger websites or community-driven platforms.
- **Drupal:** A highly customizable and scalable CMS favored by developers and enterprise-level websites.

Choosing the right CMS depends on your specific needs and technical skills. For most users, WordPress strikes the perfect balance between ease of use, flexibility, and extensive customization options, making it an excellent choice for beginners and experienced website creators alike.

Benefits of Using WordPress

WordPress offers a multitude of benefits that make it an ideal choice for building websites, regardless of your technical expertise or the type of website you envision. Let's delve into some of the key advantages:

Ease of Use

WordPress is renowned for its user-friendly interface, making it accessible to beginners and seasoned professionals alike. The intuitive dashboard provides a centralized hub for managing all aspects of your website. With its drag-and-drop functionality and visual editors, you can effortlessly create and edit pages, add content, and customize the layout without needing to write any code.

Flexibility

Whether you're starting a personal blog, launching an online store, or building a corporate website, WordPress has got you covered. Its adaptability allows it to cater to a wide range of websites, making it a versatile solution for diverse needs. With thousands of themes and plugins available, you can easily tailor your website's design and functionality to suit your specific requirements.

Customization

The extensive library of themes and plugins is one of WordPress's greatest strengths. Themes provide the visual foundation for your website, while plugins add extra features and functionality. With thousands of free and premium options available, you can find the perfect combination to create a unique and engaging website that reflects your brand and personality.

Community and Support

WordPress boasts a vast and vibrant community of users, developers, and enthusiasts. This global network offers invaluable support, resources, and tutorials to help you troubleshoot issues, learn new techniques, and stay up-to-date with the latest trends. You can find answers to your questions in forums, blogs, and online communities, ensuring you're never alone on your WordPress journey.

SEO-Friendliness

Search engine optimization (SEO) is crucial for getting your website noticed by potential visitors. WordPress is built with SEO best practices in mind, making it easier for search engines like Google to crawl and index your website. Additionally, numerous SEO plugins are available to further enhance your website's visibility and improve its ranking in search results.

Cost-Effectiveness

WordPress itself is an open-source platform, meaning it's free to download, use, and modify. While you may need to invest in web hosting, a domain name, and potentially premium themes or plugins, the overall cost of building a website with WordPress is often significantly lower than using proprietary platforms or hiring a web developer.

Why WordPress is the Top Choice

WordPress has emerged as the undisputed leader in the world of content management systems (CMS), and for good reason. The combination of its numerous benefits makes it the preferred platform for millions of website creators worldwide.

Market Dominance

WordPress's popularity is undeniable, with a staggering market share of over 40% of all websites on the internet. This widespread adoption speaks volumes about its effectiveness, reliability, and user satisfaction. By choosing WordPress, you're joining a vast community of users who have successfully built and maintained their websites using this powerful platform.

Global Community

The WordPress community is a vibrant and supportive network of users, developers, designers, and enthusiasts from all corners of the globe. This active community continuously contributes to the platform's growth and improvement, ensuring that it remains at the forefront of web development trends. Whether you need help with troubleshooting, customization, or simply seeking inspiration, the WordPress community is always ready to lend a helping hand.

Continuous Development

WordPress is not a stagnant platform; it's constantly evolving and improving. Regular updates bring new features, enhanced security, and improved performance, keeping your website up-to-date and future-proof. The dedicated team of developers and contributors ensures that WordPress remains a cutting-edge solution for website building.

A Future-Proof Choice

Choosing WordPress for your website means investing in a platform that is not only powerful and versatile today but also poised for continued growth and innovation in the future. Its open-source nature, extensive customization options, and thriving community make it a reliable and sustainable choice for building your online presence.

In summary, WordPress is the top choice for website creation due to its:

- **Ease of Use:** User-friendly interface and intuitive features.
- **Flexibility:** Adaptability to various website types and needs.
- **Customization:** Vast library of themes and plugins for endless possibilities.
- **Community and Support:** A global network of helpful users and resources.
- **SEO-Friendliness:** Built-in features and plugins for better search engine visibility.
- **Cost-Effectiveness:** Free to use with many free resources available.
- **Market Dominance:** The most popular CMS with a proven track record.
- **Global Community:** A vibrant and supportive network of users.
- **Continuous Development:** Regular updates and improvements for a future-proof solution.

Chapter Summary

In this chapter, we explored the world of WordPress and why it stands as the premier choice for building websites. We started by defining WordPress as a versatile content management system (CMS) that has evolved beyond its blogging origins to cater to a wide array of website types.

We delved into the concept of content management systems, explaining how they simplify website creation and management by separating content from design and functionality. We highlighted the ease of use and flexibility that CMS platforms offer, empowering users to create and update their websites without technical expertise.

Next, we explored the myriad benefits of using WordPress. Its intuitive interface, vast customization options through themes and plugins, vibrant community support, SEO-friendliness, and cost-effectiveness make it a compelling choice for both beginners and experienced website creators.

Finally, we summarized the key reasons why WordPress reigns supreme in the CMS landscape. Its market dominance, active global community, continuous development, and future-proof nature solidify its position as the leading platform for building websites of all kinds.

By choosing WordPress, you're not just selecting a tool; you're joining a thriving ecosystem that empowers you to create, manage, and grow your online presence with confidence and ease.

Choosing a Domain Name and Web Hosting

Outline

- What is a Domain Name?
- Importance of Choosing the Right Domain Name
- Factors to Consider When Choosing a Domain Name
- What is Web Hosting?
- Types of Web Hosting
- Factors to Consider When Choosing a Web Hosting Provider
- Recommended Web Hosting Providers for WordPress
- Chapter Summary

What is a Domain Name?

In the vast landscape of the internet, every website needs a unique address to be found and accessed. This address is known as a domain name. It's the human-readable form of an IP address (a series of numbers that identifies a device on a network), making it much easier for us to remember and type into our web browsers.

Think of a domain name like a street address for your website. Just as you use a street address to find a physical location, you use a domain name to locate a website on the internet. For example, the domain name "www.google.com" directs you to the homepage of Google's website, while "www.amazon.com" takes you to Amazon's online store.

Domain names are essential for several reasons:

- **Identity:** They provide a unique identity for your website, making it stand out from the millions of others online.
- **Branding:** A well-chosen domain name can reinforce your brand and make it more memorable for visitors.
- **Accessibility:** They make it easy for users to find and access your website by simply typing the name into their browser's address bar.
- **Professionalism:** A custom domain name adds credibility and professionalism to your online presence, especially for businesses.

A typical domain name consists of two main parts:

1. **Second-Level Domain (SLD):** This is the unique name you choose for your website, such as "google" or "amazon" in the examples above.
2. **Top-Level Domain (TLD):** This is the extension that follows the SLD, such as ".com," ".org," ".net," or country-specific extensions like ".in" for India or ".uk" for the United Kingdom.

When choosing a domain name, it's crucial to select one that is relevant to your website's content, easy to remember, and available for registration.

Importance of Choosing the Right Domain Name

Your domain name is more than just a web address; it's a fundamental component of your website's identity and branding. A carefully chosen domain name can significantly impact your online success in several ways:

Memorability and Findability

A domain name that is easy to remember and spell will make it much easier for users to find your website. If your domain name is complex or difficult to recall, potential visitors might give up on trying to access your site. A memorable domain name, on the other hand, can stick in people's minds and encourage them to return in the future.

Brand Credibility and Professionalism

Your domain name is often the first impression visitors have of your brand. A professional and relevant domain name can instantly boost your credibility and make you appear more trustworthy. Conversely, a poorly chosen domain name can undermine your brand image and deter potential customers.

For example, if you're running a serious business, using a free domain with an unfamiliar extension (e.g., [invalid URL removed]) might not convey the level of professionalism you desire. Investing in a custom domain with a reputable extension like ".com" can significantly enhance your brand's image.

Search Engine Optimization (SEO)

While the exact impact of domain names on SEO is a subject of ongoing debate, there's no doubt that a well-optimized domain name can contribute to your website's visibility in search engine results. Including relevant keywords in your domain name can signal to search engines what your website is about, potentially improving your ranking for those keywords.

However, it's important to note that SEO is a multifaceted process, and a good domain name alone won't guarantee top rankings. You'll still need to focus on creating high-quality content, building backlinks, and optimizing other aspects of your website.

In conclusion, choosing the right domain name is a crucial step in building a successful online presence. It's an investment in your brand's identity, memorability, and credibility. By taking the time to select a domain name that aligns with your brand and resonates with your target audience, you can set your website up for long-term success.

Factors to Consider When Choosing a Domain Name

Choosing the perfect domain name for your website requires careful consideration of several key factors. By evaluating each of these factors, you can make an informed decision that aligns with your brand and goals.

Relevance

The most crucial factor in choosing a domain name is its relevance to your website's content or your brand. Ideally, your domain name should give visitors a clear idea of what your website is about. If you're a bakery, for instance, incorporating words like "bakery," "cakes," or "pastries" into your domain name makes sense.

A relevant domain name not only helps users understand your website's purpose but also contributes to your brand identity and SEO efforts. It's easier for people to remember a domain name that reflects your brand, and it can signal to search engines what your website is about, potentially improving your search rankings.

Memorability

A memorable domain name is one that sticks in people's minds long after they've visited your website. Short, catchy, and easy-to-spell domain names are generally more memorable than long, complex ones. Avoid using hyphens or numbers, as they can make your domain name harder to remember and type.

Consider using a domain name that is easy to pronounce and spell, as this will make it easier for people to share your website with others through word-of-mouth. A memorable domain name can also help your brand stand out in a crowded online space.

Availability

Before you get too attached to a domain name idea, it's essential to check its availability. Many popular domain names are already registered, so you may need to get creative or consider alternative extensions.

Several domain registrars offer domain name search tools that allow you to check the availability of your desired domain name. If your first choice is unavailable, these tools often suggest similar or related domain names that might be available.

Extensions

The domain name extension, also known as the top-level domain (TLD), is the suffix that follows the dot at the end of your domain name (e.g., ".com," ".org," ".net"). While ".com" is the most popular and widely recognized TLD, there are many other options available.

Consider the purpose of your website when choosing a TLD. For example, ".org" is often used by non-profit organizations, while ".edu" is reserved for educational institutions. If you're targeting a specific country, you might consider a country-code TLD (ccTLD) like ".in" for India or ".au" for Australia.

Here are some common TLDs and their general uses:

- **.com:** Commercial businesses
- **.org:** Non-profit organizations
- **.net:** Network-related businesses
- **.edu:** Educational institutions
- **.gov:** Government agencies
- **.info:** Informational websites
- **.biz:** Businesses
- **.co:** Companies, corporations, and communities

Choosing the right TLD can contribute to your brand identity and make it clear to users what type of website they can expect to find.

What is Web Hosting?

Web hosting is a fundamental service that enables your website to be visible and accessible on the internet. Think of it as renting space on a powerful computer (server) connected to the internet 24/7. Your website's files, including its HTML code, images, videos, and other content, are stored on this server.

When someone types your domain name into their browser, their computer sends a request to the server hosting your website. The server then responds by sending back the requested files, allowing the visitor to view and interact with your website.

Why Do You Need Web Hosting?

Without web hosting, your website would simply exist as files on your computer, inaccessible to anyone else. Web hosting providers not only store your website's files but also provide the necessary infrastructure and technologies to ensure its smooth operation and availability.

This includes:

- **Server Maintenance:** Keeping the server hardware and software up-to-date and secure.
- **Bandwidth:** Allocating the necessary data transfer capacity to handle website traffic.
- **Uptime:** Ensuring that your website is accessible online most of the time.
- **Security:** Protecting your website from hackers and malware.
- **Technical Support:** Providing assistance if you encounter any issues with your website or hosting.

Choosing the Right Web Hosting

Selecting the right web hosting provider is crucial for your website's success. Different types of web hosting cater to different needs and budgets. In the next section, we'll explore the various types of web hosting available to help you make an informed decision.

Types of Web Hosting

When it comes to web hosting, there are various options available, each with its own set of features, advantages, and disadvantages. Understanding these different types is crucial for selecting the right hosting solution that aligns with your website's needs and budget.

Shared Hosting

Shared hosting is the most affordable and common type of web hosting. In this setup, multiple websites share the resources of a single server. This means that your website shares the server's CPU, memory, and storage with other websites hosted on the same server.

Pros:

- **Cost-effective:** Shared hosting is the most budget-friendly option, making it suitable for small websites or those just starting.
- **Easy to manage:** Hosting providers typically handle server maintenance and security, requiring minimal technical expertise from the website owner.

Cons:

- **Limited resources:** Since you're sharing resources with other websites, your website's performance may be affected if another website on the server experiences a traffic spike.
- **Security concerns:** A security vulnerability on one website can potentially impact other websites on the same server.

VPS Hosting (Virtual Private Server)

VPS hosting offers a middle ground between shared hosting and dedicated hosting. With VPS hosting, your website still shares a physical server with other websites, but it gets its own dedicated portion of the server's resources. This means you have more control and better performance than shared hosting.

Pros:

- **Better performance:** Your website has dedicated resources, leading to faster loading times and better overall performance.
- **More control:** You have root access to your virtual server, allowing you to install custom software and configurations.
- **Scalability:** You can easily upgrade your resources as your website grows.

Cons:

- **More expensive than shared hosting:** VPS hosting typically costs more than shared hosting.
- **Requires some technical knowledge:** Managing a VPS may require some technical expertise, although many providers offer managed VPS plans.

Dedicated Hosting

Dedicated hosting is the most powerful and expensive type of web hosting. With dedicated hosting, your website gets an entire server to itself. This provides the highest level of performance, security, and control.

Pros:

- **Maximum performance:** Your website has all the server's resources at its disposal, ensuring optimal performance even during traffic spikes.
- **Complete control:** You have full control over the server's configuration and can install any software you need.
- **Enhanced security:** Dedicated hosting is more secure than shared or VPS hosting because your website is not sharing resources with other websites.

Cons:

- **Most expensive:** Dedicated hosting is the most costly option, making it suitable for large websites with high traffic volumes.
- **Requires technical expertise:** Managing a dedicated server requires a high level of technical knowledge.

Managed WordPress Hosting

Managed WordPress hosting is a specialized hosting service designed specifically for WordPress websites. These hosting providers offer features and optimizations that cater to the unique needs of WordPress, making it easier to manage and maintain your website.

Pros:

- **Optimized for WordPress:** Managed WordPress hosting providers offer features like automatic updates, caching, and security enhancements specifically tailored for WordPress.
- **Improved performance:** The hosting environment is optimized for WordPress, leading to faster loading times and better overall performance.
- **Expert support:** Managed WordPress hosting providers typically offer expert support from WordPress specialists.

Cons:

- **More expensive than shared hosting:** Managed WordPress hosting is more costly than basic shared hosting.
- **Limited flexibility:** Some managed WordPress hosting providers have restrictions on the plugins or themes you can use.

Choosing the right type of web hosting is crucial for your website's success. Consider your website's size, traffic, budget, and technical expertise when making your decision. In the next section, we'll discuss the key factors to consider when choosing a web hosting provider.

Factors to Consider When Choosing a Web Hosting Provider

Selecting the right web hosting provider is a crucial decision that can significantly impact your website's performance, security, and overall success. Here are the key factors to consider when making your choice:

Reliability and Uptime

Your website's uptime, or the percentage of time it's available online, is critical for user experience and business continuity. A reliable web hosting provider should offer a high uptime guarantee, ideally 99.9% or higher. This means your website will be accessible to visitors almost all the time, minimizing downtime and potential revenue loss.

Performance and Speed

Website speed plays a vital role in user satisfaction and search engine rankings. Slow-loading websites can frustrate visitors and lead to higher bounce rates. Look for a web hosting provider that offers fast server response times, utilizes caching technologies, and has a Content Delivery Network (CDN) to distribute your website's content across multiple servers for faster loading in different geographical locations.

Customer Support

When technical issues arise (and they inevitably will), you need a web hosting provider with reliable and responsive customer support. Ensure the provider offers 24/7 support through various channels like phone, email, or live chat. Check online reviews and forums to gauge the provider's reputation for customer service.

Security

Website security is paramount to protect your data and your visitors' information. Choose a web hosting provider that prioritizes security by offering features like SSL certificates (for encrypting data transmitted between your website and visitors), firewalls (to block malicious traffic), malware scanning and removal, and regular backups of your website's data.

Pricing

Web hosting plans come in various price ranges, depending on the type of hosting, features, and resources offered. While it's tempting to choose the cheapest option, consider your website's specific needs and future growth potential. Don't overpay for features you won't use, but be wary of extremely cheap plans that might compromise on performance or security. Compare pricing plans from different providers and choose one that offers the best value for your budget and requirements.

Recommended Web Hosting Providers for WordPress

Selecting the ideal web hosting provider for your WordPress website can be a daunting task, given the plethora of options available. To simplify your decision-making process, we've compiled a list of highly recommended providers renowned for their exceptional support for WordPress websites:

1. **Bluehost:** A popular choice for beginners, Bluehost offers affordable shared hosting plans specifically optimized for WordPress. Their plans include features like one-click WordPress installation, free SSL certificates, and 24/7 customer support.
2. **SiteGround:** Known for its fast and reliable hosting, SiteGround provides various hosting options, including shared, cloud, and dedicated hosting. They offer WordPress-specific features like automatic updates, daily backups, and advanced caching for improved performance.
3. **WP Engine:** A premium managed WordPress hosting provider, WP Engine offers top-notch performance, security, and scalability. Their plans include features like automatic backups, malware scanning, and a staging environment for testing changes before going live.
4. **Kinsta:** Another premium managed WordPress hosting provider, Kinsta is known for its exceptional speed and reliability. They utilize Google Cloud Platform's infrastructure and offer features like automatic scaling, daily backups, and a global CDN.

Key Features:

Provider	Key Features
Bluehost	One-click WordPress installation, free SSL certificate, 24/7 support
SiteGround	Automatic updates, daily backups, advanced caching, free CDN
WP Engine	Automatic backups, malware scanning, staging environment, global CDN
Kinsta	Automatic scaling, daily backups, Google Cloud Platform, global CDN

These are just a few examples of the many excellent web hosting providers available for WordPress websites. It's essential to research and compare different providers to find the one that best suits your specific needs and budget. Consider factors like performance, reliability, customer support, security features, and pricing when making your decision.

Chapter Summary

In this chapter, we explored the fundamental concepts of domain names and web hosting, essential components for establishing your online presence. We learned that a domain name is the unique address of your website, while web hosting is the service that makes your website accessible on the internet.

We discussed the importance of choosing a suitable domain name, emphasizing its impact on brand identity, memorability, and SEO. We also highlighted the key factors to consider when selecting a domain name, such as relevance, memorability, availability, and extension.

Next, we delved into web hosting, explaining its role in storing and delivering your website's files to visitors worldwide. We explored the different types of web hosting available, including shared hosting, VPS hosting, dedicated hosting, and managed WordPress hosting, each with its own advantages and drawbacks.

Finally, we outlined the crucial factors to consider when choosing a web hosting provider, such as reliability, performance, customer support, security, and pricing. We also recommended several reputable web hosting providers that excel in supporting WordPress websites, providing you with a starting point for your research.

By understanding the concepts and factors discussed in this chapter, you are now equipped with the knowledge to make informed decisions about your domain name and web hosting, laying a solid foundation for your WordPress website.

Installing WordPress: Step-by-Step Guide

Outline

- Before You Begin
- Installing WordPress via Web Hosting Control Panel (cPanel or Similar)
- Installing WordPress Manually
- Chapter Summary

Before You Begin

Before you embark on your WordPress installation journey, ensure you have the following prerequisites in place:

- **A Registered Domain Name:** Your domain name is your website's unique address on the internet. Make sure you have registered a domain name that reflects your brand or website's purpose. Popular domain registrars include Namecheap, GoDaddy, and Google Domains.
- **A Web Hosting Account with WordPress Compatibility:** Web hosting is a service that stores your website's files and makes them accessible online. Choose a web hosting provider that explicitly supports WordPress installations. Many providers offer specialized WordPress hosting plans with features optimized for WordPress websites.
- **Access to Your Web Hosting Control Panel:** Your web hosting control panel is a web-based interface where you can manage various aspects of your hosting account, including installing WordPress. Most hosting providers use cPanel or a similar control panel. Ensure you have the login credentials (username and password) for your control panel.

Having these three elements in place will set the stage for a smooth and successful WordPress installation. In the following sections, we'll guide you through the installation process using your web hosting control panel, as well as the manual installation method for those who prefer a more hands-on approach.

Installing WordPress via Web Hosting Control Panel (cPanel or Similar)

Most web hosting providers offer a simplified WordPress installation process directly through their control panel, eliminating the need for manual setup. This streamlined approach makes it incredibly easy for beginners to get their WordPress websites up and running in a matter of minutes.

While the exact steps may vary slightly depending on your web hosting provider, the general process remains consistent:

1. **Log in to Your Web Hosting Control Panel:** Start by accessing your web hosting control panel using the login credentials provided by your hosting provider. The most common control panel is cPanel, but some providers may use their own custom interfaces.
2. **Locate the WordPress Installer:** Once you're logged in, look for the WordPress installer. It's typically found in a section called "Website," "Applications," or "Softaculous Apps Installer."
3. **Launch the Installer:** Click on the WordPress installer icon or link. This will usually open a new page or window with the WordPress installation wizard.
4. **Enter Website Details:** The installation wizard will prompt you to enter some basic information about your website, such as:
    - **Site Name:** The name you want to display on your website.

- **Site Description:** A brief description of your website's purpose.
- **Admin Username:** The username you'll use to log in to your WordPress dashboard.
- **Admin Password:** A strong password for your WordPress admin account.
- **Admin Email:** The email address associated with your WordPress admin account.

5. **Select Installation Directory:** Choose the domain where you want to install WordPress. If you want to install WordPress directly on your main domain (e.g., [invalid URL removed]), leave the installation directory field blank. If you want to install it in a subdirectory (e.g., [invalid URL removed]), enter the subdirectory name.
6. **Initiate Installation:** Once you've filled in all the necessary details, click on the "Install" or "Install Now" button. The installer will then take care of downloading and setting up WordPress for you.
7. **Installation Complete:** After a few minutes, the installation process should be complete. You'll receive a confirmation message with your website's URL and login credentials.

Note: Some web hosting providers may offer additional options or settings during the installation process. Feel free to explore these options if you're familiar with them. However, if you're unsure, it's usually safe to stick with the default settings.

Let's take a look at the specific steps for two popular web hosting providers:

- **Bluehost:** Bluehost's WordPress installer is called "Mojo Marketplace." Look for the Mojo Marketplace icon in your cPanel dashboard and click on it. Then, find the WordPress icon and click on "Install." Follow the on-screen instructions to complete the installation.
- **SiteGround:** SiteGround offers a custom WordPress installer called "Site Tools." Log in to your SiteGround account and navigate to "Websites." Select the website you want to install WordPress on and click on "Site Tools." Then, go to "WordPress" > "Install & Manage" and click on "Install New WordPress."

By following these simple steps, you can quickly and easily install WordPress on your web hosting account, even if you have no prior technical experience. Now that you have WordPress installed, you're ready to start building your dream website!

Installing WordPress Manually

While most web hosting providers offer simplified one-click WordPress installations, opting for a manual installation provides you with greater control over the process and a deeper understanding of how WordPress works. However, manual installation requires some technical knowledge and involves working with files, databases, and FTP (File Transfer Protocol).

If you're comfortable with these aspects or prefer a more hands-on approach, follow these step-by-step instructions to install WordPress manually:

1. **Download WordPress:** Visit the official WordPress website (https://wordpress.org/download/) and download the latest version of WordPress. It will be a ZIP file.
2. **Extract the Files:** Locate the downloaded ZIP file on your computer and extract its contents to a folder. This folder will contain all the necessary files for your WordPress installation.
3. **Create a Database and User:** Log in to your web hosting control panel (usually cPanel or a similar interface) and locate the MySQL Databases section. Create a new database for your WordPress installation and assign a strong password. Make note of the database name, username, and password, as you'll need them later.
4. **Upload WordPress Files:** Connect to your web hosting server using an FTP client (like FileZilla) or your hosting provider's file manager. Upload the extracted WordPress files to the root directory of your website (usually the `public_html` folder).
5. **Run the Installation Script:** Open your web browser and navigate to your website's URL (e.g., `http://www.yourdomain.com`). This should trigger the WordPress installation script. You'll be

asked to select a language and then enter the database name, username, and password you created earlier.
6. **Complete the Installation:** Follow the on-screen instructions to complete the installation process. You'll be prompted to set up your website's title, admin username, and password. Once completed, you'll be able to log in to your WordPress dashboard and start building your website.

Important Considerations:

- **wp-config.php:** The wp-config.php file is a critical WordPress configuration file. During the manual installation, you'll need to edit this file to enter your database details. Make sure to handle this file with care, as incorrect modifications can cause errors.
- **Database Management:** Familiarize yourself with basic database management tasks, such as creating a database and user, assigning permissions, and importing/exporting data.
- **FTP or File Manager:** Learn how to use an FTP client or your hosting provider's file manager to upload and manage files on your server.

If you encounter any difficulties during the manual installation process, consult your web hosting provider's documentation or seek help from online WordPress forums and communities.

Chapter Summary

In this chapter, we delved into the process of installing WordPress, a crucial step in creating your website. We first discussed the prerequisites for installation, emphasizing the importance of having a registered domain name, a compatible web hosting account, and access to your hosting control panel.

We then presented two methods for installing WordPress:

1. **Installing via Web Hosting Control Panel:** We outlined a simplified installation process using your web hosting provider's control panel, such as cPanel. We provided general step-by-step instructions and mentioned specific steps for popular providers like Bluehost and SiteGround.
2. **Installing Manually:** We explained the manual installation process, which offers more control but requires some technical knowledge. We outlined the steps involved, including downloading WordPress, creating a database, uploading files via FTP, and running the installation script. We also emphasized the importance of handling configuration files and database management carefully.

By the end of this chapter, you should have a functional WordPress installation on your web hosting account, ready for customization and content creation. Whether you chose the simplified or manual installation method, you have taken a significant step towards building your dream website.

In the next chapter, we will explore the WordPress dashboard, your command center for managing and customizing your website.

The WordPress Dashboard: Your Command Center

Outline

- Accessing Your WordPress Dashboard
- Main Navigation Menu
- The Dashboard Home Screen
- Updates Section
- Posts Section
- Media Section
- Pages Section
- Comments Section
- Appearance Section
- Plugins Section
- Users Section
- Tools Section
- Settings Section
- Chapter Summary

Accessing Your WordPress Dashboard

Once WordPress is successfully installed on your web hosting account, it's time to access your dashboard, the central hub where you'll manage and control your website.

The Dashboard URL

The WordPress dashboard is typically accessed by adding "/wp-admin" to the end of your website's domain name. For example:

http://www.yourdomain.com/wp-admin

Replace "[invalid URL removed]" with your actual domain name. This URL will take you to the WordPress login page.

Login Credentials

On the login page, you'll be prompted to enter your admin username and password. These are the credentials you created during the installation process. If you used a one-click installer provided by your web hosting provider, they may have sent you an email containing your login details.

Important Security Tip: It's crucial to choose a strong and unique password for your WordPress admin account. Avoid using easily guessable passwords like "123456" or "password." A strong password should include a combination of uppercase and lowercase letters, numbers, and symbols.

Troubleshooting Login Issues

If you're having trouble logging in, double-check that you're entering the correct username and password. If you've forgotten your password, click on the "Lost your password?" link on the login page. You'll receive an email with instructions on how to reset your password.

Dashboard Overview

Once you've successfully logged in, you'll be greeted by the WordPress dashboard. This is where you'll find all the tools and features you need to manage your website. In the following sections, we'll take a closer look at the different sections of the dashboard and how to use them to customize and control your website.

Main Navigation Menu

The WordPress dashboard features a main navigation menu on the left-hand side, providing easy access to all the essential areas of your website. This menu acts as your central control panel, allowing you to navigate seamlessly between different sections and perform various tasks.

The main sections of the navigation menu include:

1. **Dashboard** (Home icon): This is the home screen of your WordPress dashboard, offering a quick overview of your website's activity, recent comments, and other essential information.
2. **Posts** (Speech bubble icon): This section is where you create and manage your blog posts. You can add new posts, edit existing ones, categorize them, and control their visibility.
3. **Media** (Image icon): The media section is your library for images, videos, audio files, and other media assets. You can upload, organize, edit, and insert media into your posts and pages.
4. **Pages** (Document icon): Unlike posts, which are typically displayed in chronological order, pages are used for static content like your About page, Contact page, or Services page. You can create and manage these pages in this section.
5. **Comments** (Chat bubble icon): If you allow comments on your blog posts, this section is where you can moderate them. You can approve, reply to, edit, trash, or mark comments as spam.
6. **Appearance** (Paintbrush icon): This section allows you to customize the look and feel of your website. You can change themes, customize menus, add widgets to your sidebar or footer, and manage other visual aspects of your site.
7. **Plugins** (Plug icon): Plugins are like apps for your WordPress website. They extend its functionality by adding features like contact forms, SEO optimization, social media sharing buttons, and much more. You can install, activate, deactivate, and update plugins in this section.
8. **Users** (People icon): If your website has multiple contributors or authors, this is where you manage user accounts and permissions. You can add new users, assign roles (such as administrator, editor, or subscriber), and edit user profiles.
9. **Tools** (Wrench icon): The tools section provides access to various utilities for importing and exporting content, managing your website's data, and performing other administrative tasks.
10. **Settings** (Gear icon): This section contains all the general settings for your WordPress website. You can configure your site's title, tagline, permalinks, language, time zone, and other important options.

Familiarizing yourself with these main sections of the navigation menu is essential for effectively managing and customizing your WordPress website. In the following sections, we'll dive deeper into each of these sections and explore their functionalities in more detail.

The Dashboard Home Screen

The dashboard home screen serves as the welcome mat to your WordPress website's backend. It provides a snapshot of your website's current status and offers quick access to essential tasks and information. Let's explore the main components of the dashboard home screen:

Welcome Message

Upon logging into your WordPress dashboard, you'll be greeted with a personalized welcome message at the top. This message typically includes your username and a warm welcome to your WordPress site. It also often features quick links to common tasks, such as creating a new post or page, customizing your site, or viewing your website.

At a Glance

The "At a Glance" section offers a concise overview of your website's content. It displays the number of published posts, pages, and comments you have. It might also show the version of WordPress you're currently using and the active theme. This section is a handy way to get a quick snapshot of your website's overall status.

Activity

The "Activity" section displays recent activity on your website. This can include new comments awaiting moderation, recently published posts, or upcoming scheduled posts. It helps you stay informed about what's happening on your site and allows you to quickly address any pending tasks, such as responding to comments or reviewing scheduled content.

Quick Draft

For those times when inspiration strikes, the "Quick Draft" section is a convenient way to jot down your ideas without leaving the dashboard. You can start typing a new blog post directly in this section, saving it as a draft for later editing and publishing. This feature is particularly useful for bloggers who want to capture their thoughts on the go.

In addition to these main components, the dashboard home screen might also display other widgets or modules, depending on the installed plugins and your WordPress configuration. For example, some plugins might add widgets for SEO stats, analytics data, or social media updates.

Familiarizing yourself with the dashboard home screen is the first step towards effectively managing your WordPress website. It provides a centralized location to monitor your website's activity, access essential tasks, and quickly create new content. As you become more comfortable with WordPress, you can customize the dashboard by adding or removing widgets to tailor it to your specific needs and preferences.

Updates Section

The Updates section in your WordPress dashboard is a crucial area that keeps your website running smoothly and securely. It notifies you whenever updates are available for the following components:

- **WordPress Core:** The core files of WordPress are regularly updated to introduce new features, improve performance, and patch security vulnerabilities.
- **Themes:** The theme you use to design your website may receive updates to fix bugs, enhance compatibility, or add new functionalities.
- **Plugins:** Plugins that extend your website's functionality are frequently updated by their developers to improve performance, fix bugs, and address security issues.

Why Updates Matter

Keeping your WordPress core, themes, and plugins up-to-date is vital for several reasons:

- **Security:** Outdated software is a prime target for hackers and malicious actors. Security vulnerabilities are often discovered and exploited in older versions of WordPress and its components. Updates often include patches to address these vulnerabilities, protecting your website from potential attacks.

- **Functionality:** Updates can introduce new features and improvements to your website's functionality, enhancing the user experience and keeping your site modern.
- **Compatibility:** Plugins and themes may need updates to remain compatible with the latest version of WordPress. Outdated components can lead to conflicts and errors that can disrupt your website's functionality.
- **Performance:** Updates often include optimizations that can improve your website's loading speed and overall performance.

How to Update Your WordPress Website

Updating your WordPress website is a straightforward process, usually involving just a few clicks. In most cases, you'll see a notification in the Updates section of your dashboard when updates are available. Simply click on the "Update Now" button to initiate the update process.

It's generally recommended to update your website regularly, ideally as soon as updates become available. However, before updating any plugins or themes, creating a backup of your website is always a good practice. This ensures that you can easily revert to a previous version if any issues arise during the update.

By keeping your WordPress website up-to-date, you can ensure its security, functionality, compatibility, and performance, providing a seamless experience for your visitors and protecting your valuable data.

Posts Section

The Posts section in your WordPress dashboard is your gateway to creating and managing the heart of your blog – your blog posts. It provides a comprehensive set of tools for crafting engaging content, organizing your posts, and controlling their visibility.

Creating a New Post

To create a new blog post, follow these simple steps:

1. **Access the Posts Section:** Navigate to the "Posts" section in your dashboard's main navigation menu.
2. **Click "Add New":** Click on the "Add New" button (or link) to open the post editor.
3. **Enter Your Title:** Start by entering a compelling title for your blog post in the title field.
4. **Write Your Content:** Use the content editor (similar to a word processor) to write your blog post. You can format text, add headings, lists, quotes, and other elements to enhance readability.
5. **Add Images and Media:** Click on the "Add Media" button to insert images, videos, or other media files into your post. You can upload new media or choose from your existing media library.
6. **Assign Categories and Tags:** Categories help organize your blog posts into broader topics, while tags provide more specific keywords for each post. Choose relevant categories and tags to improve your website's navigation and searchability.
7. **Set a Featured Image:** A featured image is the main image associated with your post. It often appears at the top of the post or in previews. Select an eye-catching image that represents your post's content.
8. **Save or Publish:** You can save your post as a draft to work on it later or click on the "Publish" button to make it live on your website.

Managing Existing Posts

The Posts section also allows you to manage your existing blog posts. You can:

- **Edit:** Click on the "Edit" link below a post's title to modify its content, title, categories, tags, or featured image.

- **Quick Edit:** Use the "Quick Edit" link for faster access to essential post details.
- **Trash:** If you want to remove a post, move it to the trash. You can restore trashed posts or permanently delete them later.
- **View:** Click on the "View" link to see how your post looks on your website.

Drafts, Published Posts, and Scheduled Posts

Understanding the different statuses of your posts is crucial for managing your content effectively:

- **Draft:** A draft post is a saved version that hasn't been published yet. You can continue working on drafts and publish them later.
- **Published:** A published post is live on your website and visible to visitors.
- **Scheduled:** A scheduled post is set to be published automatically at a specific date and time in the future.

By mastering the Posts section, you can effortlessly create, manage, and organize your blog content, ensuring that your website remains engaging and informative for your audience.

Media Section

The Media section in your WordPress dashboard serves as the central repository for all your media files, including images, videos, audio clips, and documents. It provides a convenient way to upload, organize, edit, and insert these files into your posts and pages.

Uploading Media Files

To upload media files to your WordPress library, follow these steps:

1. **Access the Media Section:** Go to the "Media" section in your dashboard's main navigation menu.
2. **Click "Add New":** Click on the "Add New" button at the top of the screen.
3. **Select Files:** A file selection dialog will open. Choose the files you want to upload from your computer. You can select multiple files at once.
4. **Start Upload:** Click on the "Open" button to start the upload process. WordPress will upload the files to your media library.

Managing Media Files

Once your media files are uploaded, you can manage them in the Media Library:

- **View:** You can view your media files in a grid or list view.
- **Search:** Use the search bar to find specific files.
- **Filter:** Filter your media by type (image, video, audio, etc.) or date.
- **Edit:** Click on a file to open its attachment details page. Here you can edit its title, caption, alt text, and description.
- **Delete:** You can delete unwanted files from your library.

Editing Image Details

Image details are important for SEO and accessibility. Here's how to edit them:

- **Title:** The title is a brief description of the image. It's often displayed when you hover over the image.
- **Caption:** The caption appears below the image and provides additional context.
- **Alt Text:** The alt text is a description of the image for visually impaired users and search engines. It should be concise and descriptive.

- **Description:** The description is a more detailed explanation of the image. It's not always visible on the front end of your website.

Inserting Media into Posts and Pages

To insert media files into your posts and pages:

1. **Place Your Cursor:** In the post or page editor, position your cursor where you want to insert the media.
2. **Click "Add Media":** Click on the "Add Media" button above the editor.
3. **Select Media:** Choose the desired media file from your library or upload a new one.
4. **Insert into Post:** Click on the "Insert into post" button.

Creating Galleries

You can create image galleries to display multiple images in an organized and visually appealing way:

1. **Create a Gallery:** In the post or page editor, click on the "Add Media" button.
2. **Select Images:** Choose the images you want to include in your gallery.
3. **Create New Gallery:** Click on the "Create new gallery" button.
4. **Arrange Images:** Drag and drop images to reorder them.
5. **Insert Gallery:** Click on the "Insert gallery" button.

By mastering the Media section, you can effectively manage your website's visual and audio content, ensuring that your posts and pages are visually engaging and informative for your audience.

Pages Section

The Pages section in your WordPress dashboard is where you craft the essential, static content that forms the backbone of your website. These pages are typically not displayed in chronological order like blog posts and often include information that remains relatively consistent, such as your "About Us" page, "Contact" page, or "Services" page.

Creating a New Page

To create a new page in WordPress, follow these steps:

1. **Access the Pages Section:** Navigate to the "Pages" section in your dashboard's main navigation menu.
2. **Click "Add New":** Click the "Add New" button (or link) to launch the page editor.
3. **Enter Your Title:** Begin by giving your page a clear and concise title in the title field. This title will usually be displayed prominently on your website.
4. **Craft Your Content:** Use the content editor, which functions similarly to a word processor, to write and format your page content. You can add text, images, videos, headings, lists, and more to create informative and visually appealing pages.
5. **Set a Featured Image (Optional):** A featured image is a visual representation of your page's content. It may be displayed as a thumbnail on your homepage or in other areas of your website. You can set a featured image by clicking on the "Set featured image" link in the sidebar.
6. **Save or Publish:** When you're satisfied with your page, you have two options:
   - **Save Draft:** If you're not ready to make your page public, save it as a draft to work on it later.
   - **Publish:** Click the "Publish" button to make your page live on your website.

Managing Existing Pages

The Pages section also allows you to manage your existing pages. You can:

- **Edit:** Click the "Edit" link below a page's title to modify its content, title, or featured image.
- **Quick Edit:** Utilize the "Quick Edit" link for swift access to modify essential page details without opening the full editor.
- **Trash:** If you want to remove a page, move it to the trash. You can restore trashed pages or permanently delete them later.
- **View:** Click the "View" link to see how your page appears on your live website.

Static Pages vs. Blog Posts

While both pages and posts contain content, they serve different purposes:

- **Static Pages:** These pages are typically timeless and provide essential information about your website or organization. Examples include "About Us," "Contact," "Services," or "Privacy Policy."
- **Blog Posts:** Blog posts are often more dynamic and timely. They are usually displayed in reverse chronological order, with the newest posts appearing first. Blog posts are ideal for sharing news, updates, opinions, or tutorials.

Understanding the distinction between static pages and blog posts will help you effectively organize your website's content and choose the appropriate format for your message.

Comments Section

The Comments section in your WordPress dashboard is where you interact with your audience and foster a sense of community on your website. It allows you to moderate and respond to comments left by visitors on your blog posts.

Accessing the Comments Section

You can access the Comments section by clicking on the "Comments" option in the main navigation menu of your dashboard. Here, you'll find a list of all the comments that have been submitted on your website.

Moderating Comments

Before a comment appears on your website, you have the option to moderate it. This means you can review the comment and decide whether to approve, reply, edit, trash, or mark it as spam.

- **Approve:** If a comment is relevant and appropriate, you can approve it to make it visible to other visitors.
- **Reply:** Engage with your readers by replying directly to their comments. This can help build a relationship with your audience and encourage further discussion.
- **Edit:** You can edit a comment to correct typos, remove inappropriate language, or clarify any misunderstandings.
- **Trash:** If a comment is irrelevant, spammy, or offensive, you can move it to the trash.
- **Spam:** Mark a comment as spam if it's clearly spam or promotional in nature. This will help train WordPress's spam filter to identify similar comments in the future.

Navigating the Comments Section

The Comments section displays comments in chronological order, with the newest comments at the top. You can use the following features to navigate and manage your comments:

- **Search:** Use the search bar to find specific comments.
- **Filter:** Filter comments by status (pending, approved, spam, trash) or by post.
- **Bulk Actions:** You can select multiple comments and perform bulk actions, such as approving, trashing, or spamming them.

Comment Settings

You can customize the comment settings for your website in the "Discussion Settings" section under "Settings." Here, you can control various aspects of comments, such as:

- Whether comments are allowed on new posts.
- Whether commenters must provide their name and email address.
- Whether comments are held for moderation before they are published.
- How many levels of nested replies are allowed.
- Whether to notify you by email when new comments are submitted.

By actively moderating and responding to comments, you can create a welcoming and engaging community on your website. Encouraging discussions and interactions can help build a loyal readership and enhance your website's overall appeal.

Appearance Section

The Appearance section of your WordPress dashboard is where you can unleash your creativity and transform the look and feel of your website. It provides a range of tools for customizing your site's design, layout, and overall aesthetic appeal.

Changing Themes

Themes are the foundation of your website's design. They dictate the layout, colors, fonts, and overall visual style. WordPress offers thousands of free and premium themes to choose from, each with its unique features and customization options.

To change your theme:

1. Navigate to "Appearance" > "Themes" in your dashboard.
2. Browse the available themes or use the search bar to find a specific one.
3. Click the "Activate" button on the theme you want to use.

Once activated, the new theme will be applied to your website, instantly changing its appearance. You can then further customize the theme's settings through the "Customize" option, which we'll discuss in more detail below.

Customizing Menus

Menus are an essential part of your website's navigation. They help visitors easily find the content they're looking for. In the Appearance section, you can create and manage your website's menus.

To customize your menus:

1. Go to "Appearance" > "Menus."
2. Create a new menu or select an existing one to edit.
3. Add menu items by selecting pages, posts, categories, or custom links.
4. Drag and drop menu items to arrange them in the desired order.
5. Assign menu locations (e.g., primary menu, footer menu) to display your menus in different areas of your website.

Adding Widgets

Widgets are small blocks of content that you can add to your website's sidebar, footer, or other widget-ready areas. They can display various types of content, such as recent posts, social media feeds, contact forms, or search bars.

To add widgets:

1. Go to "Appearance" > "Widgets."
2. Select the widget you want to add and drag it to the desired widget area.
3. Configure the widget's settings (if applicable).

Customizing Header and Background

Your website's header and background are prominent visual elements that can significantly impact its overall look. Many themes allow you to customize the header and background through the "Customize" option.

To customize your header and background:

1. Go to "Appearance" > "Customize."
2. Look for the "Header" and "Background" sections in the customizer.
3. Upload your own images or choose from the theme's available options.
4. Adjust the settings (e.g., header layout, background color) to achieve your desired look.

By exploring the Appearance section and utilizing its various customization options, you can create a visually stunning and unique website that reflects your brand and captures your audience's attention.

Plugins Section

Think of plugins as the apps of your WordPress website. They are software extensions that add new features and functionality, allowing you to tailor your site to your specific needs. From contact forms and SEO optimization to social media integration and e-commerce capabilities, plugins offer endless possibilities for enhancing your website's power and versatility.

Adding Plugins

1. **Access the Plugins Section:** Navigate to the "Plugins" section in your dashboard's main navigation menu.
2. **Click "Add New":** Click on the "Add New" button at the top of the screen to open the plugin repository.
3. **Search for Plugins:** Use the search bar to find plugins by name or functionality. You can also browse through featured, popular, or recommended plugins.
4. **Install:** Once you find a plugin you want to add, click the "Install Now" button. WordPress will download and install the plugin for you.
5. **Activate:** After installation, click the "Activate" button to enable the plugin on your website.

Activating and Deactivating Plugins

- **Activating:** To enable a plugin's functionality, click the "Activate" link below its name in the plugins list.
- **Deactivating:** To disable a plugin without deleting it, click the "Deactivate" link. Deactivating a plugin is useful for troubleshooting or when you don't need a particular feature temporarily.

Updating Plugins

Plugins, like WordPress core and themes, receive regular updates to improve their performance, fix bugs, and address security vulnerabilities. It's crucial to keep your plugins updated to ensure the smooth and secure operation of your website.

1. **Check for Updates:** The Plugins section will display notifications for available updates. You can also manually check for updates by clicking the "Update Available" link.

2. **Update:** To update a plugin, click the "Update Now" link below its name. WordPress will automatically update the plugin to the latest version.

Choosing and Managing Plugins Wisely

While plugins offer incredible flexibility, it's important to choose and manage them wisely. Installing too many plugins can slow down your website and potentially cause conflicts.

- **Research:** Before installing a plugin, research its features, reviews, and compatibility with your WordPress version and other plugins.
- **Essential Plugins:** Focus on installing plugins that are essential for your website's functionality and goals.
- **Regular Updates:** Keep your plugins updated to ensure optimal performance and security.
- **Deactivate Unused Plugins:** If you're not using a plugin, deactivate it to reduce unnecessary load on your website.

By carefully selecting and managing plugins, you can unlock the full potential of WordPress and create a website that is tailored to your unique needs and goals.

Users Section

The Users section of your WordPress dashboard allows you to manage the individuals who have access to your website and the permissions they have. This is especially important if you have a team of contributors or want to grant limited access to certain individuals.

User Roles

WordPress comes with a set of predefined user roles, each with different capabilities:

- **Administrator:** Has complete control over the website, including managing other users, installing plugins, and changing themes.
- **Editor:** Can publish and manage posts and pages, as well as manage other users' posts.
- **Author:** Can publish and manage their own posts.
- **Contributor:** Can write and manage their own posts but cannot publish them.
- **Subscriber:** Can only read comments and manage their profile.

Understanding these roles is crucial for assigning appropriate permissions to users based on their responsibilities.

Adding a New User

To add a new user to your WordPress website:

1. Go to "Users" > "Add New" in your dashboard.
2. Fill out the user's information, including their username, email address, and name (optional).
3. Select the appropriate user role from the dropdown menu.
4. Click the "Add New User" button.

The new user will receive an email with instructions on how to set their password and log in to your website.

Editing User Profiles

You can edit user profiles to update their information or change their roles:

1. Go to "Users" > "All Users" in your dashboard.

2. Click on the username of the user you want to edit.
3. Make the necessary changes to their information or role.
4. Click the "Update User" button.

Managing User Permissions

In addition to the predefined user roles, you can also use plugins to create custom user roles with specific permissions. This can be useful if you need more granular control over what different users can do on your website.

Best Practices for User Management

- **Assign roles carefully:** Only give users the permissions they need to perform their tasks.
- **Use strong passwords:** Encourage users to create strong passwords and change them regularly.
- **Limit admin accounts:** Avoid having too many administrators, as this can increase the risk of security breaches.
- **Monitor user activity:** Keep an eye on user activity to ensure that no one is abusing their permissions.

By managing user accounts and permissions effectively, you can ensure that your website is secure and that only authorized individuals have access to sensitive areas.

Tools Section

The Tools section in your WordPress dashboard offers a collection of utilities to help you manage various aspects of your website's data and content. Let's briefly explore some of the essential tools you'll find here:

- **Available Tools:**
    - **Import:** This tool allows you to import content from other platforms or websites into your WordPress site. You can import posts, pages, comments, and other data from sources like Blogger, LiveJournal, or even another WordPress website.
    - **Export:** If you need to create a backup of your WordPress content or transfer it to another platform, the export tool enables you to export your posts, pages, comments, and other data in an XML format.
    - **Site Health:** This tool provides a comprehensive overview of your website's health, including performance, security, and configuration checks. It helps identify potential issues and suggests solutions to improve your site's overall health.
    - **Export Personal Data:** In compliance with data protection regulations like GDPR, this tool allows you to export personal data associated with a specific user, such as their profile information, posts, and comments.
    - **Erase Personal Data:** This tool allows you to erase personal data associated with a specific user, in compliance with data protection regulations.

These are just a few of the tools available in the WordPress Tools section. Depending on your installed plugins, you might find additional tools for tasks like managing redirects, optimizing your database, or repairing corrupted files.

The Tools section is an invaluable resource for website administrators, providing them with the tools they need to manage their data effectively, ensure their website's health, and comply with data protection regulations.

Settings Section

The Settings section in your WordPress dashboard is where you fine-tune the core configurations that govern how your website functions and appears. It's divided into several categories, each focusing on specific aspects of your site:

General Settings

Here, you can configure fundamental details about your website, such as:

- Site Title: The name of your website, displayed in the browser tab and often used in search results.
- Tagline: A brief description of your website that appears alongside the title.
- WordPress Address (URL): The URL where your WordPress core files are installed.
- Site Address (URL): The URL visitors use to access your website.
- Administration Email Address: The email address where WordPress notifications are sent.
- Membership: Control whether anyone can register on your site to become a user.
- New User Default Role: Choose the default role assigned to new users.
- Site Language: Select the language for your website's interface and content.
- Timezone: Set the correct time zone for your website.
- Date Format: Choose how dates are displayed on your website.
- Time Format: Choose how times are displayed on your website.

Writing Settings

This section allows you to configure settings related to writing and publishing posts, such as:

- Default Post Category: Set the default category for new posts.
- Default Post Format: Choose the default format for new posts (standard, aside, gallery, etc.).
- Post via email: Configure settings for posting to your blog via email.
- Update Services: Manage services that are notified when you update your blog.

Reading Settings

Here, you can control how your website's homepage and blog posts are displayed:

- Your homepage displays: Choose whether your homepage shows your latest posts or a static page.
- Blog pages show at most: Set the maximum number of posts displayed per page.
- Syndication feeds show the most recent: Control the number of items included in your RSS feeds.
- For each article in a feed, show: Choose whether to display summaries or full text in your RSS feeds.
- Search Engine Visibility: Discourage search engines from indexing your site (not recommended for most websites).

Discussion Settings

This section allows you to manage comments and trackbacks/pingbacks on your website:

- Default article settings: Control whether comments and pingbacks are allowed on new articles.
- Other comment settings: Set rules for comment moderation, avatars, and email notifications.
- Before a comment appears: Choose whether comments should be manually approved or held in moderation.
- Comment Moderation: Set parameters for automatically holding comments for moderation based on links or keywords.
- Comment Blacklist: List words, IP addresses, or email addresses that will trigger automatic comment moderation.
- Avatars: Control whether to display avatars for commenters.

Media Settings

Here, you can configure settings for image sizes and file uploads:

- Image sizes: Define the default sizes for thumbnail, medium, and large images.
- Uploading Files: Choose whether to organize uploads into month- and year-based folders.

Permalinks Settings

Permalinks are the permanent URLs for your individual blog posts and pages. You can choose a permalink structure that is SEO-friendly and easy for users to understand.

By exploring and customizing these settings, you can tailor your WordPress website to meet your specific needs and preferences, ensuring it functions optimally and delivers a seamless user experience.

Chapter Summary

In this chapter, we delved into the WordPress dashboard, your command center for managing and customizing your website. We learned how to access the dashboard using your website's URL and admin credentials.

We explored the main navigation menu, which provides access to all essential areas of your WordPress website, including posts, media, pages, comments, appearance, plugins, users, tools, and settings.

We also examined the dashboard home screen, highlighting key components like the welcome message, "At a Glance" summary, activity feed, and quick draft section.

We then discussed the importance of the Updates section for keeping your website secure, functional, and compatible with the latest versions of WordPress, themes, and plugins.

The Posts section was explored in detail, explaining how to create, manage, and organize your blog posts using categories, tags, and featured images. We also highlighted the differences between drafts, published posts, and scheduled posts.

Next, we covered the Media section, which allows you to upload, manage, and edit media files, including images, videos, and audio. We explained how to edit image details and create galleries to showcase your media.

In the Pages section, we learned how to create and manage static pages, such as "About Us" or "Contact" pages, which differ from blog posts in their purpose and structure.

The Comments section was explained as a means to interact with your audience and moderate comments on your blog posts. We detailed how to approve, reply, edit, trash, or spam comments.

We then explored the Appearance section, where you can customize your website's look and feel by changing themes, customizing menus, adding widgets, and managing the header and background.

The Plugins section was described as the place to add, activate, deactivate, and update plugins to extend your website's functionality. We emphasized the importance of choosing plugins carefully and keeping them updated.

The Users section was explained as the tool for managing user accounts and permissions, highlighting the different user roles and how to assign them.

Finally, we provided an overview of the Tools section, which contains various utilities for importing and exporting content, checking site health, and exporting personal data, and the Settings section, where you can configure various aspects of your website's functionality and appearance. By mastering the WordPress dashboard, you gain complete control over your website and can create a unique online presence that reflects your brand and goals.

Themes: The Foundation of Your Website's Design

Outline

- What is a WordPress Theme?
- Why Themes are Important
- Types of WordPress Themes
- Key Features to Look for in a Theme
- How to Choose the Right Theme for Your Website
- Installing and Activating a Theme
- Customizing Your Theme
- Chapter Summary

What is a WordPress Theme?

A WordPress theme is, in essence, the skin of your website. It's a collection of files that work together to dictate the visual appearance and layout of your content. These files include templates, which define the structure of different pages (like the homepage, blog posts, and pages), stylesheets (CSS), which control the colors, fonts, and overall styling, and sometimes scripts (JavaScript), which add interactive elements or functionality.

Think of a theme as a pre-designed template that you can apply to your website. It provides a consistent look and feel across all your pages, ensuring a cohesive user experience. Themes can range from simple and minimalist to complex and feature-rich, catering to a wide variety of website styles and purposes.

How Themes Control Your Website's Appearance

- **Layout:** Themes determine the overall layout of your website, including the placement of headers, footers, sidebars, navigation menus, and content areas.
- **Colors:** Themes define the color palette used throughout your website, including background colors, text colors, and link colors.
- **Fonts:** Themes specify the fonts used for headings, body text, and other elements, ensuring a consistent and legible typography.
- **Images and Media:** Themes control how images and other media (like videos and audio) are displayed on your website, including their size, placement, and styling.
- **Overall Styling:** Themes incorporate various CSS styles to create a unique visual identity for your website, including effects like shadows, borders, animations, and transitions.

The Importance of Choosing the Right Theme

Selecting the right theme is a crucial step in creating a successful website. A well-designed theme not only enhances your website's visual appeal but also improves its usability, accessibility, and overall user experience.

In the following sections, we'll delve deeper into the different types of WordPress themes, the key features to look for, and how to choose the perfect theme for your website.

Why Themes are Important

Choosing the right WordPress theme is a pivotal decision in your website creation journey. A theme isn't merely a cosmetic choice; it significantly impacts the functionality, user experience, and overall success of your website. Let's delve into the reasons why themes are so important:

Enhance User Experience

A well-designed theme plays a crucial role in enhancing the user experience (UX) on your website. It provides a clear and organized layout that guides visitors through your content seamlessly. Intuitive navigation menus, well-structured pages, and visually appealing elements make it easy for users to find what they're looking for and stay engaged with your site. A positive UX can lead to increased time spent on your site, lower bounce rates, and higher conversions.

Establish a Consistent Brand Identity

Your website is a digital representation of your brand. A theme that aligns with your brand's personality and values helps establish a consistent and recognizable identity. The colors, fonts, and overall design style should resonate with your target audience and reinforce your brand message. A cohesive visual identity builds trust and credibility with your visitors, making them more likely to engage with your content and become loyal customers or followers.

Improve Website Accessibility

Accessibility is a critical aspect of web design, ensuring that your website is usable by people with disabilities. A good theme adheres to web accessibility standards, making it easier for users with visual, auditory, or motor impairments to navigate and interact with your content. This not only makes your website more inclusive but also improves its search engine optimization (SEO), as accessible websites tend to rank higher in search results.

Optimize for Different Devices and Screen Sizes

In today's mobile-first world, it's crucial for your website to adapt seamlessly to different devices and screen sizes. A responsive theme automatically adjusts its layout and content to fit the screen of the device being used, whether it's a desktop computer, tablet, or smartphone. This ensures that your website looks and functions optimally across all devices, providing a consistent and enjoyable experience for every visitor.

Types of WordPress Themes

When it comes to selecting a WordPress theme, you have a vast array of options to choose from, each catering to different needs, budgets, and levels of customization. The three main types of WordPress themes are:

Free Themes

Free themes are readily available in the official WordPress Theme Directory. This extensive repository offers thousands of themes, many of which are created by talented developers and designers. Free themes are an excellent choice for beginners or those on a tight budget. They provide a basic foundation for your website's design and functionality, and many of them can be customized to a certain extent.

However, free themes often have limitations in terms of features, customization options, and support. They may not offer the same level of advanced functionality or design flexibility as premium themes. Additionally, support for free themes is typically limited to community forums, which may not always provide timely or comprehensive assistance.

Premium Themes

Premium themes are purchased from third-party developers and marketplaces. These themes offer a wider range of features, more extensive customization options, and often come with dedicated customer support. Premium themes are typically designed with a focus on specific niches or industries, offering tailored solutions for businesses, bloggers, e-commerce stores, and more.

Some of the advantages of premium themes include:

- **Advanced Features:** Premium themes often include features like drag-and-drop page builders, advanced theme options panels, custom widgets, and integration with popular plugins.
- **Enhanced Customization:** They offer more flexibility to personalize your website's design, including custom colors, fonts, layouts, and other visual elements.
- **Professional Support:** Premium theme developers typically provide dedicated customer support to help you with installation, customization, and troubleshooting issues.
- **Regular Updates:** Premium themes are regularly updated to ensure compatibility with the latest WordPress versions and to add new features or improvements.

The cost of premium themes can vary widely, from a few dollars to several hundred dollars. However, investing in a high-quality premium theme can save you time and effort in the long run, as it often comes with a wealth of built-in features and customization options.

Custom Themes

Custom themes are developed specifically for a website, providing the highest level of customization and unique design tailored to the client's specific requirements. These themes are typically built by professional web developers and designers who work closely with the client to understand their brand, goals, and target audience.

Custom themes offer unparalleled flexibility and control over every aspect of your website's design and functionality. They are ideal for businesses or individuals who want a truly unique and bespoke online presence that stands out from the crowd.

However, custom themes are the most expensive option, as they require significant time and resources to develop. They are typically best suited for larger businesses or organizations with specific design and functionality requirements that cannot be met by free or premium themes.

Key Features to Look for in a Theme

With the abundance of WordPress themes available, it's essential to prioritize certain features to ensure your chosen theme not only looks great but also functions effectively and provides a seamless experience for your visitors. Here are the key features to consider:

Responsiveness

In today's mobile-centric world, responsiveness is non-negotiable. A responsive theme automatically adjusts its layout and content to fit the screen size of the device being used, whether it's a desktop computer, tablet, or smartphone. This ensures that your website looks great and is easy to use on any device, providing a consistent user experience and improving your SEO rankings.

Customization Options

Your website should reflect your brand's unique identity. Look for a theme that offers ample customization options, allowing you to personalize colors, fonts, layouts, header styles, and other visual elements. A theme with a flexible design and extensive customization capabilities empowers you to create a website that truly represents your brand.

SEO Friendliness

Search engine optimization (SEO) is crucial for attracting organic traffic to your website. A well-coded and SEO-friendly theme follows best practices for search engine crawlers, making it easier for them to index your content and rank it higher in search results. Look for themes that prioritize clean code, proper heading structures, fast loading times, and mobile responsiveness, as these factors all contribute to better SEO performance.

Browser Compatibility

Your website's visitors will be using various web browsers, including Chrome, Firefox, Safari, and Edge. It's essential to choose a theme that works seamlessly across all major browsers, ensuring a consistent experience for everyone. Test the theme's demo on different browsers to verify its compatibility before making your final decision.

Page Builders Integration

If you plan to use a page builder like Elementor to customize your website's design, ensure that your chosen theme is compatible with it. Many premium themes are specifically designed to integrate seamlessly with popular page builders, offering a user-friendly drag-and-drop interface for creating unique page layouts and designs.

Performance and Speed

Website speed is a critical factor for user experience and SEO. Slow-loading websites can frustrate visitors and lead to higher bounce rates. Look for a theme that is optimized for speed, with features like lightweight code, optimized images, and minimal use of external scripts. Test the theme's demo using online speed test tools to assess its performance before purchasing.

Security

Website security is of paramount importance to protect your data and your visitors' information. Choose a theme from a reputable developer who regularly updates their themes to address security vulnerabilities and ensure compatibility with the latest WordPress versions. Avoid downloading themes from untrusted sources, as they may contain malicious code that could compromise your website's security.

How to Choose the Right Theme for Your Website

Selecting the perfect WordPress theme for your website is akin to choosing the right outfit for a special occasion. It should not only look good but also fit well and serve its purpose. Here's a guide to help you navigate the vast world of WordPress themes and find the one that suits your needs:

Website Purpose

Begin by defining the primary purpose of your website. Are you creating a personal blog, a business website, an online portfolio, or an e-commerce store? Different types of websites have distinct requirements. A blog theme, for instance, might prioritize readability and post layouts, while an e-commerce theme would focus on product display and shopping cart functionality. Choosing a theme tailored to your website's purpose ensures it has the necessary features and design elements to support your content effectively.

Design Preferences

Your website's design is a visual representation of your brand or personality. Consider your aesthetic preferences and brand identity when choosing a theme. Do you prefer a minimalist, modern design or a more vibrant, colorful one? Look for themes that resonate with your style and create a visual experience that aligns with your overall message.

Features and Functionality

Make a list of the specific features you need for your website. Do you require e-commerce integration to sell products or services? Do you need a contact form, a booking system, or a portfolio gallery? Ensure the theme you choose offers the necessary features or can be easily extended with plugins to meet your requirements.

Budget

WordPress themes come in both free and premium versions. Free themes are a great starting point, especially for personal projects or budget-conscious beginners. However, premium themes often offer more advanced features, customization options, and dedicated support. Determine your budget and weigh the benefits of both free and premium themes before making a decision.

Reviews and Ratings

Before finalizing your choice, take the time to read online reviews and ratings from other users. These reviews can provide valuable insights into the theme's quality, ease of use, customization options, and the level of support provided by the developer. Look for themes with positive reviews and high ratings to ensure you're investing in a reliable and well-supported product.

Additional Tips

- **Demo and Documentation:** Explore the theme's demo to see how it looks and functions in a real-world setting. Check the documentation for detailed instructions on installation and customization.
- **Community and Support:** Choose a theme from a reputable developer who offers active community support and regular updates.
- **Flexibility:** Opt for a theme that allows you to make changes and modifications easily, even if you don't have extensive coding knowledge.

By carefully considering these factors, you can confidently select a WordPress theme that not only enhances your website's visual appeal but also empowers you to create a functional and user-friendly online presence.

Installing and Activating a Theme

Once you've chosen the perfect theme for your WordPress website, the next step is to install and activate it. Fortunately, WordPress makes this process simple and straightforward. Here's a step-by-step guide:

1. **Access the Themes Section:**
    - Log in to your WordPress dashboard.
    - Navigate to the "Appearance" section in the main navigation menu on the left-hand side.
    - Click on "Themes."
2. **Add New Theme:**
    - On the "Themes" page, click on the "Add New" button at the top. This will open the WordPress Theme Directory, where you can browse and search for thousands of free themes.
3. **Search or Browse:**
    - If you already have a specific theme in mind, use the search bar at the top right to find it by name.
    - Alternatively, you can browse through the featured, popular, or latest themes to discover new options.
    - You can also filter themes by subject, features, and layout to narrow down your choices.
4. **Preview and Install:**

- When you find a theme you like, hover over its thumbnail to see the "Details & Preview" button.
- Click on this button to preview how the theme would look on your website.
- If you're satisfied with the preview, click on the "Install" button. WordPress will download and install the theme for you.
5. **Activate:**
   - Once the installation is complete, the "Install" button will change to "Activate." Click on the "Activate" button to apply the theme to your website.
   - Your website's appearance will immediately change to reflect the new theme.

Additional Notes:

- **Installing a Premium Theme:** If you've purchased a premium theme from a third-party marketplace, you won't find it in the WordPress Theme Directory. Instead, you'll need to upload the theme's ZIP file. To do this, click on the "Upload Theme" button at the top of the "Themes" page, choose the ZIP file, and click on "Install Now." After the installation is complete, click on "Activate."
- **Live Preview:** Before activating a new theme, you can use the "Live Preview" feature to see how it will look on your actual website without making any permanent changes. This allows you to experiment with different themes and see how they complement your content.

By following these simple steps, you can easily install and activate a new WordPress theme, giving your website a fresh look and feel in no time.

Customizing Your Theme

Once you've activated a WordPress theme, it's time to personalize it to match your brand and preferences. Most themes offer a range of customization options through two primary methods: the WordPress Customizer and the theme's own settings panel.

WordPress Customizer

The WordPress Customizer is a powerful built-in tool that allows you to make real-time changes to your website's appearance. You can preview your customizations live before publishing them, ensuring that your website looks exactly how you want it.

To access the Customizer:

1. Navigate to "Appearance" > "Customize" in your dashboard.
2. A new window or sidebar will open, displaying various customization options.
3. The available options will depend on your chosen theme, but typically include:
- **Site Identity:** Change your site title, tagline, and logo.
- **Colors:** Modify the colors used for your website's background, text, links, and other elements.
- **Menus:** Create and manage your website's navigation menus.
- **Widgets:** Add, remove, or rearrange widgets in your sidebar, footer, or other widget areas.
- **Homepage Settings:** Choose whether to display your latest posts or a static page on your homepage.
- **Additional CSS:** Add custom CSS code to further personalize your website's appearance.

Theme Settings Panel

Some themes also provide a separate settings panel, usually accessible from the "Appearance" menu. This panel may offer additional customization options not available in the Customizer, such as layout choices, typography settings, or pre-designed color schemes.

Customizing Your Theme: Step-by-Step

Here's a breakdown of how to customize some common aspects of your website using either the Customizer or the theme settings panel:

- **Site Title and Tagline:** In the Customizer (or theme settings panel), locate the "Site Identity" section. Here, you can change your site title, which usually appears in the header, and the tagline, which is a brief description of your website.
- **Logo:** Look for the "Logo" option and upload your custom logo image. You might also be able to adjust its size and placement.
- **Colors:** Explore the "Colors" section to modify the color scheme of your website. You can typically change the background color, text color, link color, and other color elements.
- **Fonts and Typography:** If your theme allows, you can choose from different font families and adjust font sizes, line heights, and letter spacing to create a unique typography style.
- **Layout:** Some themes offer layout options, such as full-width or boxed layouts, sidebar placement, and header styles. Experiment with these options to find a layout that suits your content and preferences.
- **Widgets:** In the "Widgets" section, you can add, remove, or rearrange widgets in different widget areas. Popular widgets include recent posts, search bars, social media feeds, and contact forms.

Previewing and Publishing Changes

Remember to preview your changes before publishing them. The Customizer and most theme settings panels allow you to see a live preview of your customizations as you make them. Once you're satisfied with your changes, click on the "Publish" button to make them live on your website.

By utilizing these customization options, you can personalize your WordPress theme to create a unique and visually appealing website that aligns with your brand and resonates with your audience.

Chapter Summary

In this chapter, we explored the world of WordPress themes, the visual foundation of your website's design. We defined a theme as a collection of files that determine your website's look and feel, controlling its layout, colors, fonts, and overall styling.

We discussed the importance of themes in enhancing user experience, establishing brand identity, improving accessibility, and optimizing for different devices. We also outlined the three main types of themes: free themes, premium themes, and custom themes, each with its own advantages and considerations.

We provided a list of key features to look for in a theme, including responsiveness, customization options, SEO friendliness, browser compatibility, page builder integration, performance, and security. We also offered guidance on choosing the right theme based on your website's purpose, design preferences, features, budget, and user reviews.

Finally, we provided step-by-step instructions on installing and activating a theme, whether it's a free theme from the WordPress Theme Directory or a premium theme from a third-party marketplace. We also explained how to customize your theme using the WordPress Customizer or the theme's settings panel, enabling you to personalize your website's appearance and create a unique online presence.

By understanding the significance of themes and mastering the process of selecting, installing, and customizing them, you are well on your way to building a visually stunning and functional WordPress website that reflects your brand and captivates your audience.

Plugins: Enhancing Your Website's Functionality

Outline

- What are WordPress Plugins?
- Why Plugins are Essential
- Types of WordPress Plugins
- How to Find and Choose Plugins
- Installing and Managing Plugins
- Essential Plugins for Every Website
- Recommended Plugins for Elementor
- Chapter Summary

What are WordPress Plugins?

WordPress plugins are like apps for your website. They are pre-built software modules that you can easily add to your WordPress site to enhance its functionality and customize it to your specific needs. Plugins are designed to seamlessly integrate with the WordPress core, extending its capabilities without requiring you to have any coding knowledge.

Think of plugins as building blocks that you can snap together to create a website that perfectly aligns with your vision. Whether you want to add a contact form, create an online store, optimize your website for search engines, or enhance its security, there's likely a plugin available to help you achieve your goals.

How Plugins Work

Plugins work by tapping into WordPress's vast collection of hooks and filters. These hooks and filters are essentially entry points that allow developers to modify or extend the default behavior of WordPress. By utilizing these hooks and filters, plugin developers can create add-ons that seamlessly integrate with your website's existing features and design.

The Power of Plugins

The true power of WordPress plugins lies in their versatility and abundance. With thousands of free and premium plugins available in the WordPress Plugin Directory and from third-party developers, you can find a plugin for almost any conceivable purpose.

Here are just a few examples of what plugins can do for your website:

- **Add Contact Forms:** Allow visitors to easily get in touch with you.
- **Create Online Stores:** Sell products or services online.
- **Optimize for SEO:** Improve your website's visibility in search engine results.
- **Enhance Security:** Protect your website from hackers and malware.
- **Add Social Media Integration:** Share your content on social media platforms.
- **Create Galleries and Sliders:** Showcase your images and videos in an attractive way.
- **Manage Events and Bookings:** Organize events and allow visitors to book appointments or reservations.
- **Create Membership Sites:** Restrict content to paying members.

The possibilities are truly endless. With plugins, you can transform your WordPress website from a simple blog into a powerful platform that caters to your specific needs and goals.

Why Plugins are Essential

Plugins are the lifeblood of your WordPress website, injecting it with a myriad of features and functionalities that go beyond the basic capabilities of the core software. They are the secret sauce that transforms your website from a simple online presence into a powerful, dynamic platform tailored to your specific needs and goals.

Essential Features at Your Fingertips

Plugins provide a vast array of essential features that every website needs. Here are a few examples:

- **Contact Forms:** Allow visitors to easily get in touch with you through a simple form, fostering communication and potential leads.
- **SEO Optimization:** Help your website rank higher in search engine results, driving organic traffic and increasing visibility.
- **Social Media Sharing:** Enable visitors to share your content on their social media networks, amplifying your reach and engagement.
- **Image Optimization:** Compress and optimize images to improve your website's loading speed, enhancing user experience and SEO.
- **Caching:** Store frequently accessed data to reduce server load and speed up your website's response time.

Beyond the Basics

Plugins not only provide essential features but also enhance various aspects of your website:

- **Performance:** Optimize your website's speed and performance with caching plugins, image optimization tools, and code minification.
- **Security:** Protect your website from hackers and malware with security plugins that offer firewalls, malware scanning, and brute-force attack protection.
- **Design:** Add visual flair and customization options with plugins that offer custom widgets, sliders, galleries, and other design elements.

Integration with Third-Party Services

Plugins enable seamless integration with various third-party services, expanding your website's capabilities even further. You can connect your site with:

- **Email Marketing Platforms:** Grow your email list and automate email campaigns.
- **Payment Gateways:** Accept online payments for products or services.
- **Social Media Networks:** Automatically share your content on social media and display social feeds on your website.
- **CRM Systems:** Manage customer relationships and track interactions.

Specialized Functionality

If you have a niche website or specific business needs, plugins offer specialized functionality to cater to your requirements. You can find plugins for:

- **E-commerce:** Create fully functional online stores with shopping carts, product catalogs, and payment processing.
- **Membership Sites:** Restrict content to paying members and create exclusive communities.
- **Learning Management Systems (LMS):** Build and deliver online courses and training programs.
- **Real Estate:** Showcase property listings and manage inquiries.
- **Restaurants:** Display menus, take online orders, and manage reservations.

With the right plugins, you can transform your WordPress website into a powerful tool that caters to your specific needs and goals.

Types of WordPress Plugins

The vast ecosystem of WordPress plugins can be categorized into three main types:

Free Plugins

Free plugins are readily available in the official WordPress Plugin Directory, a treasure trove of over 60,000 plugins. These plugins are developed and maintained by a community of developers and enthusiasts, offering a wide range of functionality, from basic features like contact forms and social media sharing buttons to more specialized tools for SEO, security, and performance optimization.

Free plugins are an excellent starting point for beginners and budget-conscious users. They provide a cost-effective way to add essential features and functionality to your website without breaking the bank. However, it's important to note that free plugins may have limitations in terms of features, customization options, and support.

Premium Plugins

Premium plugins are purchased from third-party developers and marketplaces. They often offer more advanced features, enhanced customization options, and dedicated customer support. Premium plugins are typically developed by professional teams who invest significant time and resources into creating high-quality products.

Some of the advantages of premium plugins include:

- **Advanced features:** Premium plugins often include more sophisticated features and functionality than their free counterparts.
- **Customization:** They usually offer more extensive customization options, allowing you to tailor the plugin to your specific needs and preferences.
- **Priority support:** Premium plugin developers typically provide dedicated customer support channels, ensuring you get timely assistance with any issues or questions.
- **Regular updates:** Premium plugins are regularly updated to ensure compatibility with the latest WordPress versions and to add new features or improvements.

The cost of premium plugins can vary depending on their complexity and functionality. However, investing in a premium plugin can be a worthwhile investment, especially if you need advanced features or require reliable support.

Custom Plugins

Custom plugins are developed specifically for a website to meet unique requirements that cannot be fulfilled by existing free or premium plugins. These plugins are typically created by professional WordPress developers who tailor the plugin's code and functionality to the specific needs of the website owner.

Custom plugins offer the highest level of flexibility and customization. They can be designed to integrate seamlessly with your website's existing design and functionality, providing a truly bespoke solution. However, custom plugins are the most expensive option, as they require the expertise of a developer and significant development time.

Choosing the right type of plugin depends on your budget, needs, and technical expertise. Free plugins are a great starting point, while premium plugins offer more advanced features and support. If you have unique requirements that cannot be met by existing plugins, a custom plugin might be the best solution, albeit a more expensive one.

How to Find and Choose Plugins

The WordPress Plugin Directory is a vast treasure trove of plugins, each designed to enhance your website in different ways. However, navigating this extensive collection can be overwhelming. Here's a guide to help you find and choose the right plugins for your website:

Finding Plugins

1. **WordPress Plugin Directory:** Start your search in the official WordPress Plugin Directory, accessible directly from your dashboard by going to "Plugins" > "Add New." This directory houses thousands of free plugins, categorized by functionality and popularity.
2. **Search Function:** Use the search bar at the top of the Plugin Directory to find plugins by name or keyword. Be specific in your search terms to narrow down the results. For example, instead of searching for "forms," you might search for "contact form" or "email subscription form."
3. **Browse Categories:** If you're not sure what you're looking for, browse through the different categories to explore various plugin types. Categories include "Popular," "Featured," "Recommended," and specific functions like "SEO," "Security," "Performance," and "E-commerce."
4. **External Resources:** In addition to the Plugin Directory, you can also find plugins on third-party marketplaces like CodeCanyon or directly from plugin developers' websites. However, be cautious when downloading plugins from external sources, as they may not be as thoroughly vetted as those in the official directory.

Choosing the Right Plugins

Once you've found some potential plugins, it's crucial to evaluate them carefully before installing them on your website. Here are some factors to consider:

1. **Reviews and Ratings:** Check the plugin's reviews and ratings to gauge its quality and user satisfaction. Look for plugins with positive reviews and high ratings.
2. **Active Installations:** The number of active installations indicates the plugin's popularity. A higher number of installations often suggests that the plugin is reliable and well-maintained.
3. **Last Updated:** Check when the plugin was last updated. Regularly updated plugins are more likely to be compatible with the latest WordPress version and have fewer bugs or security vulnerabilities.
4. **Compatibility:** Ensure the plugin is compatible with your WordPress version and any other plugins you have installed. Incompatibility can lead to conflicts and errors on your website.
5. **Features:** Carefully review the plugin's features and ensure they align with your specific needs and requirements.
6. **Support:** Check if the plugin developer offers support in case you encounter any issues or have questions. Premium plugins often come with dedicated support channels.

By following these guidelines, you can confidently choose plugins that will enhance your website's functionality, improve its performance, and provide a seamless experience for your visitors.

Installing and Managing Plugins

Once you've found the perfect plugin to enhance your WordPress website, installing and managing it is a breeze. Follow these step-by-step instructions:

Installing a Plugin

1. **Access the Plugins Section:**

- Log in to your WordPress dashboard.
- Navigate to the "Plugins" section in the main navigation menu.
- Click on "Add New."
2. **Search for the Plugin:**
    - Use the search bar at the top right to find the plugin by its name or keyword.
3. **Install the Plugin:**
    - Once you locate the desired plugin, click on the "Install Now" button next to its name.
    - WordPress will automatically download and install the plugin.
    - After a few moments, you should see a message indicating that the installation was successful.
4. **Activate the Plugin:**
    - After successful installation, the "Install Now" button will change to "Activate." Click on this button to activate the plugin and enable its features on your website.
    - Some plugins may require additional configuration after activation. Follow the on-screen instructions or refer to the plugin's documentation for guidance.

Activating and Deactivating Plugins

- **Activating:** To enable a plugin's functionality, navigate to "Plugins" > "Installed Plugins" and locate the plugin you want to activate. Click on the "Activate" link below its name.
- **Deactivating:** To temporarily disable a plugin without deleting it, go to "Plugins" > "Installed Plugins" and click on the "Deactivate" link below the plugin's name. This can be useful for troubleshooting compatibility issues or if you no longer need the plugin's features.

Updating Plugins

Regularly updating your plugins is crucial for maintaining your website's security, performance, and compatibility with the latest WordPress version.

1. **Check for Updates:**
    - WordPress automatically checks for plugin updates and displays a notification in the dashboard if updates are available.
    - You can also manually check for updates by going to "Plugins" > "Installed Plugins" and clicking on the "Update Available" link.
2. **Update:**
    - To update a plugin, simply click on the "Update Now" link below its name. WordPress will handle the update process automatically.
    - It's generally a good practice to back up your website before updating plugins, especially if you're making major updates.

By diligently installing, activating, deactivating, and updating plugins, you can ensure that your WordPress website remains functional, secure, and up-to-date with the latest features and improvements.

Essential Plugins for Every Website

While the world of WordPress plugins is vast and varied, there are a few essential plugins that every website should consider installing to enhance its functionality, security, and performance. These plugins provide core features that are crucial for a successful online presence.

Yoast SEO

Search Engine Optimization (SEO) is the practice of optimizing your website to rank higher in search engine results pages (SERPs). Yoast SEO is a powerful and user-friendly plugin that guides you through the process of optimizing your content, meta descriptions, and technical aspects of your website to improve its visibility and attract more organic traffic.

Wordfence Security

Website security is a top priority for every website owner. Wordfence Security is a comprehensive security plugin that protects your WordPress site from various threats, including malware, hackers, and brute-force attacks. It offers features like a web application firewall, malware scanner, login security, and security scans to identify and fix vulnerabilities.

UpdraftPlus

Regular backups of your website's data are essential to safeguard your content and configuration in case of unforeseen events like server failures, hacking attempts, or accidental deletions. UpdraftPlus is a popular backup plugin that allows you to create automatic backups of your entire WordPress site and store them in secure locations like cloud storage services or your own computer.

WPForms Lite

Contact forms are a crucial communication channel for your website visitors. WPForms Lite is a user-friendly drag-and-drop form builder that allows you to create various types of forms, including contact forms, survey forms, registration forms, and more. It's a simple yet effective way to engage with your audience and collect valuable information.

Smush

Image optimization is essential for improving your website's speed and performance. Large, unoptimized images can significantly slow down your site, leading to a poor user experience and lower search engine rankings. Smush is a popular image optimization plugin that automatically compresses and optimizes your images without sacrificing quality, resulting in faster loading times and a smoother user experience.

Recommended Plugins for Elementor

While Elementor itself offers a wide array of features for designing and building websites, its capabilities can be further expanded by using additional plugins. Here are some highly recommended plugins that seamlessly integrate with Elementor and elevate your website building experience:

Essential Addons for Elementor

This popular freemium plugin adds a rich collection of over 80+ creative elements and extensions to your Elementor toolkit. From advanced parallax effects and post carousels to interactive flip boxes and animated headlines, Essential Addons empowers you to create visually stunning and engaging web pages.

Premium Addons for Elementor

If you're looking for even more advanced features and creative elements, Premium Addons for Elementor is a top-notch choice. This premium plugin boasts an extensive library of over 60+ unique widgets and extensions, including cross-site copy-paste, section particles, advanced maps, and more. With Premium Addons, you can elevate your website's design to the next level and craft truly captivating user experiences.

Elementor Pro

For the most comprehensive and powerful Elementor experience, upgrading to Elementor Pro is a worthwhile investment. This premium version unlocks a wealth of additional features, including:

- **Theme Builder:** Design and customize every aspect of your website, including headers, footers, single post/page templates, archive pages, and more.
- **Popup Builder:** Create engaging popups to capture leads, promote offers, or deliver targeted messages to your visitors.
- **WooCommerce Builder:** Design and build your online store with Elementor's intuitive drag-and-drop interface.
- **Global Widgets:** Create custom widgets that can be reused across your entire website.
- **Custom Fonts:** Upload and use your own fonts to match your brand identity.

Elementor Pro is a game-changer for those who want to unleash the full potential of Elementor and create pixel-perfect websites with ease.

Crocoblock

Crocoblock is not a single plugin but a suite of plugins designed to supercharge your Elementor website building experience. It includes a variety of plugins for dynamic content, custom post types, interactive elements, and more. With Crocoblock, you can build complex websites with advanced functionality without writing any code.

Whether you're a beginner or an experienced web developer, these recommended plugins for Elementor can significantly enhance your creativity and productivity, allowing you to craft stunning, functional, and user-friendly websites that leave a lasting impression.

Chapter Summary

In this chapter, we explored the world of WordPress plugins and their pivotal role in enhancing your website's functionality. We defined plugins as software extensions that add new features and capabilities to your WordPress site without requiring any coding knowledge.

We discussed the importance of plugins in providing essential features, enhancing your website's performance, security, and design, integrating with third-party services, and offering specialized functionality for various niches.

We also provided an overview of the different types of WordPress plugins available: free plugins, premium plugins, and custom plugins, each catering to different needs and budgets.

Additionally, we outlined a step-by-step guide on how to find, install, activate, deactivate, and update plugins through the WordPress dashboard. We emphasized the importance of choosing plugins carefully, checking compatibility, reading reviews, and keeping them updated.

We also recommended several essential plugins that every WordPress website should consider, including Yoast SEO for search engine optimization, Wordfence Security for protection against threats, UpdraftPlus for backups, WPForms Lite for creating contact forms, and Smush for image optimization.

Furthermore, we provided a list of recommended plugins that work seamlessly with Elementor, such as Essential Addons for Elementor, Premium Addons for Elementor, Elementor Pro, and Crocoblock, which can further enhance your website building experience.

By understanding the power and versatility of plugins, you can unlock the full potential of WordPress and create a website that is not only visually appealing but also functional, secure, and tailored to your specific needs.

7 Core Settings and Configurations

Outline

- General Settings
- Writing Settings
- Reading Settings
- Discussion Settings
- Media Settings
- Permalinks Settings
- Chapter Summary

General Settings

The General Settings section in your WordPress dashboard serves as the control center for your website's fundamental information. It allows you to define your site's identity, contact details, language, timezone, and other essential settings. Let's delve into each of these settings:

Site Title: This is the name of your website, which is prominently displayed in the browser tab and often appears in search engine results. To set or change your site title, simply enter the desired name in the "Site Title" field. Make sure it's concise, descriptive, and relevant to your website's content.

Tagline: A tagline is a short phrase that accompanies your site title, providing a brief description or slogan for your website. It can be a catchy phrase that encapsulates your brand's essence or a concise summary of what your website offers. You can add or edit your tagline in the "Tagline" field.

WordPress Address (URL): This setting defines the address where your core WordPress files are installed. In most cases, you won't need to change this unless you're moving your WordPress installation to a different directory or server.

Site Address (URL): This is the URL that visitors use to access your website. It should typically be the same as your domain name (e.g., "[invalid URL removed]"). If you need to change your website's address, you can modify it here.

Administration Email Address: This is the email address where WordPress will send important notifications, such as new user registrations, password reset requests, and plugin updates. Make sure to use an email address that you regularly check.

Membership: This setting allows you to control whether visitors can register as users on your website. If you're running a blog or a community-driven site, you might want to enable this option. However, if you only want to publish content without allowing user registrations, you can disable it.

New User Default Role: If you allow user registrations, you can choose the default role assigned to new users. The available roles typically include Subscriber, Contributor, Author, Editor, and Administrator, each with varying levels of access and capabilities.

Site Language: WordPress supports multiple languages. You can choose the default language for your website's interface and content from the dropdown menu. This setting can be overridden by multilingual plugins if you want to create a multilingual website.

Timezone: Setting the correct timezone is crucial for ensuring accurate timestamps on your posts, comments, and other time-sensitive content. Select your website's geographical location from the dropdown menu to automatically set the appropriate timezone.

Date Format: WordPress offers various date formats to choose from. You can select the format that best suits your preferences and the conventions of your target audience.

Time Format: Similar to date formats, you can choose how times are displayed on your website, such as 12-hour or 24-hour format.

Writing Settings

The Writing Settings section in your WordPress dashboard allows you to define default settings that streamline the process of creating and publishing blog posts. These settings help you maintain consistency and save time when drafting new content.

Default Post Category:

This setting allows you to choose a default category for new posts. Categories are essential for organizing your blog posts into broader topics, making it easier for visitors to navigate your content. By selecting a default category, you ensure that all new posts are automatically assigned to that category unless you manually choose a different one. This saves you the step of assigning a category each time you create a new post.

To set the default post category, simply select the desired category from the dropdown menu in the "Default Post Category" field.

Default Post Format:

WordPress offers various post formats to cater to different types of content:

- **Standard:** The default format for typical blog posts with text and images.
- **Aside:** Short, note-like posts, often used for quick thoughts or updates.
- **Gallery:** A format designed for showcasing a collection of images.
- **Link:** A format for sharing links to external content with a brief introduction.
- **Image:** A format for posts that primarily consist of a single image.
- **Quote:** A format for highlighting a quote or excerpt.
- **Status:** A format for sharing short status updates, similar to social media posts.
- **Video:** A format for embedding videos from platforms like YouTube or Vimeo.
- **Audio:** A format for embedding audio files, such as podcasts or music.
- **Chat:** A format for displaying a conversation or dialogue.

You can choose the default post format from the dropdown menu. However, you can always change the format for individual posts later when creating or editing them.

Post via email:

This setting allows you to publish posts to your blog via email. You'll need to configure a secret email address provided by WordPress and send your blog posts to that address. This feature is useful for those who prefer writing in their email client or want to publish posts remotely.

To set up "Post via email," you'll need to configure your email settings and follow the instructions provided by WordPress. Keep in mind that this feature may have security implications, so it's essential to use a strong password for your email account and take precautions to prevent unauthorized access.

Update Services:

Whenever you publish a new post, WordPress can automatically notify various update services about your new content. These services help distribute your content to other websites and platforms, potentially increasing your reach.

You can manage the list of update services in the "Update Services" field. Simply enter the URLs of the services you want to notify, separated by commas.

Reading Settings

The Reading Settings section in your WordPress dashboard allows you to customize how your website's homepage and blog posts are presented to your visitors. These settings influence how your content is organized and displayed, affecting both user experience and how search engines index your site.

Your homepage displays:

This setting determines what visitors see when they first land on your website's homepage. You have two primary options:

- **Your latest posts:** This is the default setting for most blogs. It means your homepage will dynamically display your most recent blog posts in reverse chronological order.
- **A static page:** This option allows you to select a specific page to serve as your homepage. This is often used for business websites or sites that prioritize showcasing specific information rather than a blog feed. You can choose any page you've created as your static homepage and optionally select a different page to display your blog posts (if you still want to maintain a blog section).

Blog pages show at most:

This setting controls the maximum number of posts displayed per page on your blog's main page and archive pages (e.g., category archives, tag archives, date archives). You can choose a number that suits your preferences and content volume. Displaying fewer posts per page can make your site load faster and improve the user experience, especially on slower connections.

Syndication feeds show the most recent:

RSS (Really Simple Syndication) feeds allow users to subscribe to your blog and receive updates whenever you publish new content. This setting determines the number of your most recent posts that are included in your RSS feeds.

For each article in a feed, show:

This setting controls whether the full text or a summary of your posts is displayed in RSS feeds. Choosing "Summary" can help reduce bandwidth usage and load times for subscribers, while "Full text" provides readers with the complete content in their feed reader.

Search Engine Visibility:

This option allows you to discourage search engines from indexing your site. It's generally not recommended to check this box unless you have a specific reason, such as a website under development or a private site that you don't want to be accessible through search engines.

By carefully adjusting these reading settings, you can tailor how your WordPress website presents its content to visitors and search engines, ensuring an optimal experience for everyone.

Discussion Settings

The Discussion Settings section in your WordPress dashboard is your control hub for managing comments and fostering discussions on your website. These settings allow you to shape the way visitors interact with your content and each other.

Default Article Settings

This section lets you control whether comments and pingbacks/trackbacks are allowed on new articles by default.

- **Other comment settings:** This area covers a range of options to refine your comments section:
  - **Comment author must fill out name and email:** Require commenters to provide their name and email address before posting.
  - **Users must be registered and logged in to comment:** Restrict commenting to registered users only.
  - **Automatically close comments on articles older than X days:** Set a time limit for comments on older posts.
  - **Enable threaded (nested) comments X levels deep:** Allow replies to comments to be nested (threaded) up to a specified number of levels.
  - **Break comments into pages with X top level comments per page and the X newest comments at the top of each page:** Divide long comment threads into multiple pages.
  - **Email me whenever:** Choose to receive email notifications for new comments, comments awaiting moderation, or replies to your comments.

Before a comment appears

Here, you decide how comments are handled before they become visible on your website:

- **Comment must be manually approved:** All comments will be held in moderation until you review and approve them.
- **Comment author must have a previously approved comment:** Allow comments from users who have had at least one comment approved in the past.

Comment Moderation

This setting allows you to automatically hold comments for moderation based on specific criteria:

- **Hold a comment in the queue if it contains X or more links:** Flag comments with excessive links as potentially spam.
- **When a comment contains any of these words in its content, name, URL, email, or IP, it will be held in the moderation queue:** Specify a list of keywords that trigger moderation.

Comment Blacklist

Create a list of words, IP addresses, or email addresses that, if found in a comment, will automatically mark it as spam. This helps filter out unwanted or abusive comments.

Avatars

Decide whether to display avatars (profile pictures) for commenters. You can choose from various avatar providers or allow users to upload their own.

By adjusting these discussion settings, you can create a comment environment that fosters constructive conversation, filters out spam, and aligns with your website's community guidelines.

Media Settings

The Media Settings section in your WordPress dashboard allows you to control how images are handled and organized within your website. These settings are particularly important for optimizing your site's performance and managing your media library efficiently.

Image Sizes

WordPress automatically generates different sizes of images when you upload them to your Media Library. These sizes include:

- Thumbnail: A smaller version of the image typically used in galleries or image previews.
- Medium: A mid-sized version of the image, often used within the content of posts or pages.
- Large: The original or a larger version of the image, used for full-size display.

You can customize the dimensions (width and height) for each of these image sizes. Setting appropriate dimensions helps optimize image loading times and ensures that images are displayed correctly across different devices and screen sizes. It's generally recommended to avoid excessively large image dimensions, as this can slow down your website.

To modify image sizes:

1. Go to "Settings" > "Media" in your WordPress dashboard.
2. Enter your desired dimensions (in pixels) for each image size: Thumbnail, Medium, and Large.
3. Click the "Save Changes" button to apply your settings.

Uploading Files

This setting controls how WordPress organizes uploaded files within your media library.

- **Organize my uploads into month- and year-based folders:** When this option is checked, WordPress will create folders based on the month and year of the upload. For example, images uploaded in July 2024 would be stored in a folder named "/wp-content/uploads/2024/07/".
- **Uncheck this option to keep all uploads in the same folder:** If you prefer to keep all your uploaded files in the same folder, you can uncheck this option.

Organizing uploads into folders can be beneficial for managing a large media library, as it creates a hierarchical structure and makes it easier to locate specific files. However, if you have a smaller number of uploads, keeping them all in the same folder might be simpler.

Permalinks Settings

Permalinks are the permanent URLs for your individual blog posts and pages. They are the web addresses that people use to access and share your content. Choosing the right permalink structure is crucial for both search engine optimization (SEO) and user-friendliness.

Why Permalinks Matter for SEO

Permalinks play a significant role in how search engines understand and index your content. A well-structured permalink can:

- **Include Keywords:** Incorporating relevant keywords in your permalink can signal to search engines what your content is about, potentially improving your search rankings for those keywords.
- **Improve Readability:** A clear and concise permalink that reflects the content of your post or page makes it easier for users and search engines to understand what the page is about.
- **Enhance Click-Through Rates:** Descriptive permalinks can entice users to click on your link in search results, as they provide a preview of the content they can expect to find.

Common Permalink Structures

WordPress offers several permalink structures to choose from:

- **Plain:** The default structure, which includes a number in the URL (e.g., `http://www.yourdomain.com/?p=123`). This structure is not SEO-friendly or user-friendly.

- **Day and name:** Includes the date and post name in the URL (e.g., `http://www.yourdomain.com/2024/07/07/sample-post/`). This structure can be useful for news websites or blogs that publish frequently.
- **Month and name:** Includes the month and post name in the URL (e.g., `http://www.yourdomain.com/2024/07/sample-post/`). This is a good option for blogs with a moderate posting frequency.
- **Post name:** The most SEO-friendly and user-friendly structure, as it only includes the post name in the URL (e.g., `http://www.yourdomain.com/sample-post/`). This structure is recommended for most websites.

Choosing the Right Permalink Structure

For most websites, the "Post name" permalink structure is the best choice. It's concise, descriptive, and includes relevant keywords. However, if you run a news website or a blog that publishes multiple posts per day, you might consider using the "Day and name" structure.

To choose a permalink structure:

1. Go to "Settings" > "Permalinks" in your WordPress dashboard.
2. Select the desired permalink structure from the available options.
3. Click the "Save Changes" button to apply your settings.

Customizing Permalinks

If you choose the "Post name" structure, you can further customize your permalinks by editing the post or page slug. The slug is the part of the URL that identifies the specific post or page. For example, in the URL `http://www.yourdomain.com/sample-post/`, the slug is "sample-post."

You can edit the slug when creating or editing a post or page. Make sure to use a slug that is descriptive and relevant to the content of the post or page.

By carefully choosing and customizing your permalink structure, you can enhance your website's SEO, improve its user-friendliness, and make it easier for visitors to find and share your content.

Chapter Summary

This chapter delved into the core settings and configurations that underpin your WordPress website. We explored the General Settings section, where you can define essential details about your site, such as its title, tagline, addresses, email, membership options, language, timezone, and date/time formats.

Next, we examined the Writing Settings, which allow you to streamline your content creation process by setting default categories, formats, and even enabling post-by-email functionality.

We then turned our attention to Reading Settings, where you can determine how your homepage and blog posts are presented to visitors, including the choice between displaying your latest posts or a static page, controlling the number of posts per page, and managing your RSS feeds.

The Discussion Settings section was covered in detail, explaining how to manage comments and discussions on your website. This includes setting default article settings, configuring comment moderation rules, and managing avatars.

We also discussed the Media Settings, which allow you to control image sizes and the organization of uploaded files in your media library. Finally, we explored the importance of permalinks, the permanent URLs for your posts and pages. We explained how permalink structure affects SEO and user-friendliness and provided guidance on choosing an optimal structure.

By mastering these core settings and configurations, you can tailor your WordPress website to your specific needs and preferences, ensuring it functions optimally and delivers a seamless experience for your visitors.

Section II:
Mastering Elementor Page Builder

Introduction to Elementor: The Power of Drag-and-Drop

Outline

- What is Elementor?
- Why Use Elementor?
- Key Features of Elementor
- Understanding the Drag-and-Drop Interface
- Elementor vs. Other Page Builders
- Installing and Activating Elementor
- Chapter Summary

What is Elementor?

Elementor is a revolutionary WordPress page builder plugin that has taken the web design world by storm. It empowers users of all skill levels, from beginners to seasoned professionals, to create stunning, professional-looking websites without writing a single line of code.

Think of Elementor as your visual web design toolbox. It provides a user-friendly, drag-and-drop interface that allows you to effortlessly arrange elements on your web pages, such as text, images, videos, buttons, and more. It eliminates the need to delve into complex HTML, CSS, or PHP code, making web design accessible to everyone.

Elementor's intuitive approach to web design has made it immensely popular, boasting over 5 million active installations and a thriving community of users and developers. Its extensive library of pre-designed templates, blocks, and widgets further simplifies the design process, enabling you to create visually appealing and functional websites with ease.

Whether you're a blogger, entrepreneur, or business owner, Elementor gives you the tools to bring your website vision to life. It's a versatile platform that can be used to build a wide range of websites, from simple blogs and portfolios to complex e-commerce stores and corporate sites. With Elementor, you can create a unique and memorable online presence that captures your brand's essence and leaves a lasting impression on your visitors.

Why Use Elementor?

Elementor has emerged as a leading choice for WordPress website builders, and for good reason. Its array of benefits makes it a compelling option for both beginners and experienced web designers alike.

Ease of Use

Elementor's intuitive drag-and-drop interface revolutionizes web design, making it accessible to users with little to no technical expertise. You can easily add, arrange, and customize elements on your pages without writing a single line of code. This user-friendly approach empowers you to take control of your website's design and create a unique online presence that reflects your vision.

Customization Options

Elementor provides an extensive library of design elements, widgets, and templates, offering endless possibilities for customizing your website. You can choose from various pre-designed blocks and sections to quickly build your pages, or you can start from scratch and craft your own unique layouts. The flexibility to mix and match elements allows you to create a website that perfectly aligns with your brand identity and aesthetic preferences.

Flexibility

Elementor's flexibility extends beyond individual pages. With the Theme Builder feature (available in Elementor Pro), you can customize every aspect of your website's design, including headers, footers, single post/page templates, archive pages, and more. This gives you complete control over your website's visual presentation, allowing you to create a cohesive and seamless user experience.

Responsive Design

In today's mobile-first world, responsive design is paramount. Elementor automatically generates responsive designs, ensuring that your website looks and functions flawlessly across all devices, from desktops and laptops to tablets and smartphones. This adaptability enhances the user experience and improves your website's search engine optimization (SEO) rankings.

Performance

Elementor is built with performance in mind. Its lightweight code and efficient rendering ensure that your website loads quickly, providing a smooth browsing experience for your visitors. Fast loading times are not only crucial for user satisfaction but also contribute to better SEO performance, as search engines prioritize websites that load quickly.

Community and Support

Elementor boasts a large and active community of users and developers who are passionate about web design. This community offers a wealth of resources, including tutorials, forums, and support channels, where you can find answers to your questions, learn new techniques, and connect with fellow Elementor users. The active community ensures that you're never alone on your Elementor journey and have access to the support you need to succeed.

Key Features of Elementor

Elementor's robust feature set is a major reason for its popularity among WordPress users. Let's take a closer look at some of its key features:

Drag-and-Drop Editor

The drag-and-drop editor is the heart of Elementor. It allows you to effortlessly add, arrange, and customize elements on your pages with a simple click and drag. You can select elements from the left-hand panel and drop them onto your page, then reposition and resize them as needed. This intuitive interface eliminates the need for coding, making web design accessible to everyone.

Live Preview

With Elementor's live preview feature, you can see the changes you make in real-time as you edit your pages. This allows you to visualize your design and make adjustments on the fly, ensuring that your website looks exactly how you want it before publishing.

Widgets

Widgets are the building blocks of your Elementor pages. They represent different content elements, such as headings, text paragraphs, images, buttons, icons, forms, and more. Elementor provides a wide array of widgets, each with its own customization options, giving you the flexibility to create unique and engaging layouts.

Templates

Elementor's template library is a treasure trove of pre-designed page layouts that you can use as a starting point for your own designs. These templates cover various purposes, from landing pages and about us pages to portfolio pages and contact forms. You can easily import a template and then customize it to match your brand and content.

Theme Builder (Elementor Pro)

If you have Elementor Pro, you unlock the powerful Theme Builder feature. This allows you to design and customize every aspect of your website's theme, including the header, footer, single post/page templates, archive pages, 404 pages, and more. With Theme Builder, you can create a truly unique and cohesive design for your entire website.

Popup Builder (Elementor Pro)

Another exclusive feature of Elementor Pro is the Popup Builder. This tool enables you to create attention-grabbing popups that can be triggered by various actions, such as clicking a button, scrolling down the page, or exiting the site. You can use popups to capture leads, promote offers, display announcements, or deliver targeted messages to your visitors.

WooCommerce Builder (Elementor Pro)

If you plan to create an online store with WooCommerce, Elementor Pro's WooCommerce Builder comes to the rescue. It allows you to design custom product pages, checkout pages, and other WooCommerce elements using Elementor's intuitive drag-and-drop interface. You can create a unique shopping experience for your customers and showcase your products in a visually appealing way.

Understanding the Drag-and-Drop Interface

The cornerstone of Elementor's user-friendliness lies in its intuitive drag-and-drop interface. This approach revolutionizes web design by allowing you to create and customize your website's layout simply by dragging elements from a panel and dropping them onto your page. No coding required!

Imagine building with virtual Lego blocks. You pick the pieces you want (headings, text, images, buttons) from the Elements Panel, drag them onto the page, and arrange them to your liking. You can then customize each element's appearance, content, and behavior through the Settings Panel.

Let's break down the main components of Elementor's interface:

Elements Panel: This panel, usually located on the left side of the screen, houses a vast collection of widgets (content elements) organized into categories. You can browse or search for the specific widget you need and simply drag it onto your page.

Content Area: This is the canvas where you build your page. It's a blank slate where you drop and arrange the elements you choose from the Elements Panel. You can resize and reposition elements with ease, creating the desired layout for your page.

Navigator: Located on the right side of the screen, the Navigator provides a hierarchical view of your page's structure. It allows you to quickly jump between different sections and widgets on your page, making it easier to edit and manage complex layouts.

Settings Panel: Each widget you add to your page comes with a Settings Panel. This panel, accessible by clicking on the widget, offers a range of customization options for that specific element. You can modify its content, style, layout, and advanced settings.

In Action

Here's a simplified example of how you might use the drag-and-drop interface to create a section on your homepage:

1. **Drag and Drop a Section Widget:** Start by dragging a "Section" widget from the Elements Panel onto the Content Area.
2. **Add a Heading Widget:** Next, drag a "Heading" widget into the Section.
3. **Enter Your Heading Text:** In the Settings Panel for the Heading widget, enter the text you want to display.
4. **Style Your Heading:** Customize the heading's font, size, color, and alignment using the Style tab in the Settings Panel.
5. **Add More Elements:** Continue adding and customizing other widgets, such as text, images, or buttons, to complete the section.

By repeating this process, you can build complex and visually appealing page layouts without needing any coding knowledge. The drag-and-drop interface empowers you to experiment, iterate, and create a website that truly reflects your vision.

Elementor vs. Other Page Builders

While Elementor is a leading contender in the realm of WordPress page builders, it's not the only option available. Several other popular page builders, like Beaver Builder, Divi, and WPBakery Page Builder, offer their own unique features and strengths. Let's briefly compare Elementor with these competitors:

Elementor

Strengths:

- **Ease of Use:** Elementor's intuitive drag-and-drop interface is widely praised for its user-friendliness, making it a great choice for beginners and non-technical users.
- **Customization:** Elementor offers a vast array of widgets, templates, and design options, allowing for extensive customization and creative freedom.
- **Theme Builder:** The Theme Builder feature (in Elementor Pro) empowers you to design custom headers, footers, and other theme elements, providing greater control over your website's overall look and feel.
- **Community and Support:** Elementor boasts a large and active community, offering abundant resources, tutorials, and support forums.

Weaknesses:

- **Performance:** While Elementor has made strides in improving performance, some users still find it to be slightly heavier than other page builders, potentially impacting website loading speed.

- **Learning Curve:** While the basic interface is user-friendly, mastering all of Elementor's advanced features and functionalities may require some time and effort.

Beaver Builder

Strengths:

- **Clean Code and Performance:** Beaver Builder is known for its clean code and lightweight design, resulting in faster loading times and better overall website performance.
- **User-Friendly Interface:** While not as visually intuitive as Elementor, Beaver Builder's interface is still relatively easy to use and understand.
- **Module System:** Beaver Builder's module system allows for greater flexibility and reusability of design elements.

Weaknesses:

- **Limited Design Options:** Compared to Elementor, Beaver Builder has a smaller selection of pre-designed templates and modules, potentially limiting your creative options.
- **Pricing:** Beaver Builder is a premium plugin with various pricing tiers, which might not be suitable for budget-conscious users.

Divi

Strengths:

- **Visual Builder:** Divi's visual builder provides a unique front-end editing experience, allowing you to see your changes in real time without switching between the backend and front end.
- **Design Flexibility:** Divi offers a wide range of design options and customization features, including custom CSS control and global elements.
- **All-Inclusive Package:** Divi comes bundled with various other tools and plugins from Elegant Themes, such as Bloom (email opt-in forms) and Monarch (social media sharing).

Weaknesses:

- **Learning Curve:** Divi's unique visual builder can have a steeper learning curve compared to the more traditional drag-and-drop interfaces of Elementor and Beaver Builder.
- **Code Bloat:** Some users have reported that Divi can generate excessive code, potentially impacting website performance.

WPBakery Page Builder

Strengths:

- **Backend and Front-End Editors:** WPBakery Page Builder offers both backend and front-end editing options, giving you flexibility in how you design your pages.
- **Large Template Library:** WPBakery Page Builder boasts a vast library of pre-designed templates and elements, providing ample design inspiration.
- **Compatibility:** WPBakery Page Builder is compatible with a wide range of themes and plugins, making it a versatile choice for many WordPress websites.

Weaknesses:

- **User Interface:** WPBakery Page Builder's interface is considered less intuitive compared to Elementor and Beaver Builder, which can make it more challenging for beginners.
- **Performance:** Some users have reported that WPBakery Page Builder can negatively impact website performance due to its code structure.

Choosing the Right Page Builder

The best page builder for you ultimately depends on your individual needs, preferences, and budget. If you prioritize ease of use and extensive customization options, Elementor might be the ideal choice. If performance is your top concern, Beaver Builder could be a better fit. If you prefer a front-end visual builder and want an all-inclusive package of tools, Divi might be the way to go. And if you need a versatile page builder with a large template library, WPBakery Page Builder could be a viable option.

Installing and Activating Elementor

Now that you've explored the power and benefits of Elementor, let's get it installed and activated on your WordPress website. Follow these simple steps:

1. **Access the Plugins Section:**
    - Log in to your WordPress dashboard.
    - Navigate to the "Plugins" section in the main navigation menu on the left-hand side.
    - Click on "Add New."
2. **Search for Elementor:**
    - In the search bar at the top right of the page, type "Elementor" and press Enter.
    - The Elementor Page Builder plugin should appear as the first result.
3. **Install Elementor:**
    - Click on the "Install Now" button next to the Elementor Page Builder plugin.
    - WordPress will automatically download and install the plugin.
    - Once the installation is complete, the "Install Now" button will be replaced with an "Activate" button.
4. **Activate Elementor:**
    - Click on the "Activate" button to enable Elementor on your website.
    - You will be redirected to the Elementor welcome screen, where you can start exploring its features and begin building your pages.

Congratulations! You've successfully installed and activated the free version of Elementor on your WordPress website. You're now ready to embark on your journey to create stunning, professional-looking web pages with ease. In the following chapters, we'll dive deeper into Elementor's interface, widgets, templates, and other powerful features to help you unleash your creativity and build your dream website.

Chapter Summary

This chapter introduced you to Elementor, a revolutionary WordPress page builder plugin that empowers you to create visually stunning websites without any coding knowledge. We explored what Elementor is and why it has become a popular choice among WordPress users due to its intuitive drag-and-drop interface, extensive customization options, and flexibility.

We highlighted the key features of Elementor, including its drag-and-drop editor, live preview, widgets, templates, Theme Builder (available in Elementor Pro), Popup Builder (available in Elementor Pro), and WooCommerce Builder (available in Elementor Pro). These features collectively enable you to design and build unique, engaging, and functional websites.

We also provided an overview of Elementor's drag-and-drop interface, explaining the main components like the Elements Panel, Content Area, Navigator, and Settings Panel, and how they work together to simplify the design process.

Additionally, we briefly compared Elementor with other popular WordPress page builders, highlighting its strengths and weaknesses in comparison to Beaver Builder, Divi, and WPBakery Page Builder. This comparison can help you make an informed decision about which page builder best suits your needs and preferences.

Finally, we provided a step-by-step guide on installing and activating the free version of Elementor, setting the stage for you to start exploring its powerful features and unleashing your creativity in the next chapters.

With Elementor at your disposal, you now have the tools to transform your WordPress website into a visually stunning masterpiece that captivates your audience and drives results.

9 The Elementor Interface: A Tour of the Essentials

Outline

- Launching the Elementor Editor
- The Elementor Panel
- The Widget Panel
- The Content Area
- The Navigator Panel
- The Settings Panel
- Responsive Mode
- Chapter Summary

Launching the Elementor Editor

Accessing the Elementor editor is a simple process that integrates seamlessly with your WordPress workflow. Here's how to get started:

1. **Navigate to Your Content:**
    - Go to either the "Pages" or "Posts" section in your WordPress dashboard.
    - This depends on whether you want to edit a static page (like your About page) or a blog post.
2. **Select the Page or Post:**
    - From the list of pages or posts, locate the one you want to edit with Elementor.
    - You can use the search bar to find it quickly if you have a lot of content.
3. **Click "Edit with Elementor":**
    - Hover over the title of the page or post you want to edit.
    - You'll see several options, including "Edit," "Quick Edit," "Trash," and "View."
    - Click on the blue button labeled "Edit with Elementor."

Alternatively, if you're already viewing the page or post on the front end of your website, you can click on the "Edit with Elementor" button in the WordPress toolbar at the top of the screen.

Once you click the "Edit with Elementor" button, the Elementor editor will launch, replacing the default WordPress editor. You'll then be presented with Elementor's intuitive drag-and-drop interface, where you can start building and customizing your page.

The Elementor Panel

The Elementor panel is the heart of the Elementor editor. It's your command center, providing you with all the tools and features you need to design and customize your web pages. Located on the left-hand side of the screen, the panel is divided into two main sections:

1. **Widget Panel:** This is where you'll find all the building blocks for your web pages, known as widgets. These widgets represent various content elements like headings, text, images, buttons, icons, forms, and more. You can easily drag and drop these widgets onto your page to create your desired layout. The Widget Panel is organized into categories, making it easy to find the specific widget you need.
2. **Navigator Panel:** This panel offers a hierarchical view of your page's structure. It displays all the sections, columns, and widgets on your page in a tree-like format. You can use the Navigator Panel to quickly navigate to any element on your page, making it easier to edit and manage complex

layouts. You can also rearrange elements within the Navigator Panel by simply dragging and dropping them.

In addition to these two main sections, the Elementor panel also includes a few other essential elements:

- **Top Bar:** Located at the top of the panel, the Top Bar contains buttons for saving your work, previewing your page, accessing Elementor settings, and more.
- **Global Settings:** This section allows you to control global settings for your entire website, such as colors, fonts, and typography.
- **Finder:** The Finder is a search bar that allows you to quickly locate specific widgets or settings within the Elementor panel.

The Elementor panel is designed to be intuitive and user-friendly, allowing you to focus on your creative vision rather than technical details. As you become more familiar with its features, you'll discover its power and versatility for creating stunning and functional web pages.

The Widget Panel

The Widget Panel in Elementor is your treasure trove of creative building blocks. It's where you'll find all the elements you need to craft your web pages, from simple text and images to more complex layouts and interactive features.

Widget Categories

The widgets in the Widget Panel are organized into several categories for easy access:

1. **Basic:** This category contains the fundamental widgets you'll use most often, such as Heading, Text Editor, Image, Video, Button, and Icon. These widgets are essential for creating the basic structure and content of your pages.
2. **Pro:** If you have Elementor Pro, you'll also have access to a collection of premium widgets. These widgets offer advanced features and functionality, such as Posts, Portfolio, Slides, Forms, and Animated Headlines. They can add a touch of sophistication and interactivity to your web pages.
3. **General:** The General category includes widgets that are useful for various purposes, such as Spacer, Divider, Google Maps, and Icon List. These widgets help you organize your content, add visual elements, and integrate with external services.
4. **Site:** This category contains widgets related to your website's structure and navigation, such as Site Logo, Site Title, Page Title, and Menu Anchor.

Examples of Widgets

Here are a few examples of widgets you'll find in the Widget Panel:

- **Heading:** Used for adding headings and titles to your pages.
- **Text Editor:** Used for adding and formatting text content.
- **Image:** Used for inserting images into your pages.
- **Video:** Used for embedding videos from YouTube, Vimeo, or other sources.
- **Button:** Used for creating clickable buttons with custom links.
- **Icon:** Used for adding icons to your pages for visual appeal and clarity.
- **Spacer:** Used for adding blank space between elements to improve layout and readability.
- **Divider:** Used for creating visual separation between sections of your page.
- **Google Maps:** Used for embedding Google Maps into your pages.
- **Icon List:** Used for creating lists with icons next to each item.

Exploring the Widget Panel

Take some time to explore the Widget Panel and familiarize yourself with the different widgets available. As you drag and drop widgets onto your page, you'll see how they interact with each other and how you can customize them to achieve your desired design.

The Content Area

The Content Area in Elementor is your blank canvas, the space where your website's visual masterpiece comes to life. It's the central area of the Elementor editor where you arrange and design the various elements that make up your page.

Think of the Content Area as a virtual whiteboard. You can drag and drop widgets (your building blocks) from the Widget Panel onto this canvas, positioning them precisely where you want them to appear. As you add more widgets, your page starts to take shape, transforming from a blank slate into a visually appealing and informative layout.

Drag-and-Drop Functionality

The drag-and-drop functionality is what makes Elementor so intuitive and user-friendly. Simply click on a widget in the Widget Panel, hold down your mouse button, and drag it over to the Content Area. Release the mouse button to drop the widget into place. You can then easily resize and reposition the widget using the handles that appear around it.

This drag-and-drop system eliminates the need for complex coding, allowing you to focus on your creative vision rather than technical details. You can experiment with different layouts, try out various combinations of widgets, and instantly see the results in the live preview.

Building Your Page Layout

The Content Area is not just a static canvas; it's designed to be flexible and adaptable to your needs. You can divide the Content Area into sections and columns to create more complex layouts. Sections are horizontal containers that can hold multiple columns, while columns are vertical containers that hold individual widgets.

By combining sections, columns, and widgets, you can create a wide range of layouts, from simple single-column designs to more intricate multi-column structures. You can also add background images or colors to sections, adjust the padding and margins between elements, and apply other styling options to create a visually appealing and user-friendly page layout.

Real-Time Preview

As you drag and drop widgets and build your page layout, you'll see your changes reflected in real-time in the Elementor editor. This live preview feature allows you to instantly visualize how your page will look to visitors, making it easy to experiment and refine your design until it's perfect.

The Navigator Panel

As you add more and more elements to your page, managing and navigating your layout can become increasingly complex. That's where the Navigator Panel comes in handy. It offers a bird's-eye view of your page's structure, displaying all the sections, columns, and widgets in a hierarchical tree-like format.

Think of the Navigator Panel as a table of contents for your page. It allows you to quickly jump to any element on your page, making it easier to edit and manage complex layouts. You can also use the Navigator Panel to rearrange elements within your page by simply dragging and dropping them.

Navigating Your Page

To navigate your page using the Navigator Panel:

1. **Open the Navigator Panel:** The Navigator Panel is usually located on the right-hand side of the screen. If it's not visible, click on the Navigator icon in the Elementor toolbar at the bottom of the screen.
2. **Browse the Hierarchy:** The Navigator Panel displays a hierarchical view of your page's structure. The top-level items are usually sections, followed by columns within those sections, and then individual widgets within the columns.
3. **Click to Select:** Click on any item in the Navigator Panel to select that element on your page. The selected element will be highlighted in the Content Area, and its settings will be displayed in the Settings Panel.

Rearranging Elements

You can rearrange elements on your page using the Navigator Panel:

1. **Click and Drag:** Click on the element you want to move in the Navigator Panel.
2. **Drag to New Position:** Drag the element to its new position in the hierarchy.
3. **Release:** Release the mouse button to drop the element in its new location.

The Navigator Panel makes it easy to reorder sections, columns, and widgets, allowing you to experiment with different layouts and quickly find the optimal structure for your page. It's a powerful tool for maintaining an organized and efficient workflow, especially when working with complex designs.

The Settings Panel

The Settings Panel is your control hub for customizing each individual widget on your Elementor page. It's where you can fine-tune the appearance, content, and behavior of every element, from headings and text to images and buttons.

Accessing the Settings Panel

To access the Settings Panel for a specific widget:

1. Click on the widget in the Content Area to select it.
2. The Settings Panel will appear on the left-hand side of the screen.

Settings Panel Tabs

The Settings Panel is divided into three main tabs:

1. **Content:** This tab controls the content of the widget. For example, in a Heading widget, you would enter the text for your heading in the Content tab. In an Image widget, you would upload or select the image you want to display.
2. **Style:** This tab controls the appearance of the widget. Here, you can customize colors, fonts, spacing, borders, shadows, and other visual aspects of the widget.
3. **Advanced:** This tab contains more advanced settings, such as margins and padding, responsive behavior, custom CSS classes, and motion effects.

Overview of Settings in Each Tab

The specific settings available in each tab will vary depending on the type of widget you're editing. However, here's a general overview of what you can expect to find:

Content Tab

- Text: Enter and format text content.
- Images: Upload or select images from your media library.
- Links: Add links to other pages or websites.
- Icons: Choose from a library of icons to add visual interest.
- Other content-specific settings: Depending on the widget, you may find additional settings for customizing its content.

Style Tab

- Typography: Choose font family, size, weight, line height, and letter spacing.
- Colors: Select colors for text, background, borders, and other elements.
- Border: Adjust border style, width, color, and radius.
- Box Shadow: Add shadow effects to your widget.
- Background: Set a background color, gradient, or image for your widget.
- Other style-specific settings: Depending on the widget, you may find additional settings for customizing its appearance.

Advanced Tab

- Margins & Padding: Control the spacing around your widget.
- Responsive: Adjust how the widget appears on different screen sizes.
- Custom CSS: Add your own CSS code to further customize the widget's appearance.
- Motion Effects: Add hover effects, entrance animations, or parallax scrolling to your widget.

Customizing Your Widgets

By exploring the Settings Panel for each widget and experimenting with the available options, you can tailor the appearance and behavior of your widgets to create a visually stunning and user-friendly website.

Responsive Mode

In today's mobile-first world, it's crucial for your website to adapt seamlessly to different screen sizes. Elementor makes this easy with its Responsive Mode, allowing you to preview and edit your page on desktop, tablet, and mobile devices. This ensures your website looks and functions perfectly on any screen, enhancing the user experience and improving your SEO.

Switching Between Responsive Modes

To switch between different responsive modes in Elementor:

1. **Responsive Mode Icon:** Locate the Responsive Mode icon in the bottom left corner of the Elementor editor. It looks like a monitor with different screen sizes displayed on it.
2. **Select a Mode:** Click on the Responsive Mode icon. A menu will appear with options for Desktop, Tablet, and Mobile.
3. **Preview and Edit:** Select the desired mode to see how your page looks on that specific screen size. You can then make adjustments to the layout, content, or styling for each mode independently.

Adjusting Your Page Layout for Each Screen Size

Elementor provides several tools to help you adjust your page layout for different screen sizes:

- **Column Width:** You can adjust the width of each column in a section for different screen sizes. For example, you might want a three-column layout on desktop to become a two-column layout on tablets and a single-column layout on mobile.
- **Visibility:** You can hide or show specific widgets based on the screen size. For example, you might want to display a large image on desktop but hide it on mobile devices.

- **Column Order:** You can change the order of columns in a section for different screen sizes. For example, you might want a sidebar to appear below the main content on mobile devices.
- **Responsive Typography:** You can adjust font sizes, line heights, and letter spacing for different screen sizes to ensure readability on smaller screens.
- **Reverse Columns:** In some cases, you might want to reverse the order of columns on smaller screens to prioritize important content.

By utilizing these tools and techniques, you can create a responsive website that adapts beautifully to any device, providing a seamless and enjoyable user experience for your visitors.

Chapter Summary

This chapter provided a comprehensive tour of the Elementor interface, equipping you with the essential knowledge to navigate and utilize this powerful page builder effectively.

We began by explaining how to launch the Elementor editor within WordPress, either by editing a page or post or by accessing it directly from the front end of your website.

We then delved into the heart of Elementor, the panel, which serves as the control center for designing and editing your pages. We described its two main sections: the Widget Panel, where you find the building blocks for your pages, and the Navigator Panel, which provides a hierarchical view of your page's structure.

We explored the Widget Panel in detail, highlighting the different categories of widgets available, such as Basic, Pro, General, and Site. We also provided examples of widgets within each category, giving you a glimpse of the diverse elements you can use to build your pages.

Next, we introduced the Content Area, the blank canvas where you arrange your widgets to create your page layouts. We explained how the drag-and-drop functionality makes it easy to add, reposition, and resize elements without any coding knowledge.

The Navigator Panel was then described as a powerful tool for navigating and rearranging the sections, columns, and widgets on your page. We outlined how to use this panel to quickly jump to specific elements and reorganize your layout.

We also delved into the Settings Panel, your control hub for customizing each widget on your page. We described the different tabs within the panel—Content, Style, and Advanced—and provided an overview of the settings available in each tab.

Finally, we explored Elementor's Responsive Mode, a crucial feature for ensuring your website looks and functions seamlessly across different devices. We explained how to switch between responsive modes and adjust your page layout for desktop, tablet, and mobile screens.

By understanding the Elementor interface and its various components, you're now equipped to create visually stunning and functional web pages with ease. The next chapter will dive deeper into specific Elementor features, starting with templates and blocks.

Templates and Blocks: Building with Pre-Designed Elements

Outline

- What are Elementor Templates?
- Types of Elementor Templates
- How to Use Elementor Templates
- What are Elementor Blocks?
- Types of Elementor Blocks
- How to Use Elementor Blocks
- Combining Templates and Blocks for Efficient Design
- Chapter Summary

What are Elementor Templates?

Elementor templates are pre-designed layouts that serve as a foundation for building your web pages. They encompass the structure, design, and content of entire pages or specific sections within a page. Think of them as blueprints or starting points that you can customize and adapt to your specific needs.

Templates are a valuable asset for both beginners and experienced web designers. They save you time and effort by eliminating the need to start from scratch. Instead of meticulously designing each element and layout, you can import a template and modify it to fit your content and brand identity.

Elementor offers a vast library of free and premium templates for various purposes, including:

- **Landing Pages:** Designed to capture leads or promote specific offers.
- **Homepages:** The main entry point of your website, showcasing your brand and key content.
- **About Us Pages:** Introducing your team, mission, and values.
- **Contact Pages:** Providing contact information and forms for visitors to get in touch.
- **Services/Product Pages:** Displaying your offerings in an organized and compelling way.
- **Portfolio Pages:** Showcasing your work or projects.
- **Blog Post Templates:** Creating consistent and visually appealing layouts for your blog articles.
- **Headers and Footers:** Designing the top and bottom sections of your website.
- **Popups:** Creating engaging popups for lead generation or special offers.

By utilizing Elementor templates, you can:

- **Accelerate Your Design Process:** Skip the initial design phase and focus on customizing a pre-designed template to match your specific requirements.
- **Ensure Professional Design:** Templates are created by experienced designers, guaranteeing a visually appealing and user-friendly layout.
- **Maintain Consistency:** Easily create multiple pages with a consistent look and feel by using the same template.
- **Experiment with Different Styles:** Explore various templates to discover new design ideas and inspiration.

In the next sections, we'll delve deeper into the different types of Elementor templates available and how to use them to create stunning and effective web pages.

Types of Elementor Templates

Elementor offers a diverse range of templates to cater to different needs and use cases. These templates are categorized based on their scope and functionality, allowing you to easily find the right template for your specific requirements.

Pages

Page templates are complete, pre-designed layouts for entire web pages. They provide a comprehensive design for all the sections of a page, including the header, body, and footer. Page templates are ideal for creating:

- **Landing Pages:** These are standalone pages designed to promote a specific product, service, or offer. Landing page templates typically have a clear call-to-action and are optimized for conversions.
- **Homepages:** Your website's homepage is its main entry point. Homepage templates are designed to showcase your brand, highlight your key offerings, and guide visitors to explore further.
- **About Us Pages:** This page introduces your company, team, mission, and values. About Us page templates provide a structured layout for presenting this information in a visually appealing way.
- **Contact Pages:** This page provides your contact information, such as your email address, phone number, and physical address. Contact page templates often include a contact form to facilitate communication with visitors.
- **Other Pages:** Elementor offers page templates for various other purposes, such as services pages, product pages, pricing pages, and FAQ pages.

Sections

Section templates are pre-designed layouts for specific sections within a page. They can be used to create headers, footers, call-to-action sections, testimonials, pricing tables, team member sections, and more. Section templates are a great way to add visual interest and functionality to your pages without having to design each section from scratch.

Popups

Popup templates are designed for creating popups that appear on your website based on specific triggers, such as clicking a button, scrolling down the page, or exiting the site. Popups can be used for various purposes, including lead generation, promoting special offers, collecting email addresses, and delivering targeted messages to your visitors.

Elementor's template library offers a wide variety of popup templates for different use cases, allowing you to create eye-catching and effective popups that engage your audience and drive conversions.

How to Use Elementor Templates

Using Elementor templates is a simple and effective way to jumpstart your web page design. Follow these steps to incorporate templates into your workflow:

1. **Open the Elementor Editor:**
   - Navigate to the page or post you want to edit in your WordPress dashboard.
   - Click the "Edit with Elementor" button to launch the Elementor editor.
2. **Access the Template Library:**
   - In the Elementor editor, locate the folder icon in the bottom-left corner. This is the button that opens the template library.
   - Click on the folder icon to reveal a vast collection of pre-designed templates.
3. **Browse or Search:**

- You can browse through the template library by category (e.g., Pages, Blocks, My Templates) or use the search bar to find a specific template.
- The search bar allows you to filter by keyword, template type, or style.
- Take your time to explore the different options and find a template that aligns with your vision and needs.

4. **Insert the Template:**
   - Once you've found a suitable template, hover over its thumbnail to see a preview and additional details.
   - Click on the "Insert" button to add the template to your page.
   - The template will be inserted at your current cursor position or at the top of the page if you're starting with a blank canvas.

5. **Customize the Template:**
   - Now that the template is in place, you can start customizing it to match your content, style, and preferences.
   - Click on any element within the template to edit its content or styling in the Elementor panel.
   - You can also add new widgets, remove existing ones, and rearrange the layout to suit your needs.
   - Remember to replace the placeholder content with your own text, images, and other media.

By following these steps, you can leverage the power of Elementor templates to create beautiful and functional web pages in a fraction of the time it would take to design them from scratch.

What are Elementor Blocks?

Elementor blocks are pre-designed combinations of widgets that form a specific section or feature on your web page. Think of them as modular building components that you can easily insert and customize to create various content sections, such as:

- **Testimonials:** Showcase positive feedback from your customers or clients.
- **Pricing Tables:** Present your pricing plans in a clear and visually appealing way.
- **Team Member Sections:** Introduce your team members with their photos and bios.
- **Call-to-Action Sections:** Encourage visitors to take specific actions, such as signing up for your newsletter or purchasing a product.
- **FAQs:** Answer common questions your visitors might have.
- **Hero Sections:** Create impactful introductory sections with headlines, images, and buttons.
- **Features Lists:** Highlight the key features and benefits of your products or services.

Blocks are designed to be modular and reusable, allowing you to quickly build complex layouts without starting from scratch. They are particularly useful when you need to create specific sections that are common to many websites, such as testimonials or pricing tables.

By using Elementor blocks, you can:

- **Save Time:** Quickly add pre-designed sections to your pages, reducing development time.
- **Ensure Consistency:** Maintain a consistent look and feel across your website by using the same blocks on different pages.
- **Simplify Customization:** Customize the content and style of each block to match your brand and message.
- **Expand Your Design Options:** Access a wide variety of blocks for different purposes, allowing you to create diverse and engaging layouts.

In the next section, we'll explore the different types of Elementor blocks available and how to use them to build your web pages.

Types of Elementor Blocks

Elementor offers a wide variety of blocks, each serving a specific purpose and design style. Understanding the different types of blocks can help you choose the right ones for your specific needs and create engaging and effective web pages.

Basic Blocks

Basic blocks are the fundamental building blocks of your web pages. They typically consist of essential elements like headings, text paragraphs, images, buttons, and icons. These blocks are versatile and can be used to create various sections, such as hero sections, about us sections, feature lists, and more.

Some examples of basic blocks include:

- **Hero Block:** A large, eye-catching section that typically appears at the top of a page, featuring a headline, subheading, image, and call-to-action button.
- **About Us Block:** A section that introduces your company, team, or mission, often including text, images, and social media links.
- **Features List Block:** A section that highlights the key features and benefits of your products or services using icons, text, and images.
- **Call-to-Action Block:** A section designed to encourage visitors to take a specific action, such as signing up for a newsletter, downloading a resource, or purchasing a product.

Advanced Blocks

Advanced blocks take your designs to the next level with more complex features and interactive elements. These blocks may include animations, hover effects, parallax scrolling, or other visual enhancements that engage your visitors and make your website more dynamic.

Some examples of advanced blocks include:

- **Animated Headlines:** Headlines that animate or change appearance on hover.
- **Image Sliders:** Display multiple images in a rotating carousel format.
- **Count Up Timers:** Create countdown timers for promotions or events.
- **Progress Bars:** Visually represent the progress of a project or goal.
- **Interactive Flip Boxes:** Reveal hidden content when a user hovers over or clicks on the box.

Custom Blocks

Custom blocks are blocks that you create yourself or save from existing templates or pages. This allows you to reuse pre-designed sections across your website, saving time and ensuring consistency in your design.

To create a custom block:

1. Design the section you want to save as a block.
2. Right-click on the section in the Navigator Panel and select "Save as Template."
3. Give your block a name and choose whether to save it as a local template (available only on your current website) or a global template (available on all your Elementor-powered websites).

Once you've saved a block as a template, you can easily insert it into any page or post by accessing the template library and selecting your custom block.

How to Use Elementor Blocks

Adding Elementor blocks to your page is a straightforward process that enhances the design and functionality of your website. Follow these steps to incorporate blocks into your workflow:

1. **Open the Elementor Editor:**
   - Navigate to the page or post you want to edit in your WordPress dashboard.
   - Click the "Edit with Elementor" button to launch the editor.
2. **Add a New Section:**
   - In the Elementor editor, click on the plus icon (+) located at the top left corner of the page. This will create a new empty section on your page.
3. **Open the Block Library:**
   - Hover over the newly created section and you will see six icons appear. Click on the middle folder icon to open the block library.
4. **Browse or Search:**
   - The block library will present you with a vast array of pre-designed blocks. You can browse through them by category or use the search bar to find a specific block.
5. **Insert the Block:**
   - Once you've found a block that suits your needs, hover over its thumbnail to see a preview and additional details.
   - Click the "Insert" button to add the block to your page. The block will be placed within the section you created.
6. **Customize the Block:**
   - Now that the block is on your page, you can customize it to match your content and style. Click on any element within the block to edit its content or styling in the Elementor panel.
   - You can modify text, replace images, adjust colors, change fonts, and rearrange elements within the block.

Remember to explore the different types of blocks available, from basic layouts to advanced interactive elements, to find the perfect building blocks for your unique website design.

Combining Templates and Blocks for Efficient Design

Templates and blocks are two powerful tools in Elementor's arsenal that, when used together, can significantly streamline your website design process and unleash your creativity. By strategically combining them, you can create unique and efficient website designs that are both visually appealing and functional.

Templates for Overall Page Layout

Templates provide the overall structure and layout for your web pages. They include the header, footer, main content area, and other key sections. By choosing a template that aligns with your website's purpose and aesthetic preferences, you establish a solid foundation for your design.

For example, if you're building a landing page, you might select a template with a hero section, features list, testimonials, and a call-to-action section. If you're creating a blog page, you might choose a template with a header, sidebar, content area, and footer.

Blocks for Specific Sections

Once you have the basic page layout in place, you can use blocks to fill in the specific sections with pre-designed content. This saves you time and effort, as you don't have to create each section from scratch.

For instance, if your landing page template has a testimonial section, you can insert a testimonial block that already includes the necessary layout and styling. You simply need to replace the placeholder content with your own testimonials. Similarly, you can use a pricing table block to showcase your pricing plans, a team member block to introduce your team, or a FAQ block to answer common questions.

Customizing Templates and Blocks

Even though templates and blocks are pre-designed, you can easily customize them to match your brand and style. You can modify colors, fonts, images, and other design elements using Elementor's intuitive editing tools. You can also add or remove widgets, rearrange layouts, and apply custom CSS to further personalize your design.

Real-World Examples

Here are a few examples of how you can combine templates and blocks to create unique and efficient website designs:

- **Homepage:** Use a homepage template as a base and then insert blocks for your hero section, services/products section, about us section, testimonials, and call-to-action.
- **Landing Page:** Start with a landing page template and then add blocks for specific features, benefits, pricing, and a lead generation form.
- **About Us Page:** Choose an about us page template and then insert blocks for your team members, company history, and mission statement.
- **Blog Page:** Use a blog page template and then add blocks for recent posts, popular posts, or categories.

By leveraging the power of templates and blocks, you can accelerate your website design process, maintain consistency across your pages, and create visually stunning and functional websites that engage your audience and achieve your business goals.

Chapter Summary

This chapter has illuminated the concept of building your website efficiently with pre-designed elements in Elementor, using templates and blocks. We began by defining Elementor templates as pre-designed layouts for entire pages or sections of pages. We then explored the different types of templates available, such as pages, sections, and popups, each serving distinct purposes in website creation.

We moved on to discuss how to harness the power of templates, providing a step-by-step guide on how to locate, insert, and customize them within the Elementor editor. This allows for a significant reduction in design time while ensuring a professional and polished look.

Next, we introduced Elementor blocks as pre-designed groups of widgets, perfect for creating specific sections within your pages. We detailed the different types of blocks, including basic, advanced, and custom blocks, emphasizing their modularity and reusability.

We then outlined the process of using Elementor blocks, explaining how to add new sections, access the block library, insert blocks, and customize them according to your needs. The chapter culminated in a discussion on the strategic combination of templates and blocks to craft efficient and unique website designs. We provided real-world examples of how this can be achieved, highlighting the flexibility and creative potential this approach offers.

By understanding the capabilities and effective use of Elementor templates and blocks, you're now equipped with powerful tools to accelerate your website design process and create a website that is both visually appealing and functional.

Widgets: The Building Blocks of Your Pages

Outline

- Introduction to Widgets
- Types of Elementor Widgets
- Basic Widgets
- Pro Widgets
- General Widgets
- Site Widgets
- Third-Party Widgets
- Using Widgets in Elementor
- Customizing Widgets
- Organizing Widgets with Inner Sections
- Chapter Summary

Introduction to Widgets

In Elementor, widgets are the fundamental elements that you use to build your website's pages and posts. They are pre-designed content modules that can be easily dragged and dropped onto your canvas, allowing you to create a wide variety of layouts and designs.

Think of widgets as the individual pieces of a puzzle. Each widget serves a specific purpose, and by combining them in different ways, you can create a complete and visually appealing website.

The Role of Widgets

Widgets are the core components of your web pages. They are responsible for displaying various types of content, such as:

- **Text:** Paragraphs, headings, lists, quotes, and other text elements.
- **Images:** Photos, illustrations, and graphics.
- **Videos:** Embedded videos from platforms like YouTube or Vimeo, or self-hosted videos.
- **Buttons:** Clickable buttons that link to other pages or sections of your website.
- **Forms:** Contact forms, subscription forms, or other interactive forms.
- **Icons:** Visual symbols that represent actions or concepts.
- **Maps:** Interactive maps from Google Maps or other providers.
- **Social Media Icons:** Links to your social media profiles.
- And much more!

The Power of Widgets

Elementor offers a vast library of widgets, each with its own unique set of features and customization options. This allows you to create virtually any type of website, from simple blogs and portfolios to complex e-commerce stores and membership sites.

The drag-and-drop interface makes it incredibly easy to add and arrange widgets on your pages. You can simply click on a widget in the Widget Panel, drag it over to your canvas, and drop it into place. You can then resize and reposition the widget to create your desired layout.

Each widget also comes with its own set of settings that allow you to customize its appearance and behavior. You can change the colors, fonts, sizes, spacing, and other properties of each widget to match your brand and style.

By mastering the art of using widgets, you can create unique and engaging web pages that capture your audience's attention and drive results.

Types of Elementor Widgets

Elementor offers a vast array of widgets to cater to your every design need. They are categorized to help you easily find the right tool for the job. Here's a breakdown of the different types of widgets available in Elementor:

Basic Widgets

These are the core building blocks that come standard with the free version of Elementor. They provide the essential elements for creating basic web pages, such as:

- **Heading:** Add titles and subtitles to your pages with various styling options.
- **Text Editor:** Craft engaging content with rich text formatting tools.
- **Image:** Insert and customize images to enhance your visuals.
- **Video:** Embed videos from YouTube, Vimeo, or other sources to make your content more interactive.
- **Button:** Create clickable buttons that link to other pages or actions.

Pro Widgets

These are advanced widgets exclusively available in Elementor Pro, the premium version of Elementor. They offer more sophisticated features and design options, including:

- **Posts:** Dynamically display your latest blog posts or custom post types in various layouts.
- **Portfolio:** Showcase your projects or creative work in a visually appealing manner.
- **Slides:** Create eye-catching slideshows with images, videos, or text.
- **Forms:** Build custom forms for lead generation, contact requests, or feedback.
- **Animated Headlines:** Add animated text effects to your headlines for added visual interest.

General Widgets

These widgets are versatile and can be used for a variety of purposes across your website:

- **Spacer:** Add spacing between elements for improved layout and readability.
- **Divider:** Create visual separation between sections with lines or shapes.
- **Icon:** Insert icons from a vast library to represent different actions or concepts.
- **Google Maps:** Embed interactive maps to display your location or provide directions.

Site Widgets

These widgets are specifically designed for building your website's structure and navigation:

- **Site Logo:** Display your website's logo in a prominent location.
- **Site Title:** Show your website's title, often used in the header.
- **Menu Anchor:** Create anchor links that allow users to jump to specific sections within a page.

Third-Party Widgets

Elementor's extensibility shines through its compatibility with third-party widgets. Many developers create widgets specifically for Elementor, adding even more features and functionality to the page builder. Popular options include:

- **Essential Addons for Elementor:** Offers a wide range of creative elements and extensions.
- **Premium Addons for Elementor:** Provides even more advanced widgets and features.

- **Crocoblock:** A suite of plugins designed to extend Elementor's capabilities for specific use cases.

By leveraging the diverse range of widgets available within Elementor and from third-party developers, you can unlock endless possibilities for designing and building a website that truly stands out.

Basic Widgets

Elementor's Basic Widgets are the fundamental building blocks for creating content on your web pages. They are essential for structuring your content, adding text and media, and guiding user interactions. Let's explore these essential widgets:

Heading

The Heading widget is your go-to tool for adding titles, subtitles, and section headers to your pages. It allows you to structure your content hierarchically, making it easier for users to scan and understand.

To customize a Heading widget:

1. **Content:** Enter the text you want to display as your heading.
2. **HTML Tag:** Choose the appropriate HTML tag for your heading (e.g., H1 for the main title, H2 for subheadings).
3. **Typography:** Select the font family, size, weight, line height, and letter spacing to match your brand's style.
4. **Color:** Choose the text color for your heading.
5. **Alignment:** Align the heading left, center, or right.

Text Editor

The Text Editor widget is where you craft the main body of your content. It functions much like a word processor, allowing you to format text, add lists, quotes, and links, and embed media like images or videos.

To use the Text Editor:

1. **Content:** Enter your text directly into the editor.
2. **Formatting:** Use the toolbar to apply formatting options like bold, italic, underline, headings, lists, and links.
3. **Media:** Click the "Add Media" button to insert images, videos, or other media into your text.

Image

The Image widget lets you add visual flair to your pages by inserting images.

To add an image:

1. **Choose Image:** Click on the "Choose Image" button to select an image from your media library or upload a new one.
2. **Image Size:** Select the appropriate image size for your layout.
3. **Alignment:** Choose how you want the image to align with your text (left, center, right).
4. **Link:** Optionally, you can add a link to the image, making it clickable.

Video

The Video widget allows you to embed videos from various sources, including YouTube, Vimeo, or your own self-hosted videos.

To embed a video:

1. **Video Source:** Choose the platform from which you want to embed the video.
2. **Video URL:** Paste the URL of the video you want to embed.
3. **Start Time:** (Optional) Specify the time (in seconds) at which you want the video to start playing.
4. **Aspect Ratio:** Choose the aspect ratio (16:9, 4:3, etc.) that best fits your layout.

Button

The Button widget is a versatile tool for creating clickable buttons that can be used for various purposes, such as calling visitors to action, linking to other pages, or triggering specific events.

To create a button:

1. **Text:** Enter the text you want to display on the button.
2. **Link:** Enter the URL you want the button to link to.
3. **Alignment:** Align the button left, center, or right.
4. **Style:** Choose a style for your button, such as solid, outline, or text.
5. **Size:** Select the desired size for your button (small, medium, large).
6. **Icon:** Optionally, you can add an icon to your button.

These basic widgets provide a solid foundation for building your web pages. As you become more familiar with Elementor, you can explore the more advanced Pro and General widgets to add even more functionality and flair to your website.

Pro Widgets

Elementor Pro takes your design capabilities to the next level with a suite of advanced widgets that unlock a world of creativity and functionality. Let's explore some of the most popular Pro widgets:

Posts

The Posts widget is a dynamic tool for showcasing your blog posts or custom post types in various layouts. You can display your posts in a list, grid, or carousel format, and customize the layout, style, and query to match your preferences. This widget is ideal for creating blog pages, news feeds, or content hubs.

Portfolio

The Portfolio widget allows you to create stunning portfolios to display your work or projects. You can choose from various layout options, such as grid, masonry, or justified, and customize the appearance of each portfolio item. The Portfolio widget is perfect for photographers, designers, artists, and other creatives who want to showcase their work online.

Slides

The Slides widget lets you create captivating slideshows with images, videos, or text. You can add multiple slides, customize transitions and animations, and control the timing and behavior of your slideshows. Slides are a great way to add visual interest and engage your visitors with dynamic content.

Forms

Forms are essential for collecting information from your website visitors. The Forms widget in Elementor Pro allows you to create custom forms for various purposes, such as lead generation, contact requests, feedback surveys, event registrations, and more. You can customize the form fields, design the layout, and integrate with popular email marketing platforms or CRM systems.

Animated Headlines

The Animated Headlines widget adds a touch of flair and dynamism to your website's headlines. You can choose from various animation effects, such as typing, fading, sliding, or rotating, to make your headlines more eye-catching and memorable. This widget is a great way to grab attention and add a bit of personality to your web pages.

General Widgets

Elementor's General Widgets are a versatile collection of tools that enhance your page's layout, visual appeal, and functionality. They add those extra touches that make your website look professional and engaging. Let's take a closer look at some of the most useful general widgets:

Spacer

The Spacer widget is a simple yet indispensable tool for managing the spacing between elements on your page. It allows you to create visual breathing room, making your content easier to read and digest. You can customize the Spacer's height or width, adjust its margins and padding, and even make it responsive to different screen sizes.

Divider

The Divider widget is a visual element that helps you create clear separation between different sections of your page. It can be a simple line, a dotted line, or a more elaborate design element. Dividers are great for organizing your content and adding a touch of visual flair to your pages. You can customize the Divider's style, thickness, color, and alignment to match your website's aesthetic.

Icon

Icons are small graphical symbols that represent actions or concepts. The Icon widget in Elementor gives you access to a vast library of icons that you can use to enhance your website's visual appeal and improve user experience. Icons can be used for navigation menus, social media links, bullet points, or simply to add decorative elements to your pages.

To use the Icon widget:

1. Drag and drop the Icon widget onto your page.
2. Choose an icon from the library.
3. Customize the icon's size, color, and alignment.
4. Optionally, you can add a link to the icon.

Google Maps

If you have a physical location or want to provide directions to your visitors, the Google Maps widget is a valuable tool. It allows you to embed an interactive Google Map directly into your page. You can customize the map's location, zoom level, style, and markers. The Google Maps widget is a great way to enhance your website's local SEO and make it easier for customers to find your business.

To embed a Google Map:

1. Drag and drop the Google Maps widget onto your page.
2. Enter your address or location in the search bar.
3. Customize the map's zoom level, style, and markers.

By incorporating these general widgets into your web page design, you can create a more visually appealing, organized, and user-friendly website that leaves a positive impression on your visitors.

Site Widgets

Site widgets are specialized Elementor widgets that help you create and manage essential elements of your website's structure and navigation. They streamline the process of adding key components like your logo, site title, and navigation links to your pages.

Site Logo

The Site Logo widget allows you to easily display your website's logo in a prominent location, typically in the header. Your logo is a visual representation of your brand, so it's important to showcase it effectively. With the Site Logo widget, you can upload your logo image, adjust its size and alignment, and add a link to your homepage.

Site Title

The Site Title widget displays your website's title, which is the name you defined in the WordPress General Settings. This widget is often used in the header alongside your logo to reinforce your brand identity. You can customize the title's typography, color, and alignment to match your website's overall design.

Menu Anchor

The Menu Anchor widget is a unique tool that allows you to create anchor links within your page content. Anchor links are specific points within a page that you can link to from your navigation menu or other internal links. This can be useful for creating one-page websites or for directing visitors to specific sections within a long page.

To use the Menu Anchor widget:

1. Drag and drop the widget into the desired location on your page.
2. Give the anchor a unique name (e.g., "services" or "contact").
3. In your navigation menu, create a custom link that links to the specific anchor (e.g., `yourwebsite.com/home/#services` or `yourwebsite.com/home/#contact`).

By utilizing these site widgets, you can enhance your website's structure, navigation, and branding, creating a cohesive and user-friendly experience for your visitors.

Third-Party Widgets

While Elementor's built-in widgets offer a wide range of functionality, the true power of Elementor lies in its extensibility. Third-party developers have created a vast ecosystem of additional widgets that seamlessly integrate with Elementor, providing even more design options and features.

These third-party widgets can be found in the WordPress Plugin Directory or on the developers' websites. They often cater to specific niches or use cases, offering specialized functionality that may not be available in Elementor's core widgets.

Here are some popular examples of third-party widget libraries for Elementor:

Essential Addons for Elementor: This freemium plugin boasts a collection of over 80 creative elements and extensions, including post grids, image carousels, countdown timers, parallax effects, and more. It's a great way to add visual flair and functionality to your website without breaking the bank.

Premium Addons for Elementor: This premium plugin offers a more extensive library of over 60 advanced widgets and extensions, including cross-site copy-paste, section particles, advanced maps, and

WooCommerce elements. It's designed for users who need more sophisticated features and customization options.

Crocoblock: Crocoblock is a suite of plugins designed to extend Elementor's functionality for various purposes. It includes plugins for dynamic content, custom post types, interactive elements, popups, and more. Crocoblock is a powerful tool for building complex websites with advanced features and functionality.

In addition to these popular options, there are countless other third-party widgets available for Elementor. By exploring these plugins, you can unlock a world of possibilities and create a truly unique and customized website that meets your specific needs and goals.

Using Widgets in Elementor

Incorporating widgets into your Elementor design is a straightforward process that involves dragging, dropping, and customizing. Here's a general overview of how to use widgets in Elementor:

1. **Drag and Drop:**
   - **Select:** Start by browsing the Widget Panel and selecting the widget you want to add to your page.
   - **Drag:** Click and hold the widget with your mouse, then drag it over to the Content Area.
   - **Drop:** Release your mouse button to drop the widget into the desired location on your page.
2. **Select and Open Settings:**
   - **Click:** Once the widget is on your page, click on it to select it.
   - **Settings Panel:** This action will open the widget's Settings Panel on the left-hand side of the screen.
3. **Customize:**
   - **Content Tab:** Use this tab to add and edit the content of your widget. For example, you'd enter your text in a Heading widget or upload an image in an Image widget.
   - **Style Tab:** This tab is where you adjust the visual appearance of your widget. You can change colors, fonts, spacing, borders, shadows, and more.
   - **Advanced Tab:** This tab offers more advanced options like margins, padding, responsive behavior, custom CSS, and motion effects.

Here's a quick example of how you might use a Heading widget:

1. **Drag and drop:** Drag the Heading widget from the Widget Panel onto the Content Area.
2. **Select and open settings:** Click on the Heading widget to open its Settings Panel.
3. **Customize:**
   - **Content:** Enter the text you want to display as your heading.
   - **Style:** Choose a font, size, color, and alignment for your heading.

Repeat this process for each widget you want to add to your page. You can easily rearrange and resize widgets by dragging and dropping them within the Content Area.

Customizing Widgets

The true power of Elementor widgets lies in their flexibility and customization options. Almost every widget in Elementor comes with a range of settings that you can adjust to control its appearance and behavior, allowing you to tailor each element to your specific design needs.

Common Customizations

Here are some examples of common customizations you can make to most widgets:

- **Typography:** Change the font family, size, weight (bold, regular, light), line height, letter spacing, and text decoration (underline, overline, strikethrough). You can also transform text to uppercase, lowercase, or capitalize.
- **Colors:** Adjust the text color, background color, border color, and hover color. You can use solid colors, gradients, or even images as backgrounds.
- **Spacing:** Control the padding (space inside the widget) and margin (space outside the widget) to create visual separation and hierarchy between elements.
- **Borders:** Add borders to your widgets and customize their width, style (solid, dashed, dotted, etc.), color, and radius (rounded corners).
- **Shadows:** Apply box shadows to create a depth effect and make your widgets stand out. You can adjust the shadow's color, blur, spread, and position.
- **Hover Effects:** Change the appearance of a widget when a user hovers over it. You can add animations, change colors, or create other visual effects.
- **Responsive Settings:** Adjust how a widget displays on different screen sizes (desktop, tablet, mobile). You can hide certain elements, change column widths, or rearrange the layout for smaller screens.

Examples of Customizing Specific Widgets

- **Heading:** Change the heading text, font, size, color, alignment, and add a background image or gradient.
- **Text Editor:** Adjust the font family, size, line height, and letter spacing for your body text. You can also add custom CSS classes for more advanced styling.
- **Image:** Change the image size, alignment, border style, and add a caption or link.
- **Button:** Customize the button text, font, size, color, background color, border, and hover effects.
- **Icon:** Choose a different icon, adjust its size and color, and add a link or hover effect.

Exploring Customization Options

The best way to familiarize yourself with the customization options available for each widget is to experiment and explore. Click on a widget and open its Settings Panel to see all the different settings you can adjust. Don't be afraid to try different combinations and see how they affect the appearance and behavior of your widgets.

Organizing Widgets with Inner Sections

As you build more complex layouts with Elementor, you might find it helpful to create nested sections within your existing sections. These nested sections, called Inner Sections, allow you to group widgets together and create more organized and visually appealing designs.

Think of Inner Sections as containers within containers. You can place multiple Inner Sections within a single parent section, each with its own set of columns and widgets. This allows you to create more intricate layouts with distinct visual hierarchies.

Adding an Inner Section

To add an Inner Section:

1. **Select the Parent Section:** Click on the section where you want to add an Inner Section.
2. **Click the Plus Icon:** Hover over the section and click on the plus icon (+) that appears.
3. **Choose "Inner Section":** Select "Inner Section" from the dropdown menu.

A new Inner Section will be added within the parent section. You can now drag and drop widgets into this Inner Section and customize its layout and styling independently of the parent section.

Rearranging Widgets within an Inner Section

To rearrange widgets within an Inner Section:

1. **Select the Inner Section:** Click on the Inner Section you want to edit.
2. **Drag and Drop:** Click and drag the widgets within the Inner Section to reorder them.
3. **Resize Columns (Optional):** If your Inner Section has multiple columns, you can resize them by dragging the column handles.

Tips for Using Inner Sections

- **Organize Content:** Use Inner Sections to group related widgets together, such as creating a separate Inner Section for testimonials within an "About Us" section.
- **Create Visual Hierarchy:** Nest Inner Sections within each other to create a layered design with distinct visual hierarchy.
- **Improve Responsiveness:** Use Inner Sections to control how your layout adapts to different screen sizes. For example, you might want to stack columns vertically on smaller screens.
- **Add Backgrounds and Styling:** Apply background colors, images, or gradients to Inner Sections to visually differentiate them from other sections.

By utilizing Inner Sections effectively, you can create more organized, visually appealing, and responsive layouts for your web pages. They provide a powerful tool for managing complex designs and ensuring that your content is presented in a clear and intuitive way.

Chapter Summary

This chapter delved into the heart of Elementor's design capabilities, focusing on widgets—the essential building blocks of your web pages. We began by introducing widgets as individual elements that serve various purposes, from displaying text and images to enabling interactive features.

We then explored the diverse types of Elementor widgets, categorizing them as Basic, Pro, General, Site, and Third-Party. Each category offers a unique set of tools to enhance your website's design and functionality.

We dove deeper into the Basic Widgets, which are the foundation of most web pages. We provided a detailed overview of commonly used widgets like Heading, Text Editor, Image, Video, and Button, explaining their purpose and usage with step-by-step instructions.

For those using Elementor Pro, we briefly introduced the Pro Widgets, highlighting their advanced features like Posts, Portfolio, Slides, Forms, and Animated Headlines. These widgets empower you to create more dynamic and engaging content.

We then explored General Widgets, which serve versatile purposes in page design. We described the functionality of the Spacer, Divider, Icon, and Google Maps widgets, illustrating how they enhance your website's layout, visual appeal, and functionality.

Next, we introduced Site Widgets, specifically designed for managing your website's structure and navigation. We highlighted the Site Logo, Site Title, and Menu Anchor widgets, explaining their roles in branding and user experience.

We also touched upon Third-Party Widgets, emphasizing Elementor's extensibility through a vast ecosystem of plugins developed by external developers. We mentioned popular options like Essential Addons for Elementor, Premium Addons for Elementor, and Crocoblock, which offer even more features and design possibilities.

The chapter provided a general overview of using widgets in Elementor, emphasizing the simplicity of dragging and dropping elements onto the page. We also delved into customizing widgets, explaining how to modify their content, style, and advanced settings to create unique and visually appealing designs.

Finally, we introduced the concept of Inner Sections, explaining how they can be used to organize widgets and create more complex layouts within your pages. We provided step-by-step instructions on adding and rearranging widgets within Inner Sections.

By mastering these fundamental concepts and techniques, you now have a solid foundation for using Elementor widgets to build stunning, functional, and user-friendly websites.

Styling: Colors, Fonts, and Making It Your Own

Outline

- Introduction to Styling in Elementor
- Understanding Global Styles
- Typography
- Colors
- Backgrounds
- Borders and Shadows
- Hover Effects
- Advanced Styling Techniques
- Best Practices for Styling Your Website
- Chapter Summary

Introduction to Styling in Elementor

Styling is the art of bringing your website's visual identity to life. It's the process of choosing the right colors, fonts, backgrounds, and other visual elements to create a cohesive and engaging user experience. With Elementor, styling your website is not only easy but also enjoyable.

Elementor's intuitive interface and comprehensive styling options empower you to transform your website's appearance without needing any coding knowledge. You can experiment with different styles, preview your changes in real-time, and create a unique design that perfectly reflects your brand.

Elementor's Styling Toolbox

Elementor provides a rich set of styling tools that allow you to customize every aspect of your website's appearance. Some of the key styling features include:

- **Colors:** Choose from a wide range of colors for your website's background, text, headings, links, buttons, and other elements. You can also create custom color palettes and use gradients for more dynamic designs.
- **Fonts:** Select from hundreds of Google Fonts or upload your own custom fonts. Customize the font size, weight, line height, and letter spacing for different elements to create a unique typography style.
- **Backgrounds:** Add background images, gradients, or videos to your sections and columns. You can also customize the background position, size, repeat, and attachment.
- **Borders and Shadows:** Add borders and shadows to your widgets to create depth and visual interest. Customize the border style, width, color, and radius, as well as the shadow's color, blur, spread, and position.
- **Hover Effects:** Create interactive hover effects that change the appearance of your widgets when a user hovers their mouse over them. You can choose from various hover effects, such as changing colors, adding animations, or scaling elements.

Global Styles and Default Settings

Elementor also allows you to define global styles for specific elements, such as headings, buttons, and images. These global styles are applied across your entire website, ensuring consistency and saving you time. You can also set default styles for new widgets, making it easier to maintain a consistent look and feel throughout your site.

With Elementor's styling capabilities, you have the freedom to create a website that is both visually appealing and unique. Whether you want a minimalist design or a bold and colorful website, Elementor provides the tools to bring your vision to life.

Understanding Global Styles

In the world of web design, consistency is key. A cohesive visual language creates a professional and polished look for your website, making it more appealing and user-friendly. Elementor's Global Styles feature is designed to help you achieve this consistency effortlessly.

What are Global Styles?

Global Styles are essentially a set of predefined styles that you can apply to specific elements across your entire website. These styles encompass various aspects of design, including typography (fonts, sizes, line heights), colors, buttons, images, and form fields.

By defining global styles, you establish a default style for each element that will be automatically applied to all instances of that element throughout your site. For example, if you set a global style for your H2 headings, all H2 headings on your website will inherit that style, ensuring a consistent look and feel.

Benefits of Global Styles

Using Global Styles offers several advantages:

- **Consistency:** Maintain a unified visual language across your entire website, enhancing brand identity and professionalism.
- **Efficiency:** Save time and effort by applying styles globally instead of customizing each element individually.
- **Easier Maintenance:** Update your website's design with a few clicks by modifying global styles, eliminating the need to manually edit each instance of an element.
- **Scalability:** As your website grows, Global Styles make it easier to manage and maintain a consistent design across multiple pages and sections.

How to Use Global Styles

To create and manage Global Styles in Elementor:

1. **Access Site Settings:** Navigate to *Elementor > Site Settings* in your WordPress dashboard.
2. **Choose a Style:** Select the type of element you want to style (e.g., Typography, Colors, Buttons).
3. **Customize:** Adjust the settings for that element, such as font family, size, color, background, border, and more.
4. **Save:** Click the "Update" button to save your changes.

You can also apply Global Styles directly from the Elementor editor. When you select a widget, you'll see a globe icon next to certain style options. Clicking on the globe icon will allow you to choose from your defined Global Styles for that element.

Overriding Global Styles

While Global Styles provide a convenient way to maintain consistency, you might want to make exceptions for specific elements. Elementor allows you to override Global Styles for individual elements by simply customizing their settings directly in the editor. This gives you the flexibility to create unique variations while still benefiting from the overall design consistency provided by Global Styles.

By understanding and utilizing Elementor's Global Styles, you can streamline your design process, ensure a cohesive visual identity for your website, and make future design updates a breeze.

Typography

Typography is the art and technique of arranging type – the letters, numbers, and symbols that make up written language – to make it legible, readable, and visually appealing when displayed. It involves choosing the right fonts, font sizes, line heights, letter spacing, and other typographic elements to create a harmonious and effective visual communication.

The Role of Typography in Web Design

Typography plays a crucial role in the overall look and feel of your website. It's not just about choosing pretty fonts; it's about creating a visual hierarchy that guides the reader's eye, conveying information clearly and effectively, and reinforcing your brand identity.

- **Readability:** The primary goal of typography is to make your content easy to read. Choosing legible fonts, appropriate font sizes, and comfortable line heights ensures that your visitors can easily consume your content without straining their eyes.
- **Visual Hierarchy:** Typography helps establish a clear visual hierarchy on your page. By using different font sizes, weights, and styles for headings, subheadings, and body text, you can guide the reader's eye and make your content more scannable and digestible.
- **Brand Identity:** Your choice of fonts and typographic styles can contribute to your brand identity. Certain fonts evoke specific emotions or associations, so choosing fonts that align with your brand's personality and values can help reinforce your message and create a cohesive brand experience.
- **User Experience:** Good typography enhances the overall user experience on your website. When your content is easy to read and visually appealing, visitors are more likely to stay on your site longer and engage with your content.

Typography in Elementor

Elementor provides a comprehensive set of typography tools that allow you to customize the fonts, sizes, colors, and other typographic elements of your website. You can choose from hundreds of Google Fonts, upload your own custom fonts, and create global font styles that can be applied across your entire site.

Next, we'll delve deeper into choosing the right fonts, pairing fonts effectively, and setting appropriate font sizes, weights, and line heights to create a typographic style that elevates your website's design and readability.

Choosing the Right Fonts

Selecting the right fonts for your website is crucial for establishing a clear visual identity and ensuring readability. The fonts you choose can significantly impact how your content is perceived and how users interact with your site. Here are some tips to guide your font selection process:

1. **Consider Your Website's Purpose and Audience:**
   The fonts you choose should align with the overall tone and purpose of your website. For instance, a professional law firm's website would typically opt for more traditional and formal fonts, while a creative agency might choose more modern and playful fonts.
   Consider your target audience as well. If your audience is primarily older adults, you might want to choose fonts that are easy to read at larger sizes. If your audience is younger and more tech-savvy, you might have more flexibility to experiment with trendier fonts.
2. **Understand the Different Types of Fonts:**
   Fonts can be broadly categorized into four main types:
     - **Serif:** Serif fonts have small lines or strokes at the ends of their characters. They are often perceived as traditional, classic, and formal. Examples include Times New Roman, Georgia, and Garamond.

- **Sans-serif:** Sans-serif fonts lack the decorative strokes found in serif fonts. They are generally considered modern, clean, and minimalist. Examples include Arial, Helvetica, and Open Sans.
- **Display:** Display fonts are designed to be used at larger sizes, such as in headlines or logos. They often have unique and eye-catching designs. Examples include Impact, Lobster, and Pacifico.
- **Script:** Script fonts mimic handwriting or calligraphy. They are often used for decorative purposes or to add a touch of elegance. Examples include Brush Script MT, Lucida Handwriting, and Lobster Two.

3. **Choose Fonts That Complement Each Other:**
   When selecting multiple fonts for your website, it's important to choose fonts that complement each other. A good rule of thumb is to choose one font for your headings and another for your body text. The heading font should be more eye-catching and distinct, while the body text font should be more readable and neutral.
   You can also use different weights (e.g., regular, bold, light) and styles (e.g., italic) of the same font family to create visual contrast and hierarchy within your content.
4. **Limit the Number of Fonts:**
   Using too many different fonts can make your website look cluttered and unprofessional. A general guideline is to use a maximum of two or three fonts on your website.
5. **Test Your Fonts:**
   Before finalizing your font choices, test them out on different devices and screen sizes to ensure they are legible and look good across various platforms.

By considering these tips and understanding the different types of fonts available, you can make informed decisions about which fonts will best suit your website's purpose, audience, and brand identity.

Font Pairing

Font pairing is the art of combining two or more fonts in a way that creates a harmonious and visually appealing design. When done right, font pairing can elevate your website's typography, enhance readability, and reinforce your brand identity.

Principles of Font Pairing

- **Contrast:** The fonts you choose should have enough contrast to create visual interest and distinguish different elements on your page. This can be achieved by pairing a serif font with a sans-serif font, or by using fonts with different weights or styles.
- **Hierarchy:** Font pairing should also establish a clear visual hierarchy. Typically, you'll use a bolder or more decorative font for headings and a more neutral and readable font for body text. This helps guide the reader's eye and makes your content easier to scan.
- **Mood and Tone:** Consider the mood and tone you want to convey with your website. Certain font pairings evoke specific emotions or associations. For example, a serif and sans-serif pairing can create a classic and elegant look, while a pairing of two sans-serif fonts might feel more modern and minimalist.

Examples of Good Font Pairings

Here are a few examples of font pairings that work well together:

- **Playfair Display (serif) and Open Sans (sans-serif):** This classic pairing is both elegant and modern. Playfair Display is a beautiful serif font that works well for headings, while Open Sans is a versatile sans-serif font that is highly readable for body text.
- **Oswald (sans-serif) and Lato (sans-serif):** This pairing of two sans-serif fonts creates a clean and minimalist look. Oswald is a bold and attention-grabbing font for headings, while Lato is a neutral and readable font for body text.

- **Roboto Slab (serif) and Montserrat (sans-serif):** This pairing offers a modern and professional look. Roboto Slab is a stylish serif font with a geometric feel, while Montserrat is a clean and versatile sans-serif font.
- **Lora (serif) and Raleway (sans-serif):** This pairing is both elegant and contemporary. Lora is a delicate and sophisticated serif font, while Raleway is a modern and versatile sans-serif font.

These are just a few examples, and there are countless other font pairings that can work well for different websites. The best way to find the perfect pairing for your site is to experiment and see what looks and feels right for your brand and audience.

Additional Tips for Font Pairing

- **Limit the number of fonts:** Using too many different fonts can make your website look cluttered and unprofessional. Stick to two or three fonts at most.
- **Use a font pairing tool:** Several online tools, such as Fontjoy and Typ.io, can help you find font pairings that work well together.
- **Test your fonts:** Before finalizing your font choices, test them out on different devices and screen sizes to ensure they are legible and look good across various platforms.

By understanding the principles of font pairing and using the right tools, you can create a visually appealing and effective typography style for your website.

Font Size, Weight, and Line Height

Beyond selecting visually appealing fonts and creating harmonious pairings, mastering font size, weight, and line height is crucial for achieving optimal readability and establishing a clear visual hierarchy on your website. These seemingly small details can significantly impact how users perceive and interact with your content.

Font Size

Font size refers to the size of the characters in your text. Choosing the right font size is essential for readability. Text that's too small can strain the reader's eyes, while text that's too large can be overwhelming and difficult to scan.

Guidelines for Font Sizes:

- **Body Text:** The ideal font size for body text is typically between 16px and 18px. This ensures comfortable reading on most devices.
- **Headings:** Headings should be progressively larger to create a visual hierarchy. H1 headings are the largest, followed by H2, H3, and so on.
- **Smaller Text:** Use smaller font sizes (14px or less) for less important text, such as captions or footnotes.

Remember that these are just general guidelines, and the ideal font sizes for your website may vary depending on your chosen fonts and your specific design. Always test your font sizes on different devices to ensure optimal readability.

Font Weight

Font weight refers to the thickness of the strokes that form the characters. Common font weights include regular, bold, light, and medium.

Guidelines for Font Weights:

- **Body Text:** Use regular or medium weight for body text to ensure readability.
- **Headings:** Use bolder weights for headings to create visual emphasis and hierarchy.

- **Accent Text:** Use bolder or lighter weights for specific words or phrases you want to emphasize within your body text.

Line Height

Line height, also known as leading, is the vertical space between lines of text. Proper line height is crucial for readability. If the line height is too tight, the text can feel cramped and difficult to read. If it's too loose, the lines can appear disconnected, making it hard for the reader to follow the flow of the text.

Guidelines for Line Height:

- **Body Text:** A good rule of thumb is to set the line height to approximately 1.5 times the font size. For example, if your body text is 16px, the line height should be around 24px.
- **Headings:** Headings can have slightly tighter line heights than body text, but avoid making them too cramped.
- **Adjust for Different Fonts:** Different fonts may require different line heights to achieve optimal readability. Experiment to find the right balance for your chosen fonts.

By paying attention to font size, weight, and line height, you can create a typographic style that not only looks good but also enhances the readability and user experience of your website. Remember to consider your website's purpose, audience, and overall design when making your typography choices.

Colors

Colors are a fundamental element of design, capable of evoking emotions, establishing moods, and communicating messages without using a single word. In web design, color choices can significantly impact your website's visual appeal, user experience, and brand perception.

The Impact of Color

- **Emotional Response:** Colors evoke different emotions and feelings. For instance, warm colors like red, orange, and yellow are often associated with energy, passion, and excitement, while cool colors like blue, green, and purple can convey calmness, trust, and professionalism.
- **Brand Identity:** Colors are a key component of your brand's visual identity. Think of Coca-Cola's iconic red or Tiffany & Co.'s signature blue. The right color palette can instantly communicate your brand's personality and values.
- **Visual Hierarchy:** Colors can be used to create visual hierarchy and guide the user's attention. For example, a bright call-to-action button can stand out against a neutral background, encouraging users to click on it.
- **Readability:** Color contrast plays a vital role in readability. Ensure sufficient contrast between text and background colors to make your content easy to read.

Choosing Your Color Palette

Selecting the right color palette for your website requires careful consideration of several factors:

- **Brand Identity:** Your color palette should align with your brand's personality and values. Consider the emotions and messages you want to convey through your brand.
- **Website Purpose:** The purpose of your website should also influence your color choices. For example, a website for a spa might use calming colors like blue and green, while a website for a tech company might use bold colors like red and black.
- **Target Audience:** Think about your target audience and the colors that appeal to them. Different demographics may respond differently to various colors.
- **Color Theory:** Understanding basic color theory can help you create harmonious and visually pleasing color palettes. The color wheel is a valuable tool for understanding color relationships and choosing complementary or analogous colors.

- **Trends:** While it's important to stay current, avoid following fleeting design trends blindly. Choose colors that will stand the test of time and remain relevant for your brand.

Applying Colors in Elementor

Elementor makes it easy to apply colors to your website's elements. You can customize the colors of your text, backgrounds, borders, buttons, and other elements through the Style tab of each widget's settings panel. You can also create global color palettes that can be applied consistently across your entire website.

By thoughtfully choosing and applying colors in Elementor, you can create a visually appealing and effective website that resonates with your audience and strengthens your brand identity.

Color Theory

Color theory is the foundation of understanding how colors interact and how to use them effectively in design. It's a complex subject, but grasping the basics can significantly improve your ability to create visually appealing and harmonious color palettes for your website.

Hue

Hue refers to the pure color itself, such as red, blue, or green. It's the most basic attribute of color and is often represented on a color wheel. The color wheel is a circular diagram that arranges hues in a logical order, with primary colors (red, yellow, blue) forming the base and secondary colors (green, orange, purple) created by mixing the primary colors.

Saturation

Saturation refers to the intensity or purity of a color. A highly saturated color appears vibrant and intense, while a desaturated color appears muted or dull. You can adjust the saturation of a color to create different moods or effects. For example, a highly saturated red might convey excitement or energy, while a desaturated red might feel more calming or sophisticated.

Value

Value, also known as lightness or darkness, refers to how light or dark a color appears. A high-value color is closer to white, while a low-value color is closer to black. Value is crucial for creating contrast and depth in your design. For example, using a light background with dark text creates high contrast and improves readability.

Creating Harmonious Color Palettes

Color theory provides various techniques for creating harmonious color palettes:

- **Complementary Colors:** These are colors that are opposite each other on the color wheel (e.g., red and green, blue and orange). Complementary colors create high contrast and visual impact.
- **Analogous Colors:** These are colors that are next to each other on the color wheel (e.g., blue, green, and yellow). Analogous colors create a harmonious and calming effect.
- **Triadic Colors:** These are three colors evenly spaced around the color wheel (e.g., red, yellow, and blue). Triadic colors create a vibrant and balanced palette.
- **Monochromatic Colors:** This involves using different shades, tints, and tones of a single hue. Monochromatic color schemes create a clean and sophisticated look.

Using Color Theory in Elementor

Elementor's color picker tool allows you to easily select colors based on their hue, saturation, and value. You can also use Elementor's pre-designed color palettes or create your own custom palettes. By understanding color theory, you can make informed decisions about which colors to use and how to combine them to create a visually appealing and effective website design.

Color Psychology

Color psychology is the study of how colors affect human emotions, perceptions, and behaviors. It delves into the subconscious associations we have with different colors and how those associations can be leveraged in web design to create specific moods and responses. By understanding the psychological impact of colors, you can make informed decisions about your website's color palette to enhance user experience and achieve your desired outcomes.

The Psychology of Colors

- **Red:** Often associated with passion, energy, excitement, and urgency. It can grab attention and encourage action but can also be perceived as aggressive if overused. Consider using red for call-to-action buttons or to highlight important elements.
- **Orange:** Represents creativity, enthusiasm, warmth, and friendliness. It can evoke a sense of optimism and encourage interaction. Use orange for playful or creative websites, or to highlight calls to action.
- **Yellow:** Symbolizes happiness, optimism, and clarity. It can be used to create a cheerful and inviting atmosphere but can also be overwhelming if used excessively. Use yellow sparingly for accents or highlights.
- **Green:** Associated with nature, growth, harmony, and balance. It can evoke a sense of calmness and tranquility. Use green for websites related to health, wellness, or the environment.
- **Blue:** Represents trust, professionalism, calmness, and security. It is often used by corporate and financial institutions to build trust. Use blue for websites that want to convey a sense of reliability and expertise.
- **Purple:** Associated with luxury, creativity, spirituality, and mystery. It can be used to create a sense of elegance and sophistication. Use purple for websites related to art, fashion, or beauty.
- **Black:** Symbolizes power, elegance, sophistication, and mystery. It can be used to create a sense of formality or to add contrast to other colors. Use black sparingly as it can be overwhelming if overused.
- **White:** Represents purity, cleanliness, simplicity, and neutrality. It can be used to create a sense of openness and spaciousness. White is often used as a background color to make other colors pop.

Applying Color Psychology to Your Website

When choosing colors for your website, consider the emotions and actions you want to evoke in your visitors. Here are some examples of how you can use color psychology in your web design:

- **E-commerce Website:** Use warm colors like red or orange for call-to-action buttons to encourage purchases.
- **Health and Wellness Website:** Use calming colors like green and blue to create a relaxing and tranquil atmosphere.
- **Corporate Website:** Use blue and white to convey a sense of professionalism and trust.
- **Creative Agency Website:** Use vibrant colors like orange and purple to showcase creativity and innovation.

Remember, color is a powerful tool that can significantly impact your website's effectiveness. By understanding color psychology and using it strategically, you can create a website that not only looks great but also resonates with your audience and drives desired actions.

Backgrounds

Backgrounds are a fundamental aspect of web design, setting the stage for your content and creating a visual atmosphere for your website. Elementor offers a variety of background options to help you craft unique and engaging page designs.

Types of Backgrounds

1. **Classic Background:** This allows you to set a single, solid color as the background for a section, column, or widget. You can choose from a wide range of colors using the color picker tool or enter a specific hex code.
2. **Gradient Background:** Gradients are a blend of two or more colors that create a gradual transition between them. Elementor allows you to customize the colors, direction, angle, and position of your gradient.
3. **Image Background:** You can use images as backgrounds to add visual interest and create a more immersive experience. Elementor lets you upload images from your media library or use external URLs. You can also adjust the image size, position, repeat, and attachment settings.
4. **Video Background:** For a truly dynamic background, you can embed videos. Elementor supports videos from YouTube, Vimeo, or your own self-hosted videos.
5. **Slideshow Background:** Create an engaging background with a slideshow of multiple images or videos. You can customize the transition effects, timing, and navigation options.

Adding and Customizing Backgrounds

To add or customize a background in Elementor:

1. **Select the Element:** Click on the section, column, or widget you want to add a background to.
2. **Navigate to Style Tab:** In the Elementor panel, go to the "Style" tab.
3. **Background Type:** Choose the desired background type (Classic, Gradient, Image, Video, or Slideshow).
4. **Customize:** Depending on the background type, you'll have different customization options. You can adjust colors, gradients, image settings, video settings, and more.

Tips for Using Backgrounds

- **Consider Readability:** Ensure that your text is easily readable against the background. Use contrasting colors or overlay a semi-transparent background on top of your image or video.
- **Optimize Image Size:** If you're using image or video backgrounds, optimize them for web use to ensure fast loading times.
- **Use Backgrounds Strategically:** Don't overuse backgrounds, as they can become distracting. Use them sparingly to highlight specific sections or create visual interest.
- **Experiment:** Try out different background types and combinations to find what works best for your website's design.

By mastering Elementor's background options, you can create visually stunning and engaging web pages that leave a lasting impression on your visitors.

Background Overlays

Background overlays are a versatile tool in Elementor that allow you to add an extra layer of visual interest and depth to your designs. They are essentially semi-transparent colored or gradient layers that you can apply on top of existing backgrounds, such as images or videos.

Adding Visual Interest

Background overlays can be used to create a variety of visual effects, such as:

- **Enhancing Readability:** If your background image or video makes it difficult to read text, you can add a semi-transparent overlay to darken or lighten the background, improving text visibility.

- **Creating Mood and Atmosphere:** Overlays can be used to set the tone of a section or page. For example, a dark overlay can create a dramatic or mysterious feel, while a light overlay can evoke a sense of airiness and optimism.
- **Highlighting Content:** By applying an overlay to a specific area, you can draw attention to certain elements, such as headlines, call-to-action buttons, or important information.

Adjusting Overlay Settings

Elementor provides several settings for customizing your background overlays:

- **Color:** Choose the color of your overlay using the color picker tool or by entering a hex code.
- **Opacity:** Adjust the transparency of the overlay. A lower opacity makes the overlay more transparent, while a higher opacity makes it more opaque.
- **Blend Mode:** Experiment with different blend modes to create unique visual effects. Blend modes determine how the overlay color interacts with the background color. Some common blend modes include Multiply, Overlay, and Soft Light.
- **Position:** Control the position of the overlay relative to the background. You can choose to position the overlay in the center, top left, top right, bottom left, or bottom right.

How to Add a Background Overlay

To add a background overlay in Elementor:

1. **Select the Element:** Click on the section, column, or widget where you want to add the overlay.
2. **Navigate to Style Tab:** In the Elementor panel, go to the "Style" tab.
3. **Background Overlay:** Locate the "Background Overlay" section and enable it.
4. **Customize:** Adjust the overlay color, opacity, blend mode, and position to achieve your desired effect.

Best Practices for Using Background Overlays

- **Use Subtlety:** Avoid using overlays that are too dark or opaque, as they can obscure your background image or video and make your text difficult to read.
- **Consider Contrast:** Ensure sufficient contrast between the overlay color and your text color to maintain readability.
- **Experiment:** Try out different overlay colors, opacities, and blend modes to find the perfect combination for your design.

By mastering the art of background overlays, you can add depth, dimension, and visual interest to your web pages, creating a more immersive and engaging user experience.

Borders and Shadows

Borders and shadows are subtle yet effective design elements that can elevate the visual appeal of your website. In Elementor, you can easily add and customize borders and shadows for your widgets, creating depth, dimension, and visual interest.

Borders

Borders are lines that surround the edges of your widgets. They can be used to visually separate elements, highlight specific areas, or simply add a decorative touch. Elementor offers various border styles, including:

- **Solid:** A continuous, uninterrupted line.
- **Dotted:** A series of dots forming a line.
- **Dashed:** A series of short dashes forming a line.

- **Double:** Two parallel lines forming a border.
- **Groove:** Creates an engraved effect, as if the content is sunken into the page.
- **Ridge:** Creates a raised effect, as if the content is protruding from the page.
- **Inset:** Creates a combination of groove and ridge effects.
- **Outset:** Creates the opposite of the inset effect.

You can also customize the border width, color, and radius (rounded corners) to match your design preferences.

Shadows

Shadows add depth and dimension to your widgets, making them appear to float above the background. Elementor offers two types of shadows:

- **Box Shadow:** Creates a rectangular shadow around the widget.
- **Text Shadow:** Applies a shadow to the text within a text-based widget.

You can customize the shadow's color, blur radius, spread radius, horizontal and vertical offsets, and position (outset or inset) to achieve the desired effect.

Adding and Customizing Borders and Shadows

To add or customize borders and shadows in Elementor:

1. **Select the Widget:** Click on the widget you want to add a border or shadow to.
2. **Navigate to the Style Tab:** In the Elementor panel, go to the "Style" tab.
3. **Border:** Find the "Border" section and choose your desired border style, width, color, and radius.
4. **Box Shadow:** Find the "Box Shadow" section and adjust the shadow's color, blur, spread, position, and offset.
5. **Text Shadow:** (For text-based widgets) Find the "Text Shadow" section and customize the shadow's color, blur, and offset.

Tips for Using Borders and Shadows

- **Use Subtlety:** Avoid overusing borders and shadows, as they can become distracting if applied excessively. Use them sparingly to highlight specific elements or create subtle visual separation.
- **Consider Contrast:** Ensure sufficient contrast between the border or shadow color and the background color to maintain readability and visual clarity.
- **Experiment:** Try out different border styles, shadow effects, and customization options to find the perfect combination for your design.
- **Preview:** Always preview your changes in different responsive modes to ensure that borders and shadows look good on all screen sizes.

By skillfully utilizing borders and shadows, you can add a touch of sophistication and visual depth to your web pages, making them more engaging and aesthetically pleasing for your visitors.

Hover Effects

Hover effects are interactive elements that add a dynamic touch to your website. They trigger visual changes when a user hovers their mouse cursor over a specific widget, creating a more engaging and interactive user experience. Elementor offers a variety of hover effects that you can easily apply to your widgets.

Types of Hover Effects

1. **Background Color Change:** This effect changes the background color of the widget when hovered over. You can choose a different color, gradient, or even an image to create a visually appealing transition.
2. **Text Color Change:** This effect changes the color of the text within the widget upon hover. It's a subtle yet effective way to highlight interactive elements and guide user attention.
3. **Border Color Change:** This effect alters the color of the widget's border when hovered over, adding a visual cue to indicate interactivity.
4. **Animation Effects:** Elementor offers a range of animation effects that can be triggered on hover, such as slide, grow, shrink, rotate, and more. These animations add a playful touch and make your website more dynamic.
5. **Transform Effects:** You can apply transform effects like scaling, skewing, or translating the widget to create more dramatic hover interactions.

Adding Hover Effects in Elementor

To add a hover effect to a widget in Elementor:

1. **Select the Widget:** Click on the widget you want to add the hover effect to.
2. **Hover Style Tab:** In the Elementor panel, go to the "Style" tab and then click on the "Hover" sub-tab.
3. **Choose Hover Effect:** Select the desired hover effect from the dropdown menu.
4. **Customize:** Depending on the chosen effect, you'll have different customization options. You can adjust colors, animation speed, transition duration, and other settings.

Best Practices for Hover Effects

- **Purposeful Use:** Use hover effects strategically to enhance user experience and guide interactions. Don't overuse them, as they can become distracting or annoying.
- **Subtlety:** In most cases, subtle hover effects work best. Avoid overly flashy or distracting animations that might detract from your content.
- **Consistency:** Maintain consistency in your hover effects across your website to create a cohesive user experience.

By incorporating hover effects into your Elementor designs, you can add an extra layer of interactivity and visual appeal to your website, making it more engaging and memorable for your visitors.

Advanced Styling Techniques

While Elementor's built-in styling options are extensive, there may be times when you need even more control over your website's appearance. That's where advanced styling techniques like custom CSS and Elementor Pro's Theme Builder come into play. These techniques allow you to achieve highly customized designs and tailor your website to your exact specifications.

Custom CSS

CSS (Cascading Style Sheets) is the language used to style web pages. It controls the look and feel of your website's elements, such as colors, fonts, layouts, and spacing. By adding custom CSS code to your website, you can override or extend the default styling of your theme and Elementor widgets.

Elementor provides a convenient way to add custom CSS within the editor. You can either add CSS code directly to a specific widget or use the "Custom CSS" field in the Advanced tab of the Elementor panel to apply styles globally.

Custom CSS is a powerful tool for experienced web designers who want to have complete control over their website's appearance. However, it requires a basic understanding of CSS syntax and principles. If you're new to CSS, there are many online resources and tutorials available to help you learn.

Theme Builder (Elementor Pro)

If you have Elementor Pro, you have access to the Theme Builder, a powerful feature that allows you to design and customize every aspect of your website's theme, including:

- **Header:** Create custom headers with your logo, navigation menu, and other elements.
- **Footer:** Design unique footers with copyright information, social media links, and contact details.
- **Single Post/Page Templates:** Customize the layout and design of individual blog posts or pages.
- **Archive Pages:** Design templates for archive pages like category archives, tag archives, author archives, and search results.
- **404 Page:** Create a custom 404 page that is both informative and visually appealing.

The Theme Builder allows you to create reusable templates for different types of content, ensuring a consistent look and feel across your entire website. It also gives you the flexibility to create dynamic templates that adapt to different content types or user roles.

Best Practices for Styling Your Website

Styling your website is a crucial aspect of creating a positive user experience and establishing a strong brand identity. By following these best practices, you can ensure that your website is visually appealing, easy to navigate, and optimized for performance:

1. **Maintain Consistency:** Consistency is key to creating a professional and polished look. Use the same fonts, colors, and design elements throughout your website to create a cohesive visual language. This helps reinforce your brand identity and makes your website easier to navigate.
2. **Use a Limited Color Palette:** Avoid overwhelming your visitors with too many colors. Choose a limited color palette (2-3 main colors and a few accent colors) that aligns with your brand and creates a harmonious look. Use color theory principles to select colors that complement each other and create a visually pleasing experience.
3. **Choose Readable Fonts:** Prioritize readability over fancy fonts. Choose fonts that are easy to read on screen, especially for body text. Use a maximum of two or three fonts on your website to avoid clutter and maintain a clean look.
4. **Create Visual Hierarchy:** Use different font sizes, weights, and styles to create a clear visual hierarchy on your pages. Headings should be larger and bolder than subheadings, and body text should be easy to scan and read. This helps users quickly understand the structure of your content and find the information they're looking for.
5. **Use White Space Effectively:** White space (or negative space) is the empty space around your content. It's essential for creating a clean and uncluttered look, making your content easier to digest. Don't be afraid to use white space generously, especially around text and images.
6. **Optimize Images:** Large, unoptimized images can significantly slow down your website's loading times. Optimize your images by compressing them and using appropriate file formats (JPEG for photos, PNG for graphics with transparency).
7. **Test Responsiveness:** Always test your website on different devices and screen sizes (desktop, tablet, mobile) to ensure it's responsive and looks good on all platforms. Use Elementor's responsive mode to preview and adjust your design for different screen sizes.

By adhering to these best practices, you can create a visually stunning and user-friendly website that leaves a positive impression on your visitors and effectively communicates your brand message.

Chapter Summary

This chapter delved into the art of styling in Elementor, guiding you through the essential tools and techniques to customize your website's visual appearance and make it truly your own.

We started by defining styling as the process of tailoring your website's look and feel using colors, fonts, backgrounds, borders, shadows, and hover effects. Elementor's intuitive interface and comprehensive styling options empower you to achieve this without needing coding knowledge.

We explored the concept of Global Styles, highlighting how they allow you to define default styles for specific elements across your website, ensuring consistency and simplifying the design process.

We delved into typography, emphasizing its importance in web design for readability, visual hierarchy, brand identity, and user experience. We provided tips for choosing the right fonts, understanding font types, creating effective font pairings, and adjusting font size, weight, and line height.

The chapter also covered the significance of colors in web design, explaining their emotional impact, role in brand identity, and contribution to visual hierarchy and readability. We introduced color theory concepts like hue, saturation, and value, and discussed how to use them to create harmonious color palettes. We also touched upon color psychology, highlighting how different colors evoke specific emotions and behaviors in website visitors.

Next, we explored the various background options available in Elementor, including solid colors, gradients, images, videos, and slideshows. We explained how to add and customize backgrounds for sections, columns, and widgets, and provided tips for using backgrounds effectively.

We also covered background overlays, describing how to use them to enhance readability, create mood and atmosphere, and highlight content. We discussed the different overlay settings, such as color, opacity, blend mode, and position, and offered best practices for their usage.

The chapter also touched upon borders and shadows, explaining how to add and customize them to enhance visual appeal and create depth. We described various border styles and shadow effects available in Elementor and provided tips for using them subtly and effectively.

Finally, we explored hover effects, describing how to create interactive elements that change appearance upon hover. We discussed different types of hover effects, such as changing colors, adding animations, or scaling elements, and provided tips for using them purposefully and consistently.

By mastering these styling techniques and adhering to best practices, you can create a visually stunning, user-friendly, and high-performing website that effectively communicates your brand message and leaves a lasting impression on your visitors.

Sections and Columns: Organizing Your Content

Outline

- What are Sections and Columns?
- Creating and Editing Sections
- Creating and Editing Columns
- Using the Column Settings
- Advanced Column Layouts
- Chapter Summary

What are Sections and Columns?

Sections and columns are the backbone of Elementor's page-building structure. They provide a framework for organizing your content in a visually appealing and logical way. Think of sections as the horizontal dividers that split your page into distinct areas, while columns are the vertical divisions within each section.

Sections

Sections are the primary building blocks of your Elementor page. They act as horizontal containers that can hold multiple columns. You can think of sections as rows in a spreadsheet or chapters in a book. Each section represents a distinct area of your page, such as a header, hero section, services section, about us section, or footer.

Sections allow you to control the overall layout of your page, including:

- **Background:** You can set a background color, gradient, image, or video for each section to visually distinguish it from other sections.
- **Height:** You can control the height of a section, making it fit to the screen, have a minimum height, or adjust to the content within it.
- **Content Width:** You can choose whether the content within a section is boxed (contained within a specific width) or full width (spanning the entire width of the browser window).
- **Stretch Section:** You can stretch a section to cover the entire screen, creating a full-screen background effect.
- **Inner Sections:** You can create nested sections within a section to further organize your content and create more complex layouts.

Columns

Columns are the vertical divisions within a section. Each section can contain one or more columns, and you can adjust the width of each column to create different layouts. For example, a two-column layout could be used to display an image on one side and text on the other, while a three-column layout could be used for a pricing table or product showcase.

Columns allow you to:

- **Organize Widgets:** Place different widgets (text, images, buttons, etc.) within each column to create a visually appealing and informative layout.
- **Control Column Widths:** Adjust the width of each column using percentages or pixels to create different layouts.
- **Add Spacing:** Control the spacing between columns to create visual separation and improve readability.

By combining sections and columns in various ways, you can create virtually any type of layout you can imagine. Whether you need a simple single-column page or a complex multi-column design, Elementor's sections and columns give you the flexibility to bring your vision to life.

Creating and Editing Sections

In Elementor, sections are the fundamental building blocks of your page layout. You can add multiple sections to your page, each serving a specific purpose and containing different content elements. Here's how to create and edit sections:

Adding a New Section

1. **Click the "+" Icon:** In the Elementor editor, click the "+" icon that appears when you hover over the top or bottom of an existing section. You can also click the "+" icon in the top-left corner of the editor to add a new section at the beginning of your page.
2. **Choose Column Structure:** A popup will appear with various column structure options. Select the number of columns you want for your new section. For example, you might choose one column for a simple text section, two columns for an image and text layout, or three columns for a pricing table.

Editing Section Settings

Once you've added a section, you can customize its appearance and behavior using the section settings panel. To access the settings panel, click on the "Edit Section" icon (a pencil icon) that appears when you hover over the section.

Here are the main section settings you can modify:

- **Layout:**
  - **Background:** Choose a background color, gradient, or image for your section. You can also add a video background or a slideshow background.
  - **Height:** Control the height of your section. You can choose "Fit to Screen" to make the section fill the entire browser window, "Min Height" to set a minimum height, or "Fit to Content" to make the section adjust to the height of its content.
  - **Content Width:** Decide whether the content within your section should be "Boxed" (contained within a specific width) or "Full Width" (spanning the entire browser window).
  - **Stretch Section:** Enable this option to make the section stretch to cover the entire screen, creating a full-screen background effect.
  - **Inner Section:** Add a nested section within your current section. This allows you to create more complex layouts with multiple columns within a single section.
- **Style:**
  - **Background Overlay:** Add a semi-transparent overlay on top of your background image or video to enhance readability or create a specific mood.
  - **Shape Divider:** Add a decorative shape divider to the top or bottom of your section to create visual interest.
  - **Typography:** Customize the typography settings for the text within your section.
  - **Border:** Add a border around your section and customize its style, width, and color.
  - **Box Shadow:** Add a shadow effect to your section to make it appear to float above the background.
- **Advanced:**
  - **Margins & Padding:** Control the spacing around your section and its content.
  - **Z-Index:** Control the stacking order of overlapping elements.
  - **CSS ID & Classes:** Add custom CSS ID and classes for advanced styling.
  - **Motion Effects:** Add hover effects, entrance animations, or parallax scrolling to your section.

By experimenting with these settings, you can create unique and visually appealing sections that effectively organize your content and enhance the overall design of your website.

Creating and Editing Columns

Columns are the vertical dividers within a section that allow you to arrange your content side-by-side. You can add multiple columns to a section, and each column can contain various widgets, such as text, images, or buttons.

Adding Columns

To add columns to a section:

1. **Select the Section:** Click on the section where you want to add columns.
2. **Click the Column Icon:** In the section's editing handle, click on the column icon (it looks like a grid with two or more squares).
3. **Choose Column Structure:** A popup will appear with various column structure options. Select the number of columns you want to add to the section.

Editing Column Widths

By default, Elementor distributes column widths evenly within a section. However, you can easily adjust the width of each column to create different layouts.

To change column widths:

1. **Select the Column:** Click on the column you want to edit.
2. **Drag the Column Handle:** Hover over the edge of the column until you see a handle (a vertical line with two arrows). Click and drag the handle to resize the column. You can also enter a specific width value in pixels or percentage.

Adjusting Column Spacing

You can control the spacing between columns to create visual separation and improve readability.

To adjust column spacing:

1. **Select the Section:** Click on the section containing the columns.
2. **Column Gap:** In the section's settings panel, locate the "Column Gap" option and adjust the slider or enter a specific value in pixels.

Tips for Working with Columns

- **Balance Content:** Distribute your content evenly across columns to avoid creating a lopsided layout.
- **Use Responsive Settings:** Adjust column widths and visibility for different screen sizes to ensure your layout looks good on all devices.
- **Experiment:** Try out different column structures and widths to find the layout that best suits your content and design preferences.

By mastering the use of columns, you can create dynamic and visually appealing layouts that effectively showcase your content and guide your visitors through your website.

Using the Column Settings

Elementor's column settings allow you to fine-tune the appearance and behavior of individual columns within a section. These settings give you granular control over the layout, styling, and responsiveness of your columns, enabling you to create visually appealing and functional designs.

Layout Settings

The Layout settings determine how the content within a column is vertically aligned. You have four options to choose from:

- **Top:** Aligns the content to the top of the column.
- **Middle:** Centers the content vertically within the column.
- **Bottom:** Aligns the content to the bottom of the column.
- **Space Between:** Distributes the content evenly within the column, with equal spacing between each element.

Choose the alignment that best suits the content within your column and the overall design of your page.

Style Settings

The Style settings allow you to customize the visual appearance of your column. You can:

- **Background Color:** Choose a background color for your column using the color picker or by entering a hex code.
- **Padding:** Adjust the padding (inner spacing) of your column to create more breathing room around its content.
- **Margin:** Control the margin (outer spacing) of your column to adjust its position relative to other columns or elements on the page.
- **Border:** Add a border around your column and customize its style, width, and color.
- **Box Shadow:** Apply a shadow effect to your column to make it stand out from the background.

Responsive Settings

Responsive design is essential for ensuring that your website looks great on all devices. Elementor's responsive settings allow you to adjust the column widths and visibility for different screen sizes (desktop, tablet, mobile).

You can set different column widths for each device, ensuring that your content is displayed optimally on smaller screens. You can also hide specific columns on certain devices if they are not necessary or would clutter the layout on smaller screens.

Advanced Settings

The Advanced settings offer more technical options for customizing your columns:

- **Z-index:** Control the stacking order of overlapping elements. A higher z-index value brings an element to the front, while a lower value sends it to the back.
- **CSS ID:** Assign a unique ID to your column, allowing you to target it with custom CSS code.
- **CSS Classes:** Add custom CSS classes to your column to apply specific styles or behaviors.

By mastering Elementor's column settings, you can create versatile and responsive layouts that adapt seamlessly to different screen sizes and devices, ensuring a positive user experience for all your visitors.

Advanced Column Layouts

Elementor's column system is inherently flexible, but you can take your layouts even further by utilizing advanced techniques. These techniques allow you to create more complex and dynamic designs that cater to your specific content and visual preferences.

Nested Columns

Nested columns are a powerful feature that allows you to create columns within columns. This means you can have multiple columns within a single parent column, enabling you to create intricate and visually interesting layouts.

To create nested columns:

1. **Add an Inner Section:** Inside an existing column, click the "+" icon and select "Inner Section." This will create a new section within the column.
2. **Choose Column Structure:** Select the desired column structure for the inner section (e.g., two columns, three columns).
3. **Add Widgets:** Drag and drop widgets into the inner columns just like you would in a regular section.

Nested columns are especially useful for creating complex layouts like multi-level menus, sidebars with multiple widgets, or product displays with varying item sizes.

Custom Column Widths

By default, Elementor distributes column widths evenly within a section. However, you can easily customize the width of each column to achieve the precise layout you desire.

To set custom column widths:

1. **Select the Column:** Click on the column you want to edit.
2. **Edit Column Width:** In the column settings panel, you'll find the "Width" option. You can either drag the slider to adjust the width visually or enter a specific value in percentage (e.g., 33%) or pixels (e.g., 300px).

Custom column widths give you greater flexibility to create unique layouts that cater to your specific content and design preferences.

Column Gap

Column gap refers to the spacing between columns within a section. You can adjust the column gap to create visual separation and improve readability.

To adjust column gap:

1. **Select the Section:** Click on the section containing the columns.
2. **Column Gap:** In the section settings panel, locate the "Column Gap" option. You can either drag the slider to adjust the gap visually or enter a specific value in pixels.

A larger column gap can make your content feel more spacious and airy, while a smaller gap creates a tighter and more compact layout. Experiment with different column gap values to find the optimal spacing for your design.

Reverse Columns

In some cases, you might want to change the order of columns on different screen sizes. For example, you might want a sidebar that appears on the right side of the main content on desktop to appear below the main content on mobile devices.

To reverse columns:

1. **Select the Section:** Click on the section containing the columns.
2. **Responsive Mode:** Switch to the responsive mode for the screen size you want to adjust (tablet or mobile).
3. **Reverse Columns:** In the section settings panel, you'll find an option to reverse the order of columns. Enable this option to change the column order for that specific screen size.

By utilizing these advanced column layout techniques, you can create dynamic and visually engaging designs that adapt seamlessly to different screen sizes and devices, ensuring a positive user experience for all your visitors.

Chapter Summary

This chapter delved into the fundamental building blocks of Elementor page design: sections and columns. We explored how these elements work together to structure your content, create visual hierarchy, and enable flexible layouts.

We began by defining sections as horizontal containers that hold multiple columns, while columns act as vertical containers for individual widgets. This hierarchical structure allows you to arrange content in a visually appealing and organized manner.

We then provided step-by-step instructions on creating and editing sections. You learned how to add new sections, customize their background, height, content width, and other settings. Additionally, you discovered how to create nested sections (Inner Sections) within existing sections for more complex layouts.

Next, we focused on creating and editing columns, explaining how to adjust their widths and spacing to achieve the desired layout. We also explored the various column settings in Elementor, including layout, style, responsive, and advanced options, giving you granular control over the appearance and behavior of your columns.

Finally, we discussed advanced column layout techniques, such as creating nested columns, setting custom column widths, adjusting column gaps, and reversing column order for different screen sizes. These techniques empower you to create more sophisticated and responsive designs that adapt to various devices and screen sizes.

By mastering sections and columns in Elementor, you unlock the ability to create diverse and engaging page layouts that effectively showcase your content and enhance the overall user experience.

Responsive Design: Optimizing for All Devices

Outline

- What is Responsive Design?
- Importance of Responsive Design
- How Elementor Handles Responsive Design
- Responsive Editing Modes in Elementor
- Device-Specific Styling
- Responsive Column Settings
- Responsive Typography
- Responsive Images
- Tips for Responsive Design with Elementor
- Testing Your Responsive Design
- Chapter Summary

What is Responsive Design?

Responsive web design is an approach to creating websites that dynamically adjust their layout, content, and functionality to fit the screen size of the device being used. Whether someone is viewing your website on a large desktop monitor, a tablet, or a smartphone, a responsive design ensures that the website automatically adapts to provide the best possible user experience.

In essence, a responsive website is like a shape-shifter, seamlessly transforming its appearance and layout to suit the device it's being viewed on. This eliminates the need for users to pinch and zoom or scroll horizontally to read content on smaller screens, making the browsing experience smooth and enjoyable.

Why is Responsive Design Important?

Responsive design is essential in today's mobile-centric world for several reasons:

- **Improved User Experience:** Responsive websites offer a consistent and user-friendly experience across all devices. This leads to increased engagement, lower bounce rates, and higher conversions.
- **Increased Mobile Traffic:** With the majority of web traffic now coming from mobile devices, having a mobile-friendly website is crucial for reaching your audience.
- **Better SEO:** Search engines like Google prioritize responsive websites in their search results, as they provide a better user experience. This can lead to higher rankings and increased organic traffic.
- **Cost-Effectiveness:** Building a single responsive website is more cost-effective than creating separate versions for different devices. It saves time and resources in development and maintenance.
- **Future-Proofing:** As new devices and screen sizes emerge, a responsive design will automatically adapt, ensuring your website remains relevant and accessible.

How Does Responsive Design Work?

Responsive design is achieved through a combination of flexible grids, flexible images, and media queries.

- **Flexible Grids:** The layout of a responsive website is built on a grid system that uses relative units (percentages) instead of fixed pixel values. This allows the layout to adjust fluidly to different screen widths.
- **Flexible Images:** Responsive images are designed to scale proportionally to the screen size. This prevents images from becoming too large on smaller screens or too small on larger screens.
- **Media Queries:** Media queries are CSS rules that apply different styles to a website based on the screen size. This allows you to create specific layouts and styles for different devices.

Elementor simplifies the process of creating responsive websites by providing intuitive tools and settings to adjust your layouts for different screen sizes. You can preview your website on desktop, tablet, and mobile devices within the editor and make device-specific adjustments to ensure optimal viewing experiences on all platforms.

Importance of Responsive Design

In today's digital landscape, where mobile devices reign supreme, responsive design is no longer a luxury but a necessity. It's a cornerstone of modern web development that ensures your website delivers a seamless and user-friendly experience across a multitude of devices and screen sizes. Let's delve into why responsive design is paramount for your website's success:

Improved User Experience

Imagine trying to navigate a website on your smartphone that was designed for a desktop computer. The text would be tiny, the images oversized, and the layout would be a jumbled mess. Frustrating, right? That's why responsive design is crucial. It ensures that your website adapts to the device being used, providing a comfortable and enjoyable experience for your visitors.

With a responsive design, your website's elements automatically resize, rearrange, and reflow to fit the screen, whether it's a widescreen monitor or a compact smartphone display. This means users can easily read your content, click on links, and navigate your site without the need for excessive zooming or scrolling. A positive user experience leads to longer visit durations, lower bounce rates, and ultimately, increased conversions.

Increased Mobile Traffic

Mobile devices have surpassed desktops as the primary means of accessing the internet. In fact, a significant majority of web traffic now originates from smartphones and tablets. If your website isn't optimized for mobile, you're missing out on a massive potential audience.

Responsive design ensures that your website is accessible and user-friendly on mobile devices, tapping into this vast mobile traffic and expanding your reach. A mobile-friendly website is no longer just a nice-to-have; it's a must-have to remain competitive in the digital landscape.

Better SEO

Search engines, like Google, recognize the importance of mobile-friendliness and prioritize responsive websites in their search results. This means that if your website isn't responsive, it's likely to rank lower in search engine rankings, making it harder for potential visitors to find you.

Responsive design is a key factor in Google's mobile-first indexing approach, which prioritizes the mobile version of your website for indexing and ranking. By investing in responsive design, you not only improve user experience but also boost your website's visibility in search engines, driving more organic traffic to your site.

Cost-Effectiveness

In the past, businesses often had to create separate websites for desktop and mobile devices, which was time-consuming and expensive to maintain. Responsive design eliminates this need by providing a single website that adapts to all devices. This not only reduces development and maintenance costs but also simplifies content management and ensures a consistent brand experience across all platforms.

Future-Proofing

The world of technology is constantly evolving, with new devices and screen sizes emerging regularly. Responsive design future-proofs your website by ensuring it automatically adapts to these new devices. This means you won't have to scramble to create new versions of your website every time a new device hits the market.

In conclusion, responsive design is a critical investment for any website owner who wants to thrive in the digital age. It improves user experience, increases mobile traffic, boosts SEO, reduces costs, and ensures your website remains relevant and accessible in the ever-changing technological landscape.

How Elementor Handles Responsive Design

Elementor simplifies the complexities of responsive design, making it accessible to users of all skill levels. It employs a multi-faceted approach that combines automatic responsiveness with manual fine-tuning options, empowering you to create websites that look stunning and function seamlessly on all devices.

Automatic Responsiveness

By default, Elementor automatically generates responsive layouts for your pages. This means that when you add widgets and design your page on a desktop screen, Elementor intelligently adjusts the layout to fit smaller screens like tablets and mobile phones. It does this by rearranging elements, resizing images, and adjusting font sizes to ensure optimal readability and usability across different devices.

Manual Fine-Tuning

While Elementor's automatic responsiveness is impressive, you might want to further refine your design for specific screen sizes. Elementor provides a range of tools and settings to give you granular control over your responsive layouts.

You can easily switch between different responsive modes within the editor, previewing how your page will look on desktop, tablet, and mobile devices. This allows you to identify areas that might need adjustments and make changes accordingly.

Elementor also offers device-specific styling options for individual widgets. You can customize the visibility, size, position, and other properties of a widget based on the screen size it's being viewed on. This gives you the flexibility to create unique layouts for different devices, ensuring that your content is presented optimally on every screen.

Responsive Design Features

Elementor provides several features that facilitate responsive design:

- **Responsive Editing Modes:** As mentioned earlier, you can switch between desktop, tablet, and mobile editing modes to preview and adjust your design for each screen size.
- **Column Settings:** You can customize column widths and order for different screen sizes, ensuring that your layouts adapt seamlessly to various devices.
- **Responsive Typography:** You can adjust font sizes, line heights, and letter spacing for different screen sizes to ensure optimal readability on smaller screens.

- **Responsive Images:** Elementor automatically resizes images for different screen sizes, improving loading times and user experience on mobile devices.
- **Hidden Elements:** You can hide specific widgets or sections on certain screen sizes if they are not necessary or would clutter the layout.

By combining Elementor's automatic responsiveness with its manual fine-tuning capabilities, you can create truly responsive websites that adapt beautifully to any device, providing a consistent and enjoyable experience for all your visitors.

Responsive Editing Modes in Elementor

Elementor makes it incredibly easy to design and fine-tune your website's layout for different screen sizes with its intuitive responsive editing modes. These modes allow you to see exactly how your page will look on various devices, ensuring a seamless user experience across desktops, tablets, and mobile phones.

The Three Responsive Modes

1. **Desktop:** This is the default mode in Elementor, representing the standard desktop or laptop screen size. You'll typically start designing your page in this mode, focusing on the layout and content that will be displayed on larger screens.
2. **Tablet:** This mode simulates the view on a tablet device, typically with a screen size around 768 pixels wide. Switching to tablet mode allows you to see how your layout adapts to a smaller screen and make necessary adjustments to optimize the user experience for tablet users.
3. **Mobile:** This mode emulates the view on a smartphone, typically with a screen width of 360 pixels or less. In this mode, you can fine-tune your layout for mobile users, ensuring that your content is readable, buttons are easily tappable, and navigation is intuitive on smaller screens.

Switching Between Modes

To switch between different responsive modes in Elementor, simply click on the Responsive Mode icon located in the bottom left corner of the Elementor editor. It looks like a monitor with three icons representing desktop, tablet, and mobile views. Clicking on this icon will open a menu where you can select the desired mode.

Once you've selected a mode, the Elementor editor will automatically resize to simulate the chosen screen size. You can then make any necessary adjustments to the layout, content, or styling specifically for that device. For example, you might want to stack columns vertically on mobile, hide certain elements, or adjust font sizes for better readability.

By toggling between these responsive modes and making device-specific customizations, you can ensure that your website delivers a consistent and user-friendly experience across all devices.

Device-Specific Styling

Elementor's device-specific styling feature is a game-changer when it comes to responsive design. It allows you to tailor the appearance and behavior of individual widgets based on the screen size they are viewed on. This means you can make a widget look and function differently on desktop, tablet, and mobile devices, ensuring an optimal experience for each user.

How It Works

When you select a widget in Elementor, you'll notice a small device icon next to certain style options in the panel. This icon indicates that you can apply different settings for that option depending on the screen size.

By clicking on the device icon, you can toggle between desktop, tablet, and mobile views. Each view allows you to customize the settings specifically for that device. For example, you can change the font size of a heading to make it larger on desktop and smaller on mobile, or you can adjust the padding of a section to create more breathing room on smaller screens.

Common Device-Specific Customizations

Here are some common customizations you can make using device-specific styling:

- **Visibility:** You can hide or show a widget entirely on certain devices. For example, you might want to display a large image on desktop but hide it on mobile to avoid cluttering the layout.
- **Size:** You can adjust the size of a widget (e.g., width, height, font size) for different screen sizes.
- **Position:** You can reposition a widget on the page based on the screen size.
- **Typography:** You can change the font family, size, weight, and line height for different devices to ensure optimal readability.
- **Colors:** You can use different color schemes for different screen sizes to create a unique visual experience for each device.
- **Background:** You can change the background image or color for different devices.
- **Margins & Padding:** You can adjust the spacing around a widget for different screen sizes.

Best Practices

When applying device-specific styling, keep the following tips in mind:

- **Start with mobile:** Design your page for mobile devices first, then adapt it for larger screens. This approach ensures that your content is optimized for the smallest screens and works its way up.
- **Prioritize content:** Focus on the most important content and make sure it's easily accessible on all devices.
- **Test thoroughly:** Preview your design on different devices and screen sizes to ensure that it looks and functions as expected.

By mastering device-specific styling in Elementor, you can create truly responsive websites that adapt seamlessly to any screen size, providing a consistent and enjoyable user experience for all your visitors.

Responsive Column Settings

Elementor's column settings give you the power to create flexible and dynamic layouts that adapt seamlessly to different screen sizes. You can easily adjust the width and order of columns for desktop, tablet, and mobile devices, ensuring your content is presented optimally on every screen.

Adjusting Column Widths

To adjust column widths for different screen sizes:

1. **Select the Column:** Click on the column you want to edit in the Elementor editor.
2. **Responsive Mode:** Click on the Responsive Mode icon in the bottom-left corner of the editor and choose the desired device (Desktop, Tablet, or Mobile).
3. **Column Width:** In the column settings panel (left-hand side), locate the "Width" option. You can either drag the slider to adjust the width visually or enter a specific value in percentage (e.g., 50%) or pixels (e.g., 300px).

Repeat these steps for each column in your section, adjusting the widths as needed for each device.

Stacking Columns Vertically

On smaller screens, like mobile devices, you might want your columns to stack vertically instead of appearing side-by-side. This can improve readability and user experience on smaller screens.

To stack columns vertically:

1. **Select the Section:** Click on the section containing the columns you want to stack.
2. **Responsive Mode:** Switch to the "Mobile" mode.
3. **Reverse Columns (Optional):** If you want to change the order in which the columns stack, you can enable the "Reverse Columns" option in the section settings panel.

Changing Column Order

You can also change the order in which columns appear on different screen sizes. This is useful if you want certain columns to be prioritized on smaller screens.

To change column order:

1. **Select the Section:** Click on the section containing the columns you want to reorder.
2. **Responsive Mode:** Switch to the desired device (Tablet or Mobile).
3. **Drag and Drop Columns:** In the Navigator Panel on the right-hand side of the editor, click and drag the columns to rearrange their order.

Tips for Responsive Column Settings

- **Start with Mobile:** Design your layout for mobile first, then adjust for tablet and desktop. This ensures your content is optimized for the smallest screens.
- **Use Percentage Widths:** Whenever possible, use percentage-based widths for your columns. This allows them to scale proportionally to different screen sizes.
- **Test on Multiple Devices:** Preview your design on various devices and screen sizes to ensure it looks and functions correctly across all platforms.

By utilizing Elementor's responsive column settings, you can create flexible and adaptable layouts that provide an optimal viewing experience for your visitors, regardless of the device they use.

Responsive Typography

Clear and legible typography is essential for a positive user experience, especially on smaller screens. Elementor allows you to fine-tune your typography settings for different devices, ensuring that your text remains readable and visually appealing across all screen sizes.

Adjusting Font Sizes

Font sizes that look perfect on a desktop screen might appear too small or too large on a mobile device. Elementor enables you to adjust font sizes individually for desktop, tablet, and mobile views.

To adjust font sizes for different screen sizes:

1. **Select the Widget:** Click on the text-based widget (e.g., Heading, Text Editor) you want to modify.
2. **Responsive Mode:** Click on the Responsive Mode icon in the bottom-left corner of the editor and choose the desired device (Desktop, Tablet, or Mobile).
3. **Typography Settings:** In the widget's Style tab, locate the typography settings. Here, you'll find options for adjusting font size, usually measured in pixels (px) or em units.
4. **Adjust Font Size:** Decrease the font size for smaller screens (tablet and mobile) to ensure readability. You can also increase the font size for desktop if needed.

Adjusting Line Height

Line height, or leading, is the vertical space between lines of text. Proper line height is crucial for readability, especially on smaller screens.

To adjust line height for different screen sizes:

1. **Select the Widget:** Click on the text-based widget you want to modify.
2. **Responsive Mode:** Choose the desired device (Desktop, Tablet, or Mobile).
3. **Typography Settings:** In the widget's Style tab, locate the line-height setting. It's usually expressed as a number (e.g., 1.5) or in pixels (px).
4. **Adjust Line Height:** Increase the line height for smaller screens to improve readability and prevent text from appearing cramped.

Adjusting Letter Spacing

Letter spacing, or tracking, is the space between individual letters. It can affect the readability and overall appearance of your text.

To adjust letter spacing for different screen sizes:

1. **Select the Widget:** Click on the text-based widget you want to modify.
2. **Responsive Mode:** Choose the desired device (Desktop, Tablet, or Mobile).
3. **Typography Settings:** In the widget's Style tab, locate the letter-spacing setting. It's usually expressed in pixels (px) or em units.
4. **Adjust Letter Spacing:** Experiment with different letter spacing values to find the optimal balance for readability and aesthetics on each screen size.

By meticulously adjusting these typography settings for different devices, you can ensure that your text remains clear, legible, and visually appealing, regardless of the screen size it's being viewed on. This attention to detail will significantly enhance the user experience and make your website more accessible to a wider audience.

Responsive Images

Elementor simplifies the process of using responsive images on your website. Responsive images are images that automatically adjust their size and resolution to fit the screen they are being viewed on. This is crucial for optimizing your website's performance, especially on mobile devices, where bandwidth and screen size can be limited.

Elementor's Automatic Image Resizing

When you upload an image to your WordPress media library and insert it into your Elementor page, Elementor automatically generates multiple versions of that image at different sizes. These different sizes cater to various screen resolutions, ensuring that the appropriate image size is served to each device.

For example, a large image might be displayed on a desktop screen, while a smaller version of the same image would be served to a mobile device. This automatic resizing prevents large images from being downloaded on smaller screens, which can significantly slow down page loading times and consume unnecessary bandwidth.

Importance of Responsive Images

Using responsive images offers several benefits for your website:

1. **Faster Loading Times:** Responsive images reduce the amount of data that needs to be downloaded, resulting in faster page loading times, especially on mobile devices with slower

connections. This improves user experience and can positively impact your website's search engine rankings.
2. **Reduced Bandwidth Usage:** By serving smaller image sizes to mobile devices, you can significantly reduce your website's bandwidth usage. This can be especially important if you have a limited hosting plan or if you're paying for bandwidth overages.
3. **Improved User Experience:** Responsive images ensure that your images are displayed correctly on all devices. This means that users won't have to zoom in or out to view your images, and they won't be overwhelmed by oversized images on smaller screens.
4. **Better SEO:** Search engines favor websites that load quickly and provide a good user experience. Responsive images contribute to both of these factors, potentially improving your website's search engine rankings.

Best Practices for Responsive Images in Elementor

- **Optimize Your Images:** Before uploading images to your WordPress media library, optimize them for web use. This includes compressing images to reduce their file size without sacrificing quality. You can use image optimization plugins like Smush or TinyPNG to streamline this process.
- **Use the Right Image Format:** Choose the appropriate image format for different types of images. JPEG is generally best for photographs, while PNG is better for images with transparency or graphics with sharp lines.
- **Set Appropriate Image Sizes:** In the Elementor image widget settings, make sure to select an appropriate image size for each device. Avoid using unnecessarily large image sizes on smaller screens.
- **Use `srcset` and `sizes` Attributes:** Elementor automatically adds `srcset` and `sizes` attributes to your image code. These attributes provide hints to the browser about which image size to download based on the screen resolution, further optimizing image delivery.

By following these best practices and utilizing Elementor's responsive image features, you can ensure that your website's images are optimized for all devices, resulting in faster loading times, improved user experience, and better search engine visibility.

Tips for Responsive Design with Elementor

Creating responsive designs with Elementor is a breeze, but here are some additional tips to help you create a truly seamless experience across all devices:

1. **Start with Mobile-First:** When designing your layout, start by optimizing it for mobile devices first. This will help you prioritize the most important content and ensure it's easily accessible on smaller screens. Then, gradually adjust your design for larger screens like tablets and desktops.
2. **Embrace Percentage-Based Widths:** Use percentage-based widths for columns and elements whenever possible. This allows your layout to scale proportionally to different screen sizes, ensuring a consistent look and feel across devices.
3. **Avoid Fixed Pixel Values:** Avoid using fixed pixel values for widths and heights, as they can lead to issues on different screen sizes. Instead, use relative units like percentages, ems, or rems, which adapt to the user's screen resolution.
4. **Utilize Media Queries:** Media queries are CSS rules that allow you to apply specific styles to different screen sizes. You can use media queries to adjust font sizes, column layouts, and other elements based on the device being used.
5. **Leverage Elementor's Responsive Controls:** Elementor offers a range of responsive controls for individual widgets, such as hiding or showing elements on specific devices, adjusting column widths, and changing the order of elements.
6. **Test, Test, Test:** Always test your website on various devices and browsers to ensure that it looks and functions correctly across all platforms. Use browser developer tools or online simulators to preview your website on different screen sizes.

7. **Optimize Images:** Large images can slow down your website's loading times, especially on mobile devices. Use Elementor's built-in image optimization tools or a dedicated image optimization plugin to compress your images and improve performance.
8. **Limit the Use of Custom Breakpoints:** While Elementor allows you to create custom breakpoints for specific screen sizes, try to use them sparingly. Stick to the default breakpoints (desktop, tablet, mobile) whenever possible to simplify your design process.
9. **Keep Your Design Simple:** Avoid overly complex layouts and animations that might not work well on smaller screens. Stick to a clean and simple design that is easy to navigate and understand on any device.

By incorporating these tips into your workflow, you can create beautiful, functional, and responsive websites with Elementor that deliver a seamless experience to your visitors, no matter what device they use.

Testing Your Responsive Design

Thorough testing is a critical final step in the responsive design process. It's essential to ensure your website looks and functions flawlessly across a variety of devices and screen sizes before making it live. While Elementor's live preview gives you a good starting point, testing on real devices is necessary to catch any potential issues that might not be apparent in the editor.

Why Test Your Responsive Design?

- **Identify and Fix Issues:** Testing allows you to identify and fix any layout problems, rendering errors, or functionality glitches that may occur on different devices.
- **Optimize User Experience:** By testing your website on various devices, you can ensure that the user experience is seamless and enjoyable, regardless of the screen size.
- **Improve SEO:** Search engines prioritize mobile-friendly websites, so testing and optimizing your responsive design can positively impact your search rankings.
- **Avoid Losing Visitors:** A website that doesn't function correctly on mobile devices can frustrate visitors and cause them to leave your site quickly.

Tools for Testing Responsive Design

1. **Browser Developer Tools:** Most modern web browsers (Chrome, Firefox, Safari, Edge) come with built-in developer tools that allow you to simulate different screen sizes and devices. Simply open your website in the browser, press F12 (or Ctrl+Shift+I on Windows/Linux or Cmd+Opt+I on macOS) to open the developer tools, and then use the device toolbar to switch between different views.
2. **Online Simulators:** There are numerous online simulators available, such as Responsinator (https://www.responsinator.com/) and Screenfly (https://quirktools.com/screenfly/), that allow you to preview your website on various devices and screen sizes.
3. **Real Devices:** While browser developer tools and online simulators are helpful, it's crucial to test your website on real devices whenever possible. This will give you the most accurate representation of how your website looks and functions on different screens.

Testing on Real Devices

To test your website on real devices:

1. **Gather Devices:** Ideally, test your website on a variety of devices, including different models of smartphones, tablets, and laptops.
2. **Access Your Website:** Open your website on each device using the browser of your choice.
3. **Test Functionality:** Navigate through your website, test all links and buttons, and ensure that all interactive elements work correctly.

4. **Check Layout and Design:** Pay attention to how your layout adapts to different screen sizes and whether any elements overlap or become difficult to read.
5. **Test Performance:** Make sure your website loads quickly and smoothly on all devices.

Tips for Testing Responsive Design

- **Focus on Mobile First:** Start your testing with the smallest screen size (mobile) and work your way up to larger screens.
- **Test Different Orientations:** Test your website in both portrait and landscape orientations on mobile devices.
- **Check Touch Interactions:** Ensure that your website is easy to navigate and interact with using touch gestures.
- **Test on Different Browsers:** Test your website on different browsers (Chrome, Firefox, Safari, Edge) to ensure cross-browser compatibility.
- **Get Feedback:** Ask friends, family, or colleagues to test your website on their devices and provide feedback.

By thoroughly testing your responsive design, you can ensure that your website delivers a seamless and enjoyable experience to all visitors, regardless of the device they use.

Chapter Summary

This chapter delved into the crucial aspect of responsive design, emphasizing its importance in creating websites that adapt seamlessly to various devices and screen sizes. We began by defining responsive design and explaining why it's essential for improving user experience, increasing mobile traffic, boosting SEO, ensuring cost-effectiveness, and future-proofing your website.

We then explored how Elementor simplifies the process of creating responsive designs by providing intuitive tools and settings. We discussed Elementor's automatic responsiveness, which adjusts layouts for different screen sizes, and the manual fine-tuning options that allow you to further customize your design.

Next, we introduced the three responsive editing modes in Elementor: Desktop, Tablet, and Mobile. We described how to switch between these modes and how they help you visualize and adjust your layout for specific screen sizes.

We also covered device-specific styling, explaining how you can apply different styles to individual widgets based on the screen size. This allows you to create unique experiences for users on different devices, ensuring optimal usability and readability.

Furthermore, we explained how to adjust column widths and order for different screen sizes, including how to stack columns vertically or change their order on smaller screens. We also discussed how to make your typography and images responsive to different screen sizes, ensuring optimal readability and performance.

Finally, we provided a list of tips for creating responsive designs with Elementor, emphasizing the importance of a mobile-first approach, using percentage-based widths, avoiding fixed pixel values, utilizing media queries, and testing your design thoroughly on various devices and browsers.

By mastering these responsive design techniques in Elementor, you can create websites that look stunning and function flawlessly on any device, providing a positive user experience and improving your website's overall success.

Section III:
Creating Essential Website Pages

Designing Your Homepage: First Impressions Matter

Outline

- The Importance of a Well-Designed Homepage
- Essential Elements of a Homepage
- Designing Your Homepage with Elementor
- Best Practices for Homepage Design
- Additional Tips for an Engaging Homepage
- Examples of Effective Homepages Built with Elementor
- Chapter Summary

The Importance of a Well-Designed Homepage

Your homepage is the digital equivalent of your business's storefront or a book's cover. It's the first impression visitors have of your brand, and it sets the tone for their entire experience on your website. A well-designed homepage can captivate visitors, spark their interest, and guide them deeper into your site, while a poorly designed one can quickly drive them away.

First Impressions Matter

Think of your homepage as a virtual handshake. It's the first interaction visitors have with your brand online, and it needs to make a positive impact. A visually appealing, well-organized, and informative homepage can instantly convey professionalism, credibility, and trustworthiness. It can spark curiosity and encourage visitors to explore your products, services, or content.

On the other hand, a cluttered, confusing, or outdated homepage can leave a negative impression. Visitors might perceive your brand as unprofessional or untrustworthy, leading them to quickly abandon your site and seek alternatives.

Engaging Visitors and Encouraging Exploration

A well-designed homepage goes beyond just looking good; it actively engages visitors and guides them towards the actions you want them to take. It uses clear calls to action, intuitive navigation, and compelling visuals to draw visitors deeper into your website.

For example, a strong headline can immediately grab attention and communicate your value proposition. High-quality images or videos can create an emotional connection and showcase your brand's personality. A well-placed call-to-action button can guide visitors towards purchasing a product, signing up for a newsletter, or contacting you for more information.

The Role of the Homepage in Your Website's Success

Your homepage plays a crucial role in your website's overall success. It's the starting point for most visitors, and it often determines whether they stay on your site or leave. A well-designed homepage can:

- **Reduce Bounce Rate:** By providing clear navigation and engaging content, you can encourage visitors to explore multiple pages on your site, reducing the bounce rate (the percentage of visitors who leave after viewing only one page).
- **Increase Conversions:** A compelling homepage with clear calls to action can guide visitors towards the actions you want them to take, such as making a purchase or filling out a contact form.
- **Improve SEO:** A well-structured homepage with relevant keywords and engaging content can help your website rank higher in search engine results, leading to more organic traffic.

In essence, your homepage is the cornerstone of your online presence. It's a powerful tool for attracting, engaging, and converting visitors into customers, clients, or followers. By investing time and effort into designing an effective homepage, you can set your website up for success and achieve your business goals.

Essential Elements of a Homepage

A well-crafted homepage is the cornerstone of an effective website. It should be designed to quickly engage visitors, communicate your brand's essence, and guide them toward further exploration or specific actions. Here are the essential elements that should be incorporated into a well-designed homepage:

Above the Fold Content

This refers to the content that is immediately visible to visitors when they land on your homepage, without having to scroll down. Given its prime real estate, it's crucial to make the most of this space. Include:

- **Compelling Headline:** A strong, concise headline that captures attention and communicates your website's main message.
- **Clear Call-to-Action (CTA) Button:** Prominently display a CTA button that encourages visitors to take a specific action, such as "Get Started," "Learn More," or "Shop Now."
- **High-Quality Visuals:** Use eye-catching images or videos that are relevant to your content and brand.

Navigation Menu

A clear and intuitive navigation menu is crucial for helping visitors find their way around your website. It should be easy to locate, logically organized, and include links to all essential pages.

Consider these types of menus:

- **Horizontal Menus:** Typically located at the top of the page, these are the most common type of navigation menu.
- **Vertical Menus:** Often used for websites with a large number of pages, vertical menus can be placed on the left or right side of the page.
- **Hamburger Menus:** These are space-saving menus that are collapsed by default and can be expanded by clicking on a "hamburger" icon (three horizontal lines). They are commonly used on mobile devices.

Hero Section

The hero section is a large banner-like area, usually at the top of the homepage, designed to capture attention and make a strong first impression. It typically includes:

- **Background Image or Video:** A visually striking image or video that sets the tone for your website.

- **Headline and Subheading:** A compelling headline and a brief subheading that summarize your website's main message or value proposition.
- **Call-to-Action Button:** A prominent button that encourages visitors to take the next step, such as exploring your services, learning more about your products, or contacting you.

About Us Section

The About Us section is your chance to introduce your brand or business to visitors. It's where you can tell your story, share your mission and values, and highlight what makes you unique. A well-crafted About Us section can build trust and credibility with your audience.

Services or Products Section

If your website offers services or products, dedicate a section on your homepage to showcase them. Use high-quality images, icons, and concise descriptions to highlight your offerings. You can also include testimonials or case studies to provide social proof and build confidence in your brand.

Testimonials or Social Proof

Testimonials or social proof are powerful tools for building trust and credibility. Display positive feedback from customers, clients, or users to demonstrate the value of your products or services. You can use text-based testimonials, video testimonials, or social media posts to showcase your social proof.

Call to Action (CTA)

Throughout your homepage, strategically place clear and compelling calls to action. These can be buttons, links, or forms that encourage visitors to take specific actions, such as subscribing to your newsletter, requesting a demo, downloading a resource, or making a purchase.

Footer

The footer is the bottom section of your website, typically containing essential information like contact details, social media links, copyright information, and links to important pages such as your privacy policy or terms of service. A well-designed footer can provide a sense of closure and make it easy for visitors to find important information or navigate to other areas of your site.

Designing Your Homepage with Elementor

Designing a captivating homepage with Elementor is a straightforward process that combines creativity with user-friendly tools. Here's a step-by-step guide to help you craft a homepage that leaves a lasting impression:

1. **Choose a Template (Optional):**
   Elementor offers a vast library of pre-designed homepage templates that cater to various industries and styles. To explore these templates:
   - Click on the folder icon in the Elementor editor.
   - Browse through the "Pages" category or use the search bar to find a template that aligns with your vision.
   - Click "Insert" to add the template to your page.
2. While using a template is optional, it can significantly accelerate the design process, especially if you're starting from scratch. Remember, you can always customize the template extensively to make it your own.
3. **Add Sections and Columns:**
   Structure your homepage by dividing it into sections and columns. Each section can represent a different content block, such as the hero section, about us, services, testimonials, etc.
   - Click the "+" icon to add a new section.

- Choose the desired column structure (e.g., one, two, or three columns).
- Drag the section's edges to adjust its height.
- Utilize the Navigator Panel to arrange sections in the desired order.

4. Elementor's flexibility allows you to experiment with different layouts to find the perfect structure for your content.
5. **Insert Widgets:**
   Now that you have the basic structure in place, it's time to populate your sections with content using Elementor widgets.
   - Drag and drop widgets from the panel onto your page.
   - Commonly used homepage widgets include:
     - **Heading:** For titles and subtitles.
     - **Text Editor:** For body text and paragraphs.
     - **Image:** For adding visuals.
     - **Video:** For embedding videos.
     - **Button:** For call-to-action buttons.
     - **Icon:** For adding visual icons.
     - **Spacer:** For adjusting spacing between elements.
6. **Customize Styling:**
   Give your homepage a unique touch by customizing the styling of each widget.
   - Click on a widget to open its settings panel.
   - In the "Style" tab, adjust colors, fonts, backgrounds, borders, and shadows to match your brand aesthetic.
   - Explore different typography options (font families, sizes, weights) to enhance readability and visual appeal.
   - Use color palettes and themes that resonate with your brand identity.
7. **Add Interactive Elements:**
   Make your homepage more engaging by incorporating interactive elements.
   - Use the "Slides" widget to create eye-catching image or video carousels.
   - Add animations or hover effects to buttons and other elements.
   - Embed videos or interactive maps to provide dynamic content.
8. **Optimize for Mobile:**
   Ensure your homepage looks and functions perfectly on all devices.
   - Switch between Elementor's responsive modes (Desktop, Tablet, Mobile) to preview and adjust your design for different screen sizes.
   - Optimize images for faster loading on mobile devices.
   - Adjust font sizes and spacing for better readability on smaller screens.

By following these steps and incorporating your creativity, you can design a homepage that not only looks stunning but also effectively communicates your message and guides visitors toward desired actions.

Best Practices for Homepage Design

Creating an effective homepage requires a strategic approach that combines aesthetics with functionality. Here are some best practices to guide your homepage design:

1. **Keep it Simple:** A cluttered homepage can overwhelm visitors and make it difficult to find the information they seek. Focus on showcasing the most important content and elements above the fold. Use clear and concise messaging, and avoid overwhelming the page with too many images, text blocks, or distracting animations.
2. **Use High-Quality Visuals:** Invest in professional photos and videos that are relevant to your content and brand. High-quality visuals can significantly enhance your website's appeal and make it look more polished and credible. Avoid using low-resolution or pixelated images, as they can detract from your website's professionalism.

3. **Highlight Your Unique Value Proposition (UVP):** Clearly communicate what sets your brand or business apart from your competitors. Your homepage should answer the question "What's in it for me?" for your visitors within seconds. Use a strong headline, a concise value proposition statement, and supporting visuals to showcase your unique strengths and benefits.
4. **Make it Easy to Navigate:** Ensure your navigation menu is clear, intuitive, and easy to use. Place it in a prominent location (usually at the top of the page) and use descriptive labels for your menu items. Consider using a sticky menu that stays visible as visitors scroll down the page.
5. **Include Social Proof:** Social proof, such as testimonials, case studies, client logos, or awards, can significantly boost your credibility and build trust with potential customers. Showcase positive feedback from satisfied customers or clients to demonstrate the value you provide.
6. **Optimize for Speed:** A fast-loading homepage is crucial for user experience and SEO. Optimize your images, minimize code and scripts, and leverage caching to ensure your homepage loads quickly. You can use online speed test tools like GTmetrix or Google PageSpeed Insights to analyze your homepage's performance and identify areas for improvement.

By adhering to these best practices, you can create a homepage that not only looks visually appealing but also functions effectively to engage your audience, build trust, and drive desired actions.

Additional Tips for an Engaging Homepage

While the essential elements provide a solid foundation, these additional tips can elevate your homepage from good to exceptional, captivating your audience and leaving a lasting impression:

Use Compelling Headlines

Your headlines are the first thing visitors see, so make them count. Craft attention-grabbing headlines that pique curiosity and entice users to learn more. Use strong verbs, ask thought-provoking questions, or offer a compelling benefit to encourage visitors to delve deeper into your website.

Tell a Story

Humans are wired for stories. By incorporating storytelling techniques into your homepage design and content, you can connect with your audience on an emotional level. Share your brand's story, highlight customer success stories, or create a narrative that resonates with your target audience's aspirations and challenges.

Use a Clear Call to Action

Don't leave your visitors wondering what to do next. Guide them towards the actions you want them to take by using clear and compelling calls to action (CTAs). Whether it's "Shop Now," "Learn More," "Get a Quote," or "Contact Us," your CTAs should be prominent, visually appealing, and strategically placed throughout your homepage.

Keep Your Content Fresh

A stagnant homepage can quickly become stale. Regularly update your content with new blog posts, product announcements, seasonal promotions, or other relevant information. This shows visitors that your website is active and up-to-date, encouraging them to return for more. You can also use Elementor's dynamic content feature to display personalized content or automatically update sections with fresh data.

Examples of Effective Homepages Built with Elementor

Let's examine a few real-world examples of homepages crafted using Elementor to glean inspiration and insights for your own designs:

1. **Apple:** Apple's homepage is a masterclass in minimalist design. It features large, high-quality product images, concise headlines, and ample white space. The focus is on the products themselves, allowing them to speak for themselves. The navigation menu is discreetly tucked away in the top right corner, ensuring that the products remain the center of attention. The overall effect is a clean, elegant, and visually stunning homepage that effectively showcases Apple's brand identity and product offerings.
2. **Airbnb:** Airbnb's homepage is all about inspiring wanderlust. It features a large search bar prominently placed at the top, inviting users to start their travel search. Below the search bar, a dynamic carousel showcases stunning destination photos and enticing headlines. The page also features curated lists of unique stays and experiences, encouraging users to explore and book. The overall design is vibrant, inviting, and visually appealing, effectively capturing the essence of travel and adventure.
3. **Mailchimp:** Mailchimp's homepage is designed to quickly communicate its value proposition and guide users towards signing up for its email marketing services. The hero section features a bold headline, a concise description of the platform's benefits, and a prominent call-to-action button. Below the hero section, the page highlights key features and testimonials from satisfied customers. The design is clean, professional, and user-friendly, making it easy for visitors to understand what Mailchimp offers and how it can benefit them.

These are just a few examples of the many effective homepages that have been built with Elementor. By studying these examples and analyzing their design elements, layout, and effectiveness, you can gain valuable insights and inspiration for creating your own captivating homepage.

Chapter Summary

This chapter delved into the art of designing an effective homepage, the virtual front door of your website. We emphasized the homepage's crucial role in creating a positive first impression, engaging visitors, and encouraging them to explore further. We outlined the essential elements that every well-designed homepage should include, such as above-the-fold content, navigation menus, hero sections, about us sections, service/product showcases, testimonials, calls to action, and footers.

Furthermore, we provided a detailed, step-by-step guide on how to use Elementor to design your homepage, from choosing a template to adding sections, columns, and widgets. We also discussed customization of styling, the addition of interactive elements, and mobile optimization.

Additionally, we presented best practices for homepage design, such as keeping it simple, using high-quality visuals, highlighting your unique value proposition, making navigation easy, including social proof, and optimizing for speed. We then offered additional tips to make your homepage more engaging, including using compelling headlines, storytelling, clear calls to action, and regularly updating your content.

Lastly, we discussed examples of effective homepages built with Elementor, analyzing their design elements, layout, and effectiveness. These examples serve as inspiration and demonstrate the versatility and potential of Elementor in creating stunning and high-performing homepages.

Armed with this knowledge and these practical tips, you are now ready to design a homepage that not only looks impressive but also effectively communicates your brand message and drives user engagement.

Building an About Us Page: Tell Your Story

Outline

- The Importance of an About Us Page
- Key Elements of an About Us Page
- Designing Your About Us Page with Elementor
- Tips for Writing Compelling About Us Content
- Chapter Summary

The Importance of an About Us Page

An About Us page is a virtual handshake, a digital introduction that offers a glimpse into the heart and soul of your brand or business. It's a crucial component of any website, serving as a bridge between you and your audience.

This page provides a unique opportunity to tell your story, share your values, and showcase your personality. It's where you can humanize your brand, connect with your audience on a personal level, and build a relationship based on trust and authenticity.

For businesses, an About Us page is essential for establishing credibility and building trust with potential customers. It's a chance to showcase your expertise, experience, and commitment to quality. By sharing your company's history, mission, and vision, you can demonstrate your passion for what you do and why customers should choose you over your competitors.

For individuals, an About Us page is a platform for self-expression and personal branding. It's a chance to share your story, your interests, and your accomplishments. Whether you're a blogger, artist, freelancer, or entrepreneur, an About Us page can help you connect with your audience and build a loyal following.

The About Us page is often one of the most visited pages on a website. Visitors are curious to learn more about the people or company behind the brand. It's where they go to find out if they resonate with your values, if they trust your expertise, and if they want to do business with you.

A well-crafted About Us page can make a significant impact on your website's success. It can:

- **Increase Engagement:** By sharing your story and values, you can connect with your audience on a deeper level, leading to increased engagement and loyalty.
- **Boost Conversions:** A compelling About Us page can build trust and credibility, making visitors more likely to take the desired action, such as making a purchase or filling out a contact form.
- **Improve SEO:** By incorporating relevant keywords and providing valuable information, you can optimize your About Us page for search engines, increasing its visibility and attracting more organic traffic.

In essence, the About Us page is a powerful tool for humanizing your brand, establishing credibility, and building trust with your audience. It's an investment in your online presence that can yield significant returns in terms of engagement, conversions, and overall brand awareness.

Key Elements of an Effective About Us Page

An effective About Us page goes beyond a dry recitation of facts and figures. It's a chance to tell a compelling story, showcase your personality, and connect with your audience on a deeper level. Here are the key elements that should be included:

Company or Personal Story

The heart of your About Us page should be the story behind your brand or yourself. This is your opportunity to share your journey, your passion, and the values that drive you. It's a chance to humanize your brand and make it relatable to your audience.

Delve into your history, explaining how you got started and what challenges you've overcome. Share your mission and vision, outlining what you hope to achieve and the impact you want to make. By revealing your story, you create an emotional connection with your audience and make them more invested in your brand.

Team Introduction

If you have a team, introduce them to your audience. Highlight their skills, experience, and passion for their work. Include photos and brief bios for each team member to make them more relatable and approachable. This helps build trust and shows that there are real people behind your brand.

Consider adding a personal touch to each bio, such as hobbies or interests, to showcase the team's personalities and create a more human connection with your audience.

Testimonials or Client Logos

Testimonials and client logos are powerful forms of social proof. They demonstrate that others have found value in your products or services and are satisfied with their experience. Displaying positive feedback from customers or showcasing the logos of well-known clients can boost your credibility and increase trust in your brand.

Consider using a variety of testimonials, such as quotes, video testimonials, or case studies, to showcase the diversity of your customer base and the positive impact you've had.

Call to Action (CTA)

An About Us page should not be a dead end. It should guide visitors towards the next step you want them to take. Include a clear and compelling call to action that directs them to a relevant action, such as:

- Contacting you for more information or a quote.
- Learning more about your services or products.
- Reading your blog or subscribing to your newsletter.
- Making a purchase or booking an appointment.

The CTA should be prominently displayed and use action-oriented language to encourage clicks.

Awards and Recognition (Optional)

If you've received any awards, certifications, or media mentions, this is the place to showcase them. These accolades can further establish your credibility and demonstrate your expertise in your field. Display them in a visually appealing way, such as logos, badges, or quotes from the recognition.

Designing Your About Us Page with Elementor

Designing an About Us page that captures the essence of your brand or personality is a breeze with Elementor. Follow these steps to craft an engaging and informative page:

1. **Choose a Template (Optional):**
   Elementor offers a variety of pre-designed About Us page templates to kickstart your design process.

- Click the folder icon within the Elementor editor to open the template library.
- Navigate to the "Pages" category and search for "About Us."
- Browse the available templates and select one that aligns with your vision.
- Click "Insert" to add the template to your page.
2. Remember, templates are just starting points. Feel free to customize them to fit your specific content and style.
3. **Add Sections and Columns:**
Structure your About Us page by dividing it into sections and columns. Each section can focus on a different aspect, like your story, team, or testimonials.
    - Click the "+" icon to add new sections.
    - Choose the number of columns for each section based on your content and layout preferences.
    - Drag and drop sections to rearrange them as needed.
4. Think of sections as chapters in a book, each telling a part of your story.
5. **Insert Widgets:**
Populate your sections with relevant content using Elementor's versatile widgets.
    - **Heading:** Use headings to clearly label each section (e.g., "Our Story," "Meet the Team," "Client Testimonials").
    - **Text Editor:** Craft engaging text content to tell your story, introduce your team, and showcase testimonials.
    - **Image:** Add photos of your team members, your workspace, or other relevant visuals.
    - **Image Gallery:** Showcase a collection of images that represent your brand or tell your story visually.
    - **Button:** Include a call-to-action button that encourages visitors to take the next step, such as "Contact Us" or "Learn More."
6. **Customize Styling:**
Make your About Us page visually appealing by customizing the style of each widget.
    - Click on a widget to access its settings panel.
    - Adjust colors, fonts, backgrounds, borders, and shadows to create a cohesive look that matches your brand identity.
    - Consider using visual elements like icons or dividers to break up text and enhance readability.
7. **Add Interactive Elements (Optional):**
Engage your visitors with interactive elements that enhance their experience.
    - **Timeline:** Use a timeline widget to visually showcase your company's history or milestones.
    - **Accordion:** Organize information into expandable sections to save space and keep the page uncluttered.
    - **Tabs:** Present different types of content in separate tabs, allowing visitors to choose what they want to see.
8. **Optimize for Mobile:**
Ensure your About Us page looks great on all devices.
    - Switch to Elementor's tablet and mobile views to preview and adjust your design for smaller screens.
    - Consider using a simpler layout or reducing the number of elements for mobile devices.
    - Test your page on real smartphones and tablets to ensure a smooth user experience.

Tips for Writing Compelling About Us Content

An About Us page is more than just a list of facts and figures; it's an opportunity to tell your story and connect with your audience on a personal level. Here are some tips to help you craft an About Us page that captivates readers and leaves a lasting impression:

Be Authentic and Transparent

Share your genuine story and values. People connect with authenticity. Don't be afraid to show your personality and let your passion shine through. Explain what drives you, what challenges you've overcome, and what makes your brand or business unique.

Highlight Your Unique Value Proposition (UVP)

Clearly communicate what sets you apart from your competitors. What makes your products or services special? What unique value do you bring to the table? Your About Us page should answer these questions and convince visitors why they should choose you over others.

Use Storytelling Techniques

Stories are powerful tools for capturing attention and building emotional connections. Craft a narrative that highlights your journey, your struggles, and your triumphs. Use vivid language, anecdotes, and personal details to engage your readers and make them feel invested in your story.

Keep it Concise and Focused

While it's important to share your story, avoid rambling or including irrelevant information. Keep your content focused and to the point. Use concise language and highlight the most important aspects of your brand or business.

Use a Conversational Tone

Write in a friendly and approachable tone. Avoid using jargon or technical language that your audience might not understand. Speak directly to your readers, as if you're having a conversation with them. This will help you build rapport and create a more personal connection.

Proofread and Edit

Before publishing your About Us page, thoroughly proofread and edit your content. Ensure that your grammar and spelling are impeccable, and your sentences are clear and concise. A well-polished About Us page reflects professionalism and attention to detail.

Additional Tips:

- **Use visuals:** Incorporate high-quality images or videos to make your About Us page more visually appealing.
- **Incorporate testimonials:** Include quotes from satisfied customers or clients to build trust and credibility.
- **Highlight your team:** Introduce your team members and showcase their expertise.
- **Keep it updated:** Regularly update your About Us page to reflect any changes in your brand or business.

By following these tips, you can create an About Us page that not only informs but also inspires and connects with your audience, leaving them with a positive and lasting impression of your brand.

Chapter Summary

This chapter delved into the creation of a compelling About Us page, a vital component of any website. We emphasized the importance of this page in introducing your brand or yourself to your audience, establishing credibility, and building trust. The About Us page is often one of the most frequented pages on a website, making it crucial to make a good impression.

We outlined the key elements that make an About Us page effective. These include sharing your company or personal story, introducing your team, incorporating testimonials or client logos, providing a clear call to action, and optionally, showcasing any awards or recognition you have received.

Furthermore, we provided a step-by-step guide on how to use Elementor to design your About Us page. This included choosing a template, adding sections and columns, inserting relevant widgets, customizing the styling to align with your brand, incorporating interactive elements, and optimizing the page for mobile devices.

Finally, we provided tips for crafting compelling About Us content. These tips emphasized authenticity, highlighting your unique value proposition, using storytelling techniques, keeping the content concise and focused, using a conversational tone, and meticulous proofreading and editing.

By following these guidelines, you can create an About Us page that not only informs your audience but also engages them, builds trust, and leaves a positive lasting impression. This page serves as a platform to showcase your brand's personality and values, ultimately contributing to your website's overall success.

Crafting a Services/Products Page: Showcase Your Offerings

Outline

- The Importance of a Compelling Services/Products Page
- Key Elements of a Services/Products Page
- Designing Your Services/Products Page with Elementor
- Tips for Effective Product/Service Descriptions
- Chapter Summary

The Importance of a Compelling Services/Products Page

In the digital age, your Services or Products page is the heart of your online business. It serves as the virtual storefront, showcasing your offerings to potential customers. Whether you're selling physical products, offering professional services, or providing digital downloads, this page is where you make your case and persuade visitors to take action.

A well-crafted Services or Products page is essential for several reasons:

- **Showcasing Your Value:** This page is your opportunity to highlight the unique value proposition of your offerings. It's where you explain how your products or services solve problems, meet needs, or enhance the lives of your customers. By clearly articulating the benefits and features, you make a compelling case for why someone should choose you.
- **Building Trust and Credibility:** A professionally designed and informative Services or Products page builds trust with potential customers. By providing detailed descriptions, high-quality visuals, and social proof like testimonials or case studies, you demonstrate your expertise and instill confidence in your brand.
- **Driving Conversions:** Ultimately, the goal of your Services or Products page is to drive conversions, whether it's making a purchase, requesting a quote, or signing up for a service. A well-structured page with clear calls to action guides visitors towards taking the desired action, turning them from casual browsers into paying customers.
- **Enhancing User Experience:** A user-friendly Services or Products page improves the overall experience for your visitors. Easy navigation, clear pricing (if applicable), and comprehensive information make it effortless for users to find what they're looking for and make informed decisions.
- **Boosting SEO:** A well-optimized Services or Products page can improve your website's search engine visibility. By incorporating relevant keywords and providing valuable information, you can attract organic traffic from people searching for the types of products or services you offer.

In the competitive online landscape, a compelling Services or Products page is not just a nice-to-have; it's a necessity for any business or individual looking to succeed in the digital marketplace. It's the platform where you can showcase your unique offerings, build trust with potential customers, and ultimately drive conversions.

Key Elements of a Services/Products Page

A well-designed Services or Products page is more than just a list of what you offer. It's a persuasive tool that showcases your value, addresses customer concerns, and guides them toward taking action. Here are the key elements that contribute to a successful page:

Clear and Concise Descriptions

Craft descriptions that are easy to understand, even for those unfamiliar with your industry. Focus on the benefits your services or products provide rather than just listing features. Clearly explain how your offerings can solve problems, meet needs, or enhance the lives of your customers. Use concise language, bullet points, and strong verbs to make your descriptions engaging and informative.

Visuals

High-quality images or videos are essential for showcasing your services or products in action. Visuals can make your offerings more tangible and appealing, helping potential customers visualize how they would use or benefit from them.

Consider using:

- **Product Photos:** Showcase your products from different angles, highlighting their features and aesthetics.
- **Lifestyle Images:** Show your products or services being used in real-life scenarios to illustrate their benefits.
- **Explainer Videos:** Create videos that demonstrate how your products work or the process of your services.
- **Customer Photos:** If applicable, showcase photos of satisfied customers using your products or benefiting from your services.

Pricing (Optional)

Whether or not to include pricing information on your Services/Products page depends on various factors, including your industry, target audience, and pricing strategy.

If you choose to display prices, make them clear, easy to find, and transparent. Consider using tables or comparison charts to make it easier for customers to compare different options. If your pricing is complex or variable, offer a way for customers to request a personalized quote.

Call to Action (CTA)

A compelling CTA is crucial for guiding visitors towards the next step you want them to take. It could be a button that says "Buy Now," "Get a Quote," "Learn More," or "Contact Us." The CTA should be prominently displayed, visually distinct, and use action-oriented language to encourage clicks.

Strategically place CTAs throughout your page, especially after each service or product description, to make it easy for visitors to take action when they are most interested.

Testimonials or Case Studies

Social proof, in the form of testimonials or case studies, can be a powerful persuasive tool. Positive feedback from satisfied customers demonstrates that your offerings are valuable and trustworthy. Include testimonials from real customers, highlighting their specific experiences and outcomes. Case studies can provide a more in-depth look at how your products or services have helped clients achieve their goals.

FAQs (Optional)

An FAQ (Frequently Asked Questions) section can be a valuable addition to your Services/Products page. It allows you to address common inquiries and concerns upfront, saving time for both you and your potential customers. Consider including questions about pricing, features, shipping, returns, or anything else that customers frequently ask about your offerings.

By incorporating these key elements into your Services/Products page, you can create a compelling and informative resource that showcases your value, builds trust, and drives conversions.

Designing Your Services/Products Page with Elementor

Elementor provides a user-friendly and flexible platform for designing a visually appealing and informative Services/Products page. Here's a step-by-step guide to help you create a page that effectively showcases your offerings:

1. **Choose a Template (Optional):**
   Elementor offers a variety of pre-designed templates specifically for services and product pages. These templates provide a starting point with different layouts and design elements.
   - Click on the folder icon in the Elementor editor to open the template library.
   - Browse the "Pages" or "Blocks" category and search for "services," "products," or related keywords.
   - Preview the templates to find one that suits your style and needs.
   - Click "Insert" to add the template to your page.
2. **Structure with Sections and Columns:**
   Divide your page into logical sections using Elementor's sections and columns. Each section can focus on a different aspect of your services or products.
   - For product pages, consider using a grid layout to display multiple products in an organized manner.
   - For service pages, a multi-column layout can be effective for showcasing different services side-by-side.
   - Use Elementor's drag-and-drop interface to easily add, remove, and rearrange sections and columns.
3. **Add Widgets:**
   Populate your sections with relevant content using Elementor's widgets. Here are some commonly used widgets for services/products pages:
   - **Heading:** Create clear and concise headings for your page title, sections, and product/service titles.
   - **Text Editor:** Craft detailed descriptions for each service or product, highlighting their benefits and features.
   - **Image:** Add high-quality images to showcase your products or services visually.
   - **Image Gallery:** Display multiple product images in an organized gallery format.
   - **Price List:** Present pricing information clearly and concisely using a price list widget.
   - **Button:** Encourage visitors to take action by adding call-to-action buttons like "Buy Now," "Learn More," or "Get a Quote."
   - **Testimonials:** Display customer testimonials using the Testimonial widget or a Text Editor widget.
4. **Customize Styling:**
   Elevate your page's visual appeal by customizing the style of each widget.
   - Use Elementor's styling options to adjust colors, fonts, backgrounds, borders, and shadows.
   - Ensure your styling is consistent with your overall website design and brand identity.
   - Consider using visual elements like icons, dividers, and background images to enhance the page's aesthetic.
5. **Add Interactive Elements (Optional):**
   Engage your visitors with interactive elements that showcase your offerings dynamically.
   - **Image Carousel:** Create an interactive slideshow of product images or service highlights.
   - **Tabs:** Use tabs to organize content and make it easier for visitors to find the information they need.
   - **Animated Headlines or Text:** Add subtle animations to your headings or text to capture attention.

6. **Optimize for Mobile:**
   With a significant portion of users browsing on mobile devices, responsive design is crucial.
   - Test your page on different screen sizes using Elementor's responsive mode (desktop, tablet, mobile).
   - Ensure that your layout adapts smoothly and all elements are easily viewable and clickable on smaller screens.
   - Consider using mobile-specific widgets or adjusting the layout for optimal mobile viewing.

By following these steps and incorporating your creativity, you can craft a visually appealing, informative, and high-converting Services/Products page that showcases your offerings effectively and drives customer engagement.

Tips for Effective Product/Service Descriptions

Your product or service descriptions are more than just informational blurbs; they are your sales pitch in written form. A well-crafted description can entice potential customers, answer their questions, and ultimately lead them to make a purchase or inquiry. Here are some tips to help you write compelling and effective descriptions:

Focus on Benefits: Customers are more interested in what your product or service can do for them than its technical specifications. Clearly explain how your offerings solve their problems, meet their needs, or enhance their lives. Use phrases like "save time," "increase productivity," "improve health," or "achieve your goals" to highlight the benefits.

Use Clear and Concise Language: Avoid using jargon or technical terms that your audience might not understand. Keep your language simple, straightforward, and easy to read. Use short sentences and paragraphs to break up the text and make it more digestible.

Highlight Key Features: While focusing on benefits is important, don't neglect to mention the key features of your products or services. These features provide tangible evidence of the value you offer. List the most important features in bullet points or a concise summary, making it easy for customers to scan and understand.

Use Persuasive Language: Employ persuasive language to encourage action. Use words and phrases that create a sense of urgency or excitement, such as "limited time offer," "exclusive deal," or "act now." Highlight the unique selling points of your offerings and use testimonials or social proof to reinforce their value.

Incorporate Keywords: If you want to improve your page's search engine optimization (SEO), include relevant keywords in your descriptions. Research the keywords your target audience is searching for and naturally incorporate them into your descriptions. However, avoid keyword stuffing, which can negatively impact your SEO.

Proofread and Edit: Thoroughly review your descriptions for grammatical errors, typos, and inconsistencies. Ensure that your writing is clear, concise, and easy to understand. Ask a friend or colleague to review your descriptions to get a fresh perspective and catch any errors you might have missed.

By following these tips, you can write product and service descriptions that are informative, engaging, and persuasive. A well-crafted description can capture attention, answer questions, build trust, and ultimately drive conversions.

Chapter Summary

This chapter focused on the essential role of a well-crafted Services/Products page in showcasing your offerings and driving customer engagement. We discussed the importance of this page as a virtual storefront or portfolio, highlighting its role in showcasing your value, building trust, and driving conversions.

We outlined the key elements that contribute to a successful Services/Products page, including clear and concise descriptions that focus on benefits, high-quality visuals, optional pricing information, compelling calls to action, testimonials or case studies for social proof, and potentially an FAQ section to address common inquiries.

We then provided a step-by-step guide on how to use Elementor to design your Services/Products page. This included choosing a template, structuring your content with sections and columns, adding relevant widgets, customizing the styling, incorporating interactive elements, and optimizing for mobile devices.

Finally, we offered tips for writing effective product or service descriptions, emphasizing the importance of focusing on benefits, using clear and concise language, highlighting key features, using persuasive language, incorporating keywords for SEO, and meticulous proofreading and editing.

By applying these principles and strategies, you can create a Services/Products page that not only effectively showcases your offerings but also encourages visitors to take action, leading to increased engagement and ultimately, business growth.

Setting Up a Blog: Share Your Expertise

Outline

- Why a Blog is Essential for Your Website
- Choosing the Right Blog Layout
- Creating and Publishing Blog Posts
- Blog Categories and Tags
- Designing Your Blog Page with Elementor
- Promoting Your Blog
- Chapter Summary

Why a Blog is Essential for Your Website

In today's digital landscape, a blog is a powerful tool that can significantly enhance your website's value and effectiveness. It goes beyond simply sharing information; it's a platform for engagement, education, and establishing your brand's authority. Here are the compelling reasons why incorporating a blog into your website is essential:

Establishing Authority and Expertise

A blog allows you to showcase your knowledge and expertise in your industry or niche. By consistently publishing high-quality, informative content, you position yourself as a thought leader and a reliable source of information. This builds trust and credibility with your audience, making them more likely to choose your products or services over your competitors.

Driving Organic Traffic

Search engines love fresh, relevant content. By creating blog posts around keywords that your target audience is searching for, you can attract organic traffic to your website. This means more potential customers discovering your brand and exploring your offerings. A well-optimized blog can significantly improve your website's visibility in search engine results pages (SERPs).

Building Relationships

A blog provides a platform for engaging with your audience and fostering a sense of community. By encouraging comments and discussions, you can create a space where your readers can interact with you and each other. This two-way communication can help you build stronger relationships with your audience, understand their needs and preferences, and gain valuable feedback.

Generating Leads and Sales

Your blog can be a powerful lead generation tool. By offering valuable content, you attract potential customers to your website. You can then subtly promote your products or services within your blog posts, guiding readers towards taking the next step, such as signing up for a newsletter, downloading a free resource, or making a purchase. A well-crafted blog can nurture leads through the sales funnel and ultimately drive conversions.

Keeping Your Website Fresh

Search engines favor websites that are regularly updated with fresh content. A blog is an ideal way to keep your website dynamic and relevant. By consistently publishing new posts, you signal to search engines that your website is active and up-to-date. This can lead to improved search rankings and increased organic traffic. Additionally, a blog can help you keep your existing audience engaged and coming back for more.

In conclusion, a blog is a valuable asset that can benefit your website in numerous ways. It can help you establish authority, drive traffic, build relationships, generate leads, and keep your website fresh. If you're not already blogging, now is the time to start!

Choosing the Right Blog Layout

Your blog's layout plays a crucial role in how your content is presented and consumed by your audience. The right layout can enhance readability, engagement, and the overall user experience. Let's explore the different blog layout options available in WordPress and Elementor, along with the factors to consider when making your choice:

Classic Blog Layout

The classic blog layout is the most traditional and familiar format. It typically features a list of blog posts arranged in reverse chronological order, with the newest posts appearing first. This layout often includes a sidebar on the right or left side of the page, where you can display widgets like recent posts, categories, tags, or a search bar.

Pros:

- Familiar and easy to navigate for most users.
- Allows for a sidebar to showcase additional information or calls to action.
- Suitable for blogs with text-heavy content.

Cons:

- Can look monotonous and lack visual appeal.
- May not be the best choice for image-heavy blogs.

Grid Layout

The grid layout arranges blog posts in a visually appealing grid format. Each post is typically represented by a thumbnail image, title, and a short excerpt. This layout is excellent for image-heavy blogs or websites that want to showcase visual content.

Pros:

- Visually appealing and engaging.
- Ideal for showcasing images and visual content.
- Can accommodate different post formats.

Cons:

- May not be suitable for text-heavy blogs.
- Can make it harder for users to scan through content quickly.

Masonry Layout

The masonry layout is a dynamic grid layout where posts of different sizes fit together like bricks. This layout creates a visually interesting and unique look, especially for blogs with a mix of image and text content.

Pros:

- Visually dynamic and engaging.
- Ideal for showcasing a variety of content formats.
- Can accommodate different post lengths.

Cons:

- Can be less predictable for users.
- May not be the best choice for text-heavy blogs.

List Layout

The list layout is a simple and clean layout where posts are listed vertically, often with a thumbnail image, title, and excerpt. This layout is straightforward and easy to navigate, making it a good choice for blogs with a focus on written content.

Pros:

- Simple and clean design.
- Easy to navigate and scan through content.
- Suitable for text-heavy blogs.

Cons:

- May lack visual appeal compared to grid or masonry layouts.

Factors to Consider When Choosing a Blog Layout

- **Website Purpose:** Consider the overall purpose of your website and how your blog fits into that purpose.
- **Content Type:** Think about the type of content you'll be publishing (e.g., text-heavy articles, image-focused posts, video content).
- **Aesthetic Preferences:** Choose a layout that aligns with your overall website design and brand identity.
- **Target Audience:** Consider your target audience's preferences and reading habits.
- **Functionality:** Some layouts offer additional features like infinite scroll or post filtering, which can enhance user experience.

By carefully evaluating these factors and experimenting with different layouts, you can find the perfect blog layout that complements your content, engages your audience, and enhances your website's overall appeal.

Creating and Publishing Blog Posts

Creating and publishing blog posts in WordPress is a user-friendly process, even for beginners. The WordPress editor (formerly known as Gutenberg) provides a streamlined interface with intuitive tools to help you craft engaging content.

1. Access the Post Editor:

- Navigate to your WordPress dashboard.
- Hover over the "Posts" tab in the left-hand menu.
- Click "Add New" to open a fresh canvas for your blog post.

2. Enter a Captivating Title:

- The title field sits at the top of the editor.

- Craft a clear, concise, and attention-grabbing title that reflects the essence of your blog post.
- Incorporate relevant keywords that your target audience might search for.

3. Write Engaging Content:

- The main content area of the editor is where you'll write your blog post.
- Use the various formatting options (bold, italic, headings, lists, quotes) to structure your content and enhance readability.
- Break down your text into shorter paragraphs for easier consumption.
- Use a conversational tone to connect with your audience.
- Proofread and edit your content thoroughly before publishing.

4. Add Images, Videos, or Other Media:

- Click the "+" icon within the editor to add blocks for various media types.
- Select "Image" to upload images from your computer or choose from your media library.
- Optimize images for web use before uploading to ensure faster loading times.
- Use the "Video" block to embed videos from platforms like YouTube or Vimeo.
- Consider adding relevant media to break up text and enhance visual appeal.

5. Assign Categories and Tags:

- Categories and tags help organize your blog content and make it easier for readers to find relevant posts.
- On the right-hand sidebar, you'll find the "Categories" and "Tags" sections.
- Select relevant categories that best fit the topic of your post.
- Add specific tags (keywords) that describe your content.

6. Choose a Featured Image:

- The featured image is the main image associated with your blog post. It often appears at the top of the post, in social media previews, or in blog listings.
- Select an eye-catching and relevant image that represents your post's content.

7. Publish Your Post:

- When you're satisfied with your post, click the "Publish" button in the top-right corner of the editor.
- You can also schedule your post to be published at a later date or time by clicking on the "Immediately" text next to the "Publish" button and selecting a date and time.

By following these steps, you can create and publish compelling blog posts that engage your audience, drive traffic to your website, and establish your authority in your field.

Blog Categories and Tags

Categories and tags are essential tools for organizing your blog content in WordPress. They help you create a structured and navigable website, making it easier for readers to find the content they're interested in. While they both serve to classify your posts, they have distinct roles and purposes:

Categories

Categories represent broad topics or groups that your blog posts fall under. They are hierarchical, meaning you can create sub-categories within parent categories. Think of categories as the main sections of a library, each housing books on a specific subject.

For example, if you have a food blog, you might have categories like "Recipes," "Restaurant Reviews," and "Cooking Tips." Within the "Recipes" category, you could have sub-categories like "Desserts," "Main Courses," and "Appetizers."

Tags

Tags are more specific keywords or phrases that describe the content of individual blog posts. They are not hierarchical and can be used to create more granular connections between posts across different categories. Think of tags as the index terms in a book, highlighting specific topics or themes within the content.

For example, a blog post about a chocolate cake recipe might be categorized under "Recipes" and "Desserts," but it could also be tagged with "chocolate," "cake," "baking," or "dessert recipes."

How to Create and Manage Categories and Tags

1. **Categories:**
    - Go to "Posts" > "Categories" in your WordPress dashboard.
    - Enter a name for your category and a slug (a URL-friendly version of the name).
    - Optionally, you can choose a parent category if you want to create a hierarchical structure.
    - Click "Add New Category" to save your changes.
2. **Tags:**
    - Go to "Posts" > "Tags" in your WordPress dashboard.
    - Enter a name for your tag and a slug.
    - Click "Add New Tag" to save your changes.

You can also create and assign categories and tags when creating or editing a blog post. In the post editor, you'll find the "Categories" and "Tags" meta boxes on the right-hand sidebar.

Best Practices for Categories and Tags

- **Use Categories Strategically:** Choose a limited number of broad categories to organize your main content areas.
- **Use Tags for Specificity:** Use tags to highlight specific keywords or phrases within your posts.
- **Don't Overuse Tags:** Avoid creating too many tags, as this can lead to clutter and confusion.
- **Maintain Consistency:** Use the same categories and tags consistently across your blog posts.

By effectively using categories and tags, you can create a well-organized blog that is easy for readers to navigate and discover relevant content.

Designing Your Blog Page with Elementor

While WordPress provides a default blog page, Elementor empowers you to create a custom blog page that aligns perfectly with your website's design and functionality. Here's how to design your unique blog page using Elementor:

1. **Create a New Page:**
    - In your WordPress dashboard, go to "Pages" > "Add New."
    - Give your page a title (e.g., "Blog" or "News").
    - Leave the content area blank for now.
2. **Assign as "Posts Page":**
    - Go to "Settings" > "Reading."
    - Under "Your homepage displays," select "A static page."
    - Choose your newly created page as the "Posts page."
    - Save your changes.
3. **Edit with Elementor:**

- Return to your newly created page.
- Click the "Edit with Elementor" button to launch the Elementor editor.
4. **Choose a Template or Build from Scratch:**
    - You can choose a pre-designed blog page template from Elementor's library for a quick start.
    - Alternatively, you can build your layout from scratch using sections, columns, and widgets.
5. **Add Widgets to Display Blog Content:**
Elementor offers several widgets specifically designed for displaying blog content:
    - **Posts Widget:** This is the most common widget for displaying a list or grid of your blog posts. You can customize the layout, style, number of posts to display, and other settings.
    - **Archive Posts Widget:** Similar to the Posts widget, but it allows you to display posts from specific archives, such as categories, tags, or author archives.
    - **Search Bar:** Add a search bar to your blog page to help visitors find specific posts.
6. You can also use other widgets like Heading, Text Editor, and Image to add additional content to your blog page, such as a welcome message, category descriptions, or featured images.
7. **Customize Styling:**
    - Click on each widget to access its settings panel and customize its appearance.
    - Change colors, fonts, backgrounds, borders, and shadows to match your website's overall design.
    - Ensure your blog page is visually consistent with the rest of your site.

By following these steps and unleashing your creativity with Elementor, you can create a custom blog page that is both visually appealing and functional, providing your readers with an enjoyable and engaging experience.

Promoting Your Blog

Creating high-quality blog content is just the first step. To maximize the impact of your blog and reach a wider audience, you need to actively promote it. Here are some effective strategies for getting your blog noticed:

Social Media

Social media platforms are powerful tools for amplifying your blog's reach. Share your blog posts on platforms like Facebook, Twitter, LinkedIn, Pinterest, and Instagram. Craft engaging social media posts that pique interest and encourage clicks. Use relevant hashtags to reach a wider audience and consider joining relevant groups or communities to share your content with like-minded individuals.

Email Marketing

Building an email listis a valuable asset for any blogger. Encourage your website visitors to subscribe to your newsletter by offering valuable content upgrades or free resources. Once you have a list of subscribers, you can send regular email newsletters featuring your latest blog posts, driving traffic back to your website.

SEO

Search engine optimization (SEO) is crucial for attracting organic traffic to your blog. Optimize your blog posts for search engines by conducting keyword research and incorporating relevant keywords into your titles, headings, and content. Craft compelling meta descriptions that entice users to click on your links in search results. Optimize your images by adding alt text and compressing them for faster loading times.

Guest Blogging

Guest blogging involves writing blog posts for other websites or blogs in your niche. This is a great way to reach a new audience, build backlinks to your website, and establish yourself as an authority in your field. Look for opportunities to contribute guest posts to reputable blogs that share a similar target audience.

Paid Advertising

Paid advertising can be a powerful tool for promoting your blog to a wider audience. Platforms like Google Ads and social media advertising platforms allow you to target specific demographics and interests, ensuring that your ads are seen by people who are most likely to be interested in your content. Consider using paid advertising to promote your most popular blog posts or to drive traffic to your blog during product launches or special events.

Additional Promotion Strategies

- **Repurpose Your Content:** Turn your blog posts into videos, podcasts, infographics, or social media posts to reach a wider audience and maximize your content's lifespan.
- **Engage with Your Audience:** Respond to comments on your blog posts and social media channels. Participate in relevant online communities and forums to connect with your audience and build relationships.
- **Collaborate with Other Bloggers:** Partner with other bloggers in your niche to cross-promote each other's content.
- **Submit Your Blog to Directories:** Submit your blog to relevant online directories to increase its visibility.
- **Analyze Your Results:** Use website analytics tools like Google Analytics to track your blog's performance and identify areas for improvement.

By implementing a combination of these promotion strategies, you can effectively increase your blog's reach, attract more readers, and establish yourself as a thought leader in your field. Remember, consistent effort and a focus on providing valuable content are key to achieving long-term success with your blog.

Chapter Summary

This chapter delved into the power of blogging as a valuable tool for enhancing your website's reach and engagement. We explored the numerous benefits of having a blog, from establishing authority and expertise to driving organic traffic, building relationships, generating leads, and keeping your website fresh and relevant.

We discussed various blog layouts available in WordPress and Elementor, such as the classic blog layout, grid layout, masonry layout, and list layout. We highlighted the factors to consider when choosing a layout, emphasizing the importance of aligning it with your website's purpose, content type, and aesthetic preferences.

We provided a step-by-step guide on creating and publishing blog posts using the WordPress editor, outlining the process from accessing the post editor to adding a title, crafting engaging content, incorporating media, assigning categories and tags, choosing a featured image, and finally, publishing your post.

We also explained the distinction between categories and tags, emphasizing their role in organizing your blog content and improving its discoverability. We provided instructions on how to create and manage categories and tags effectively.

Furthermore, we guided you through designing a custom blog page with Elementor, explaining how to create a new page, assign it as your "Posts page," and utilize templates or build your layout from scratch using sections, columns, and widgets.

Finally, we discussed various strategies for promoting your blog and increasing its reach. We explored the power of social media, email marketing, SEO, guest blogging, and paid advertising, offering tips and insights to help you reach a wider audience and achieve your blogging goals.

By implementing the strategies and best practices outlined in this chapter, you can harness the full potential of your blog, turning it into a powerful engine for driving traffic, engagement, and growth for your website.

Creating a Contact Page: Make It Easy to Reach You

Outline

- The Importance of a Contact Page
- Key Elements of a Contact Page
- Creating Your Contact Page with Elementor
- Advanced Contact Form Features with Elementor Pro
- Chapter Summary

The Importance of a Contact Page

In the digital age, a well-designed contact page is a vital component of any website. It serves as a bridge between you and your website visitors, facilitating communication and fostering engagement. Regardless of your website's purpose, a contact page offers numerous benefits that can significantly impact your online success.

A Gateway to Communication

A contact page provides a clear and convenient way for visitors to get in touch with you. Whether they have questions, feedback, inquiries, or want to learn more about your products or services, the contact page is the designated channel for communication. By making it easy for visitors to reach out, you encourage interaction and create opportunities for building relationships.

Increased User Engagement

A contact page can boost user engagement on your website. When visitors know they can easily contact you, they are more likely to spend time exploring your site and interacting with your content. It shows that you value their feedback and are open to communication, which can lead to a more positive user experience.

Building Trust and Credibility

Having a visible and accessible contact page builds trust and credibility with your audience. It signals that you are a legitimate business or individual who is open and transparent. When visitors see that you are easy to reach, they are more likely to trust your brand and consider doing business with you.

Generating Leads

A contact page can be a valuable lead generation tool. Many visitors who land on your contact page are already interested in your products or services. By providing a simple way for them to get in touch, you can capture their contact information and initiate a conversation that could potentially lead to a sale or collaboration.

Handling Customer Inquiries

A contact page is not just for potential customers; it's also essential for handling customer inquiries and support requests. By providing a dedicated channel for customer communication, you can address their concerns promptly and efficiently, leading to higher customer satisfaction and loyalty.

Gathering Feedback

Your contact page can also serve as a platform for gathering valuable feedback from your audience. This feedback can help you understand your customers' needs and preferences, identify areas where you can improve, and make informed decisions about your website's content and design.

In conclusion, a contact page is a vital tool for establishing a strong online presence. It facilitates communication, increases engagement, builds trust, generates leads, and helps you gather valuable feedback. By investing time and effort in creating a user-friendly and informative contact page, you can significantly enhance your website's effectiveness and achieve your online goals.

Key Elements of a Contact Page

A well-designed contact page is not just a formality; it's a strategic tool for engaging with your audience and building relationships. To maximize its effectiveness, ensure your contact page includes these essential elements:

Contact Information

The most fundamental element of a contact page is clear and accurate contact information. This typically includes:

- **Business Address:** If you have a physical location, providing your address allows visitors to find you easily. This is especially important for businesses that rely on foot traffic, such as retail stores or restaurants.
- **Phone Number:** Include a phone number that visitors can call to speak with you directly. This can be a landline, mobile number, or a virtual phone number.
- **Email Address:** Provide a professional email address that visitors can use to send you inquiries or feedback. Avoid using generic email addresses like [invalid email address]

Make sure your contact information is prominently displayed on the page, easy to read, and clickable (for phone numbers and email addresses).

Contact Form

A contact form is a convenient way for visitors to send you messages directly from your website. It eliminates the need for them to open their email client or copy and paste your email address. Contact forms also allow you to collect specific information from users, such as their name, email address, and the nature of their inquiry, streamlining your communication process.

When designing your contact form, keep it simple and user-friendly. Include essential fields like name, email, and message, but avoid asking for too much information, as this can deter users from filling out the form.

Map (Optional)

If your business has a physical location, consider embedding a map on your contact page. This can help visitors visualize your location and make it easier for them to find you. You can use the Google Maps widget in Elementor to embed a map with customizable markers and styling.

Additional Information (Optional)

In addition to the essential contact information and form, you can also include additional details that might be relevant to your visitors, such as:

- **Business Hours:** Let visitors know when you are available to answer phone calls or emails.
- **Social Media Links:** Provide links to your social media profiles for additional channels of communication.

- **Brief FAQ Section:** Answer common questions upfront to save time and provide quick solutions for visitors.

By incorporating these key elements into your contact page, you can create a welcoming and informative resource that encourages visitors to get in touch and engage with your brand. A well-designed contact page is an essential tool for building relationships, generating leads, and providing excellent customer service.

Creating Your Contact Page with Elementor

Building an effective contact page in Elementor is a user-friendly process that involves a few simple steps:

1. **Create a New Page:**
   - From your WordPress dashboard, go to "Pages" > "Add New."
   - Title the page "Contact Us" or a similar name that reflects its purpose.
2. **Edit with Elementor:**
   - Click on the blue "Edit with Elementor" button at the top of the page to launch the Elementor editor.
3. **Choose a Template (Optional):**
   - Elementor's template library offers pre-designed contact page templates that you can use as a starting point.
   - Click the folder icon in the editor, browse the "Pages" category, and search for "contact."
   - If you find a template you like, click "Insert" to add it to your page.
4. **Add Sections and Columns:**
   - Divide your page into sections using the "+" icon. A common approach is to have a section for your contact form and another for your contact information.
   - Add columns to each section if you want to display content side-by-side. For example, a two-column layout can be used to display your contact form on one side and your address and phone number on the other.
5. **Insert Widgets:**
   - **Heading:** Drag and drop the Heading widget onto your page to add your page title (e.g., "Contact Us").
   - **Text Editor:** Use the Text Editor widget to provide additional information or instructions above your contact form.
   - **Contact Form:** Use the Form widget or a third-party plugin like WPForms to create your contact form. Customize the form fields (e.g., name, email, message) to collect the information you need.
   - **Google Maps:** If your business has a physical location, drag and drop the Google Maps widget onto your page and enter your address to display a map.
6. **Customize Styling:**
   - Click on each widget to access its settings panel and customize its appearance.
   - Change colors, fonts, backgrounds, and other styles to match your website's overall design.
   - Consider adding a background image or gradient to your contact page for a more visually engaging look.
   - Ensure the form is visually distinct and easy to find.

By following these steps, you can create a professional and user-friendly contact page that makes it easy for visitors to get in touch with you.

Advanced Contact Form Features with Elementor Pro

Elementor Pro takes your contact forms to the next level with advanced features that streamline lead management, enhance user experience, and enable deeper customization.

Form Submissions

With Elementor Pro, you can easily view and manage form submissions directly within your WordPress dashboard. No need to rely on external email clients or third-party plugins to access your leads. You can view a list of all submissions, filter them by date or form, and even export them to a CSV file for further analysis.

Integrations

Elementor Pro seamlessly integrates with popular email marketing platforms like Mailchimp, ActiveCampaign, and GetResponse. This allows you to automatically add new leads from your contact forms to your email lists, nurturing them with targeted campaigns and turning them into customers.

Additionally, Elementor Pro integrates with CRM (Customer Relationship Management) systems like HubSpot and Salesforce, enabling you to manage your leads and customer interactions more effectively. You can track lead sources, assign leads to sales representatives, and create automated workflows to streamline your sales process.

Conditional Logic

Conditional logic adds a layer of interactivity and personalization to your contact forms. It allows you to show or hide specific form fields based on the user's input. For example, you can ask users if they are interested in a particular service and then display additional fields related to that service only if they answer "yes."

Conditional logic can make your forms more user-friendly and relevant, as users only see the fields that are pertinent to them. It can also help you collect more targeted information from your leads.

Custom Styling

Elementor Pro offers advanced styling options for your contact forms, allowing you to create truly unique and visually appealing designs. You can customize the colors, fonts, spacing, borders, shadows, and other visual elements of your form to match your website's branding.

You can also create custom form fields with different input types, such as dropdowns, checkboxes, radio buttons, and file uploads. This allows you to tailor your forms to collect the specific information you need from your users.

By leveraging Elementor Pro's advanced contact form features, you can create more effective, engaging, and personalized forms that drive leads, improve user experience, and seamlessly integrate with your marketing and sales processes.

Chapter Summary

This chapter illuminated the crucial role of the contact page in fostering communication and engagement on your website. It serves as a bridge, making it easy for visitors to connect with you, ask questions, provide feedback, or express interest in your products or services.

We emphasized that a well-designed contact page not only increases user engagement and builds trust but also serves as a valuable lead generation tool. It allows you to gather information from potential customers and address customer inquiries effectively.

We then outlined the key elements that constitute an effective contact page: clear and accurate contact information, a user-friendly contact form, an optional map for physical locations, and additional information like business hours, social media links, or a brief FAQ section.

Furthermore, we provided a step-by-step guide on how to create a contact page using Elementor, detailing how to choose a template, structure the page with sections and columns, insert widgets like Heading, Text Editor, Contact Form, and Google Maps, and finally, customize the styling to match your website's aesthetic.

For those using Elementor Pro, we delved into the advanced contact form features it offers. These include the ability to view and manage form submissions directly within WordPress, integrations with email marketing platforms and CRM systems, conditional logic for dynamic form fields, and enhanced custom styling options.

By following these guidelines and leveraging Elementor's capabilities, you can create a contact page that effectively facilitates communication with your audience, builds trust, and generates valuable leads, ultimately contributing to the success of your website.

Section IV:
Advanced Elementor Techniques

Dynamic Content: Personalization and Automation

Outline

- What is Dynamic Content?
- Benefits of Using Dynamic Content
- Types of Dynamic Content in Elementor
- How to Use Dynamic Content in Elementor
- Dynamic Content Examples
- Best Practices for Using Dynamic Content
- Troubleshooting Dynamic Content Issues
- Chapter Summary

What is Dynamic Content?

Dynamic content refers to website content that adapts and changes based on various factors, such as user data, behavior, preferences, location, or other variables. Unlike static content, which remains fixed for all visitors, dynamic content delivers a personalized and tailored experience to each user.

Imagine visiting an e-commerce website that greets you by name and recommends products based on your browsing history. Or a news website that displays articles relevant to your interests and location. These are examples of dynamic content in action, creating a more engaging and relevant experience for each user.

In contrast, static content remains the same regardless of who is viewing it. This could be a standard welcome message, a generic product listing, or a news article that is displayed to everyone in the same way.

Examples of Dynamic Content

Dynamic content can take many forms, including:

- **Personalized Greetings:** Websites can use the user's name or location to create personalized greetings, making them feel more welcomed and valued. For example, "Welcome back, [User Name]!" or "Hello from [User Location]!"
- **Product Recommendations:** E-commerce sites can display product recommendations based on a user's browsing history, purchase history, or demographic information. This can help users discover new products they might be interested in and increase sales.
- **Targeted Messages:** Websites can display different messages or calls to action based on user segments or behaviors. For example, a website might display a special offer to first-time visitors or a reminder to complete a purchase to returning visitors who have abandoned their shopping carts.
- **Dynamic Forms:** Forms can be customized to show or hide specific fields based on user input. For example, a contact form might ask for additional information if the user selects a specific inquiry type.

- **Real-Time Updates:** Websites can display real-time data, such as stock prices, weather forecasts, or news updates.

The Power of Dynamic Content

Dynamic content is a powerful tool that can significantly enhance your website's effectiveness. By tailoring the content to each individual user, you can create a more engaging, relevant, and personalized experience. This can lead to increased user satisfaction, longer visit durations, higher conversion rates, and improved brand loyalty.

In the next sections, we'll explore how Elementor empowers you to create and manage dynamic content on your WordPress website, opening up a world of possibilities for personalization and automation.

Benefits of Using Dynamic Content

Dynamic content is a game-changer for website owners who want to create a more personalized, engaging, and effective online presence. By leveraging dynamic content, you can reap the following benefits:

Personalization

The ability to tailor the website experience to individual users is a powerful tool for engagement and conversion. Dynamic content allows you to display information, offers, or recommendations that are relevant to each user's interests, preferences, or behavior. This personalization makes visitors feel seen and understood, increasing their likelihood of staying on your site, interacting with your content, and ultimately converting into customers or clients.

Improved Conversions

By delivering targeted content and offers that are more likely to resonate with specific users, you can significantly improve your website's conversion rates. Instead of showing generic messages to everyone, dynamic content allows you to personalize your calls to action, product recommendations, and other elements based on user data and behavior. This targeted approach can lead to higher click-through rates, more leads, and increased sales.

Enhanced User Experience

Dynamic content makes your website more interactive and engaging. By displaying personalized greetings, relevant content, and real-time updates, you can create a more dynamic and immersive experience for your visitors. This can lead to increased time spent on your site, lower bounce rates, and a more positive overall perception of your brand.

Automation

Dynamic content can save you valuable time and resources by automating content updates and personalization. Instead of manually updating content for different user segments or scenarios, you can set up rules and conditions that automatically trigger the display of relevant content. This frees up your time to focus on other important aspects of your business while still providing a personalized experience for your visitors.

In conclusion, incorporating dynamic content into your website is a strategic move that can yield significant benefits. By personalizing the user experience, improving conversions, enhancing engagement, and automating content updates, you can create a website that is more effective, efficient, and ultimately, more successful.

Types of Dynamic Content in Elementor

Elementor offers a variety of dynamic content options to enhance your website's personalization and interactivity. These features allow you to display content that adapts and changes based on various factors, creating a more tailored experience for each user.

Dynamic Text

With Elementor's Dynamic Text feature, you can display text that changes based on different conditions or variables. This could include:

- **User Data:** Display the user's name, email address, or other information they've provided.
- **Website Settings:** Show your website's name, tagline, or other settings.
- **Date and Time:** Display the current date, time, or upcoming events.
- **Post/Page Data:** Show the title, author, or excerpt of a post or page.
- **Custom Fields:** Pull data from custom fields you've created to display personalized information.

Dynamic Images

Similar to dynamic text, you can also display different images based on user preferences, actions, or other variables. This could include:

- **User-Selected Images:** Allow users to choose their profile picture or avatar.
- **Featured Images:** Display the featured image of a specific post or page.
- **Product Images:** Show different product images based on the user's selection or preferences.

Dynamic Fields

Dynamic Fields allow you to pull data from various sources, such as custom fields, WooCommerce product attributes, or ACF fields, and display it on your page. This is a powerful way to create personalized content, such as:

- **User Profiles:** Display customized information based on the user's profile data.
- **Product Details:** Show specific product attributes or variations based on the user's selection.
- **Custom Post Types:** Display data from custom post types you've created for specific content.

Dynamic Templates

Dynamic Templates are reusable templates that can be populated with dynamic content. You can create a template for a specific section or page element, and then use it multiple times on your website. The template will automatically pull in the relevant dynamic content based on the context it's used in.

For example, you could create a dynamic template for a blog post excerpt that displays the post title, featured image, and a short excerpt. Then, you can insert this template on your homepage, archive pages, or anywhere else you want to display a list of blog posts.

By leveraging these dynamic content options in Elementor, you can create a more personalized and engaging experience for your website visitors. You can tailor the content to their interests and preferences, leading to increased engagement, higher conversions, and a more positive overall perception of your brand.

How to Use Dynamic Content in Elementor

Elementor's intuitive interface makes it remarkably easy to harness the power of dynamic content and personalize your website without writing a single line of code. Here's a step-by-step guide to get you started:

1. **Select the Widget:** Start by identifying the widget where you want to incorporate dynamic content. This could be a Heading widget to display a personalized greeting, an Image widget to show different images based on user preferences, or any other widget that can benefit from dynamic data.
2. **Look for the "Dynamic" Tag:** Once you've selected the widget, navigate to its settings panel. In most widgets, you'll find a "Dynamic" tag icon. Click on this icon to reveal the dynamic content options.
3. **Choose the Type of Dynamic Content:** Elementor offers various types of dynamic content, including:
   - **Text:** Display text that changes based on user data, website settings, or other dynamic sources.
   - **Image:** Show different images based on user preferences or conditions.
   - **URL:** Dynamically generate URLs for buttons or links.
   - **Number:** Display dynamic numbers, such as post counts or product prices.
   - **HTML:** Insert custom HTML code that can be dynamically populated with data.
   - **Shortcode:** Include dynamic shortcodes from other plugins or themes.
4. Select the type of dynamic content that best suits your needs.
5. **Select the Source of Your Dynamic Data:** Choose the source from which you want to pull your dynamic data. Elementor offers a wide range of options, including:
   - **Site:** Website title, logo, description, etc.
   - **Author:** Author name, bio, profile picture, etc.
   - **Post/Page:** Title, content, featured image, meta data, etc.
   - **User:** User name, email, registration date, etc.
   - **Archive:** Current archive title, URL, etc.
   - **Comments:** Number of comments, latest comment, etc.
   - **Custom Fields:** Data from custom fields you've created for posts or pages.
   - **WooCommerce:** Product details, prices, categories, etc. (if you have WooCommerce installed).
   - **ACF:** Data from Advanced Custom Fields (if you have ACF installed).
6. **Configure Additional Settings:** Depending on the type of dynamic content you've chosen, you might have additional settings to configure, such as:
   - **Filters:** Filter the dynamic content based on specific conditions (e.g., display a certain message only to logged-in users).
   - **Fallback:** Specify a default value to display if the dynamic data is not available.
   - **Format:** Control how the dynamic content is formatted (e.g., date format, number format).

By following these steps, you can easily add dynamic content to your Elementor widgets, creating a more personalized and engaging experience for your website visitors.

Dynamic Content Examples

Dynamic content can be applied across a variety of websites to create personalized experiences, improve engagement, and boost conversions. Here are some practical examples of how dynamic content can be leveraged on different types of websites:

E-commerce Websites

- **Personalized Product Recommendations:** Utilize customer data and browsing behavior to showcase tailored product suggestions. For example, if a customer frequently views running shoes, display recommendations for similar products or accessories.

- **Recently Viewed Items:** Keep track of products a customer has recently viewed and display them in a "Recently Viewed" section. This simplifies their browsing experience and encourages them to revisit items they might have forgotten about.
- **Targeted Discounts:** Offer personalized discounts or promotions based on customer demographics, purchase history, or loyalty status. This incentivizes purchases and fosters customer loyalty.

Blogs

- **Related Posts:** Suggest articles that are relevant to the topic a user is currently reading. This encourages visitors to explore more of your content and spend more time on your website.
- **Author Information:** Display the author's name, bio, and social media links at the end of a blog post. This helps personalize the content and establish the author as an authority in their field.
- **Personalized Greetings:** Greet returning visitors by name (e.g., "Welcome back, [User Name]!"). This simple gesture can make them feel valued and appreciated.

Membership Sites

- **Member-Specific Content:** Restrict access to certain content or features to paying members only. This incentivizes membership sign-ups and creates a sense of exclusivity.
- **Account Details:** Display personalized account details, such as membership level, billing information, and renewal dates.
- **Personalized Offers:** Offer exclusive discounts or promotions to members based on their subscription level or interests.

These are just a few examples of how dynamic content can be used to enhance your website's user experience and achieve your business goals. By understanding the different types of dynamic content available in Elementor and applying them strategically, you can create a more personalized and engaging website that resonates with your audience and drives results.

Best Practices for Using Dynamic Content

Dynamic content is a powerful tool, but like any tool, it needs to be used wisely to achieve the desired results. Here are some best practices to help you leverage dynamic content effectively:

1. **Use Dynamic Content Sparingly and Strategically:**
   Don't overdo it with dynamic content. Too much personalization can feel intrusive or overwhelming to users. Focus on using dynamic content in areas where it can have the most impact, such as personalized greetings, product recommendations, and targeted calls to action.
2. **Ensure Relevance to the User and Context:**
   Dynamic content should always be relevant to the user and the context in which it's displayed. For example, showing a returning visitor a welcome back message is appropriate, but displaying a first-time visitor offer to someone who has already made a purchase would be confusing and irrelevant.
3. **Test Thoroughly:**
   Before launching your dynamic content, thoroughly test it on different devices and browsers to ensure it works as expected. Check that the correct content is displayed based on the conditions you've set up, and verify that there are no errors or glitches.
4. **Consider A/B Testing:**
   A/B testing involves creating two or more versions of your dynamic content and comparing their performance. This can help you determine which version resonates best with your audience and drives the most conversions. You can use Elementor's built-in A/B testing feature or a third-party tool to conduct your tests.

5. **Keep it Simple:**
   Start with simple dynamic content implementations and gradually add more complexity as you become more familiar with the feature. Don't try to do too much at once, as this can lead to confusion and errors.
6. **Measure and Optimize:**
   Track the performance of your dynamic content using analytics tools like Google Analytics. Monitor metrics like engagement, conversions, and bounce rates to see how dynamic content is impacting your website's goals. Use this data to refine your strategy and optimize your dynamic content for maximum effectiveness.

By adhering to these best practices, you can harness the power of dynamic content to create a more personalized and engaging website experience for your visitors, ultimately driving better results for your business.

Troubleshooting Dynamic Content Issues

While Elementor's dynamic content is a powerful tool, you might encounter some hiccups along the way. Here are common issues users face and how to address them:

Dynamic Content Not Displaying Correctly

This is a frequent issue, often caused by incorrect setup or missing data. Here's what to check:

- **Dynamic Tag Setup:** Double-check that you've correctly inserted the dynamic tag into the widget's settings. Ensure the tag is associated with the correct field or data source.
- **Data Source Availability:** Verify that the data source you've selected (e.g., custom field, user data) is actually populated with data. If the data is missing, the dynamic content won't have anything to display.
- **Conditions and Restrictions:** If you've set up conditions or restrictions for your dynamic content, ensure they are configured correctly. For instance, if you've set a condition to show specific content only to logged-in users, make sure you're logged in when testing.
- **Caching:** If you're using a caching plugin, clear your cache to ensure the latest version of your page is displayed.

Performance Issues

Dynamic content can sometimes affect your website's loading speed, especially if you're pulling in a large amount of data or using complex queries. Here are some tips to optimize performance:

- **Caching:** Use a caching plugin to store the results of dynamic content queries, reducing the need to generate them on every page load.
- **Limit Queries:** Avoid using too many dynamic content elements on a single page. If possible, combine multiple queries into one to reduce server load.
- **Optimize Images:** If you're using dynamic images, ensure they are optimized for web use to minimize file size and improve loading times.
- **Use Lazy Loading:** Consider implementing lazy loading for dynamic images, which means images are only loaded when they come into the user's viewport, reducing the initial page load time.

Compatibility Issues

In rare cases, dynamic content might conflict with certain themes or plugins. If you experience issues, try the following:

- **Deactivate Other Plugins:** Temporarily deactivate other plugins to see if they are causing conflicts with Elementor's dynamic content feature.

- **Switch to a Default Theme:** If you suspect your theme is causing issues, try switching to a default WordPress theme like Twenty Twenty-Three to see if the problem persists.
- **Contact Elementor Support:** If you're still experiencing issues, reach out to Elementor's support team for assistance.

By troubleshooting these common issues, you can ensure that your dynamic content functions smoothly and delivers a seamless personalized experience for your website visitors.

Chapter Summary

This chapter has illuminated the power of dynamic content to elevate your WordPress website's personalization and automation capabilities. We began by defining dynamic content as website content that adapts and changes based on user interactions or specific conditions, differentiating it from static content. We explored the benefits of dynamic content, including personalization, improved conversions, enhanced user experience, and automation, showcasing its potential to revolutionize your website's effectiveness.

We then delved into the different types of dynamic content that Elementor offers, such as Dynamic Text, Dynamic Images, Dynamic Fields, and Dynamic Templates. Each of these tools provides a unique way to personalize your website's content and deliver a tailored experience to each visitor.

Furthermore, we provided a step-by-step guide on how to use dynamic content in Elementor, outlining the process of selecting a widget, choosing the type of dynamic content, selecting the data source, and configuring additional settings.

To solidify your understanding, we presented practical examples of how dynamic content can be applied to various types of websites, including e-commerce sites, blogs, and membership sites.

We also offered best practices for effectively using dynamic content, emphasizing the importance of using it strategically, ensuring relevance to the user and context, thoroughly testing, considering A/B testing, keeping implementations simple, and continuously measuring and optimizing.

Finally, we addressed common troubleshooting issues you might encounter when using dynamic content, such as incorrect display, performance issues, and compatibility problems. By following the suggested solutions, you can ensure that your dynamic content functions smoothly and delivers a seamless personalized experience to your website visitors.

By mastering the concepts and techniques covered in this chapter, you can unlock the full potential of dynamic content in Elementor and create a website that truly resonates with your audience, leading to increased engagement, conversions, and overall success.

21. Popups: Engaging Visitors with Targeted Messages

Outline

- What are Popups?
- Benefits of Using Popups
- Types of Popups
- Creating Popups with Elementor (Pro)
- Targeting and Triggering Popups
- Designing Effective Popups
- Popup Best Practices and Considerations
- Examples of Effective Popups
- Measuring Popup Performance
- Chapter Summary

What are Popups?

Popups are interactive windows or overlays that appear on top of your website's main content, capturing the visitor's attention and prompting them to take a specific action. They are a powerful tool in your website's arsenal, allowing you to deliver targeted messages, promote offers, collect email addresses, or simply provide additional information.

Popups are typically triggered by specific user actions or conditions, such as scrolling to a certain point on a page, clicking a button, or attempting to exit the website. When triggered, they emerge from the background, often with an animation or effect to further grab the visitor's focus.

While some people might find popups intrusive, when used strategically and respectfully, they can be a highly effective way to engage your audience and achieve your marketing goals. They can help you:

- **Capture Leads:** Collect email addresses and other valuable information from visitors, building your email list and potential customer base.
- **Drive Sales:** Promote special offers, discounts, or new products to boost sales and conversions.
- **Increase Engagement:** Share relevant content, surveys, or quizzes to keep visitors engaged and interested in your brand.
- **Reduce Bounce Rate:** Offer incentives or exclusive content to entice visitors to stay on your website longer.

With Elementor Pro, you have a powerful popup builder at your disposal. You can easily create and customize various types of popups, target them to specific audiences or pages, and track their performance to optimize their effectiveness.

Benefits of Using Popups

Popups, when used thoughtfully and strategically, can be a valuable tool in your website engagement strategy. Here are some key benefits of incorporating popups into your website:

Increased Conversions

Popups are incredibly effective at driving conversions, whether it's getting visitors to sign up for your newsletter, download a free resource, or purchase a product. By presenting targeted offers or calls to action at the right moment, you can nudge visitors towards taking the desired action. For example, an exit-intent popup offering a discount code can entice a user who is about to leave your website to complete a purchase.

Lead Generation

Popups are a popular method for collecting email addresses and other valuable information from visitors. By offering something of value, such as a discount code, free ebook, or exclusive content, you can incentivize visitors to share their email address. This allows you to build your email list and nurture leads with targeted email campaigns, ultimately converting them into customers.

Reduced Bounce Rate

Popups can help reduce your website's bounce rate, which is the percentage of visitors who leave your site after viewing only one page. By engaging visitors with relevant content or offers through popups, you can encourage them to explore your website further. For example, a popup offering a helpful guide or resource related to the content they are currently viewing can entice them to click and stay on your site longer.

Improved User Experience

Contrary to popular belief, popups can enhance the user experience when used strategically. By providing timely and relevant information, guidance, or offers, you can make the user's journey through your website more enjoyable and productive. For instance, a popup offering a discount code on a product a user has been viewing can be seen as helpful rather than intrusive.

However, it's crucial to use popups judiciously and avoid bombarding visitors with too many or irrelevant popups, as this can lead to a negative experience and drive them away.

Types of Popups

Elementor Pro's Popup Builder offers a variety of popup types to suit your specific needs and design preferences. Each type has its own unique characteristics and advantages, allowing you to choose the format that best aligns with your goals and target audience.

Lightbox Popups

Lightbox popups are the most common type of popup. They appear in a modal window that overlays the main content of your website, dimming the background to focus attention on the popup. Lightbox popups are versatile and can be used for various purposes, such as email sign-up forms, promotional offers, announcements, or even displaying additional content.

Full-Screen Popups

Full-screen popups, as the name suggests, cover the entire browser window, creating a truly immersive experience. They are ideal for capturing attention and delivering impactful messages. You can use full-screen popups to showcase a new product, highlight a special offer, or present a survey or questionnaire.

Slide-in Popups

Slide-in popups subtly emerge from the side or bottom of the screen, making them less intrusive than lightbox or full-screen popups. They are a good choice for displaying calls to action, promoting social media channels, or offering discounts without disrupting the user's browsing experience.

Bar Popups

Bar popups are smaller and less obtrusive than other types of popups. They typically appear as a thin bar at the top or bottom of the screen and are often used to display announcements, notifications, or cookie consent messages. Bar popups can be easily dismissed by the user, making them a less disruptive option for delivering important information.

Choosing the Right Popup Type

The best type of popup for your website depends on your specific goals and target audience. Consider the following factors when making your choice:

- **Purpose:** What is the main goal of your popup? Are you trying to capture leads, promote a product, or deliver an announcement?
- **Audience:** Who are you targeting with your popup? What type of popup is most likely to appeal to them?
- **Content:** What type of content are you including in your popup? Some types of content are better suited for certain popup formats.
- **Design:** How do you want your popup to look and feel? Choose a style that aligns with your brand and website's aesthetic.

By carefully considering these factors, you can choose the right popup type that effectively engages your audience, delivers your message, and drives the desired action.

Creating Popups with Elementor (Pro)

Elementor Pro's Popup Builder is a powerful tool that lets you design and implement engaging popups to capture leads, promote offers, or deliver targeted messages. Follow these steps to create your first popup:

1. **Access the Popup Builder:**
   From your WordPress dashboard, navigate to *Templates > Popups*. This will take you to the Popup Builder interface.
2. **Add New Popup:**
   Click the "Add New Popup" button. A window will appear prompting you to name your popup and select a type (lightbox, full-screen, slide-in, or bar). Choose the type that best suits your purpose and click "Create Template."
3. **Choose a Template (Optional):**
   Elementor Pro offers a library of pre-designed popup templates to get you started quickly. You can browse these templates, preview them, and choose one that aligns with your design vision. Alternatively, you can start from scratch with a blank canvas.
4. **Design Your Popup:**
   If you chose a template, customize it to match your branding and message. If you're starting from scratch, use Elementor's drag-and-drop editor to add widgets like headings, text, images, forms, buttons, and more. Arrange them to create an eye-catching and effective layout.
5. **Customize Popup Settings:**
   In the Popup Settings panel, you can control various aspects of your popup, including:
   - **Layout:** Set the width and height of the popup, choose its position on the screen, and add entrance and exit animations.
   - **Styles:** Customize the colors, typography, background, and borders of your popup to match your website's design.
   - **Advanced:** Configure advanced settings like close button behavior, overlay effects, and prevent closing on click (not recommended for user experience).
6. **Publish Your Popup:**
   Once you're satisfied with your design and settings, click the "Publish" button to save your popup. You'll then be able to set display conditions and triggers to determine when and where your popup will appear on your website.

Remember, effective popups are clear, concise, and visually appealing. Keep your message focused, use a strong call-to-action, and offer something of value to entice visitors to interact with your popup.

Targeting and Triggering Popups

The true power of popups lies in their ability to be targeted and triggered strategically. Elementor Pro offers a robust set of targeting and triggering options, allowing you to display the right popup to the right audience at the right time.

Targeting Popups

Targeting ensures that your popups are only shown to specific segments of your audience based on their behavior, demographics, or other criteria. This helps you deliver more personalized and relevant messages, increasing the chances of engagement and conversion.

In Elementor Pro, you can target popups based on:

- **User Behavior:** Show popups based on user actions, such as scrolling to a certain point on a page, clicking on a specific link, or spending a certain amount of time on your website.
- **User Demographics:** Target popups based on the user's location, language, device, or referral source.
- **Page-Specific Targeting:** Display specific popups on specific pages or posts.
- **User Roles:** Show popups only to logged-in users or users with specific roles (e.g., subscribers, customers).
- **Advanced Rules:** Create complex targeting rules using multiple conditions and logic operators (AND, OR, NOT).

Triggering Popups

Triggers determine when a popup should appear on your website. Elementor Pro offers a variety of triggers, including:

- **On Page Load:** The popup appears as soon as the page loads.
- **After a Few Seconds:** The popup appears after a specified amount of time.
- **On Scroll:** The popup appears when the user scrolls to a certain point on the page.
- **On Click:** The popup appears when the user clicks on a specific element, such as a button or link.
- **On Exit Intent:** The popup appears when the user is about to leave your website.

You can combine multiple triggers to create more specific conditions for your popups. For example, you could show a popup only to new visitors who have scrolled to the bottom of the page.

Setting up Targeting and Triggers

To set up targeting and triggers for your popups in Elementor Pro:

1. Go to *Templates > Popups* and select the popup you want to edit.
2. Click on the "Settings" tab in the Elementor panel.
3. In the "Conditions" section, choose the targeting options that you want to apply.
4. In the "Triggers" section, select the trigger(s) for when you want the popup to appear.

By mastering targeting and triggering in Elementor Pro, you can deliver personalized messages and offers to your website visitors, increasing engagement, conversions, and overall user experience.

Designing Effective Popups

A well-designed popup can be a powerful tool for engaging your website visitors and achieving your marketing goals. However, a poorly designed popup can be annoying and drive visitors away. Here are some tips to help you design effective popups that capture attention and drive conversions:

Keep it Simple and Concise

Avoid overwhelming visitors with too much text or information. Get straight to the point and clearly communicate your message or offer. Use short sentences, bullet points, and concise language to make your popup easy to read and understand.

Use a Clear Call to Action

Your popup should have a single, clear call to action (CTA). Make it obvious what you want visitors to do, whether it's subscribing to your newsletter, downloading a free ebook, or making a purchase. Use action-oriented language for your CTA button, such as "Get Started," "Sign Up Now," or "Download Your Free Guide."

Use High-Quality Visuals

Images or videos can make your popup more visually appealing and engaging. Choose high-quality visuals that are relevant to your message or offer. For example, if you're promoting a product, use a product image. If you're offering a discount, use an image that conveys excitement or urgency.

Offer an Incentive

To entice visitors to take action, consider offering an incentive. This could be a discount code, a free ebook, access to exclusive content, or entry into a contest. The incentive should be something that your target audience finds valuable and relevant to their interests.

Additional Tips

- Use a visually appealing design that matches your website's branding.
- Keep your popup mobile-friendly and responsive.
- Use contrasting colors to make your CTA button stand out.
- Test different popup designs and CTAs to see what works best for your audience.
- Use exit-intent technology to trigger popups when visitors are about to leave your website.

By following these tips, you can create popups that are not only visually appealing but also effective at achieving your goals. Whether you're looking to capture leads, promote offers, or simply engage your audience, a well-designed popup can be a valuable asset in your marketing toolkit.

Popup Best Practices and Considerations

Popups can be a valuable tool, but their effectiveness hinges on using them responsibly and strategically. Here are some best practices to ensure your popups enhance user experience rather than hindering it:

1. **Don't Overuse Popups:** Bombarding visitors with too many popups can create a frustrating experience and drive them away from your site. Be selective and only use popups when they serve a clear purpose and offer real value to your audience.
2. **Consider Timing and Frequency:** The timing of your popup is crucial. Don't display it immediately when a visitor lands on your page; give them some time to explore your content first. Additionally, limit the frequency with which you show popups to the same visitor. If someone has already seen a popup, don't show it to them again for a certain period.

3. **Make it Easy to Close:** Always provide a clear and obvious way for visitors to close the popup, such as an "X" button or a "No thanks" link. Don't force visitors to interact with the popup; give them the option to dismiss it if they are not interested.
4. **Respect User Privacy:** Be transparent about how you collect and use user data. If you're using a popup to collect email addresses, clearly state your privacy policy and how you intend to use the information. Obtain explicit consent before adding users to your email list.
5. **Comply with Regulations:** If you're targeting users in regions with data protection regulations like GDPR (General Data Protection Regulation) or CCPA (California Consumer Privacy Act), ensure your popup practices comply with these laws. This includes obtaining consent for data collection and providing options for users to manage their data.
6. **Design for Mobile:** Ensure your popups are optimized for mobile devices. They should be easy to read, navigate, and close on smaller screens. Consider using a simpler design or a different popup type for mobile users.
7. **Test and Optimize:** Regularly test your popups to see how they perform. Track metrics like impressions, views, conversions, and close rates. Use this data to optimize your popup designs, content, targeting, and triggers for better results.

By following these best practices, you can create popups that are effective, engaging, and respectful of your visitors' time and privacy.

Examples of Effective Popups

Let's delve into some real-world examples of popups that effectively engage users and achieve their intended goals across different website types:

E-commerce: Exit-Intent Popup Offering a Discount Code

- **Type:** Lightbox popup
- **Trigger:** Exit-intent (triggered when the user's mouse cursor moves towards the browser's close button or back button)
- **Goal:** Prevent cart abandonment and incentivize purchase
- **Design:** Clean and simple design with a clear headline, discount code, and call-to-action button.
- **Effectiveness:** Exit-intent popups can be highly effective at reducing cart abandonment rates by offering a last-minute incentive to complete the purchase.

Blog: Slide-in Popup Inviting Visitors to Subscribe to a Newsletter

- **Type:** Slide-in popup
- **Trigger:** Time on page or scroll depth (e.g., after the user has read 50% of the article)
- **Goal:** Increase newsletter subscriptions and build an email list
- **Design:** Visually appealing design with a compelling headline, brief description of the newsletter's benefits, and a clear sign-up form.
- **Effectiveness:** Slide-in popups are less intrusive than lightbox popups, making them a good choice for capturing email addresses without disrupting the reading experience.

Service-Based Business: Lightbox Popup Offering a Free Consultation or Quote

- **Type:** Lightbox popup
- **Trigger:** Time on page or click trigger (e.g., when the user clicks on a "Get a Quote" button)
- **Goal:** Generate leads and capture contact information
- **Design:** Professional and trustworthy design with a clear headline, brief description of the service offered, and a form to request a consultation or quote.
- **Effectiveness:** Lightbox popups are effective at capturing attention and can be used to promote high-value offers like consultations or quotes.

These are just a few examples of how popups can be used creatively and effectively on different types of websites. By tailoring your popup design, targeting, and triggers to your specific audience and goals, you can create popups that enhance user engagement and drive conversions.

Measuring Popup Performance

Tracking the performance of your popups is crucial for understanding their effectiveness and identifying areas for improvement. Elementor Pro offers built-in analytics that provide valuable insights into your popup's performance. You can also integrate your popups with Google Analytics for even more comprehensive tracking.

Key Metrics to Track

1. **Impressions:** The number of times your popup is displayed to visitors.
2. **Views:** The number of times visitors actually see and interact with your popup (e.g., by reading the content or clicking on a button).
3. **Conversions:** The number of visitors who complete the desired action on your popup (e.g., submitting a form, clicking a link, making a purchase).
4. **Conversion Rate:** The percentage of views that result in conversions. This is calculated by dividing the number of conversions by the number of views.
5. **Close Rate:** The percentage of views that result in the popup being closed without taking any action.

Using Elementor Pro's Built-in Analytics

Elementor Pro provides a simple and intuitive way to track your popup's performance. To access the analytics:

1. Go to *Templates* > *Popups* and select the popup you want to analyze.
2. Click on the "Analytics" tab.
3. You'll see a summary of your popup's performance, including impressions, views, conversions, and conversion rate.

You can also view detailed statistics for each individual trigger and targeting condition you've set up. This allows you to see which triggers and targeting options are most effective and which ones need improvement.

Integrating with Google Analytics

To get even more in-depth insights into your popup's performance, you can integrate Elementor Pro with Google Analytics. This allows you to track popup events, such as impressions, views, and conversions, alongside other website data.

To integrate Elementor Pro with Google Analytics:

1. Install and activate the Google Analytics plugin for WordPress.
2. Go to *Elementor* > *Settings* > *Integrations* and enable the Google Analytics integration.
3. Enter your Google Analytics tracking ID.

Once the integration is set up, you can view your popup data in your Google Analytics account.

Using Data to Optimize Your Popups

The data you collect from Elementor Pro's analytics or Google Analytics can help you identify areas where you can improve your popup's performance. For example, if your popup has a low conversion rate, you might try changing the design, the offer, or the targeting conditions. By analyzing your data and making data-driven decisions, you can optimize your popups to achieve better results.

Here are some tips for optimizing your popups based on data:

- **Test different designs:** Experiment with different layouts, colors, images, and CTAs to see what resonates best with your audience.
- **Optimize your targeting:** Make sure you're targeting the right audience with the right message.
- **Experiment with different triggers:** Try different triggers to see when is the best time to show your popup.
- **Analyze your close rate:** If your close rate is high, it might indicate that your popup is too intrusive or irrelevant. Try making it less obtrusive or targeting it more specifically.
- **Track conversions over time:** Monitor your popup's performance over time to see if it's improving or declining.

Chapter Summary

This chapter illuminated the art of using popups to effectively engage website visitors and drive conversions. We started by defining popups and highlighting their benefits, such as increasing conversions, generating leads, reducing bounce rate, and improving user experience. We then explored the different types of popups available in Elementor Pro, including lightbox, full-screen, slide-in, and bar popups, each with unique characteristics and use cases.

We provided a step-by-step guide on creating popups with Elementor Pro, emphasizing the importance of choosing the right template, designing an eye-catching layout, and customizing settings for optimal performance.

The chapter also delved into the power of targeting and triggering popups. We discussed various targeting options, such as user behavior, demographics, page-specific targeting, and advanced rules, allowing you to deliver the right message to the right audience. We also explored different triggers, including on page load, after a few seconds, on scroll, on click, and on exit intent, to control when your popups appear.

We then offered tips for designing effective popups, emphasizing simplicity, clear calls to action, high-quality visuals, and enticing incentives. These tips will help you create popups that capture attention and drive desired actions.

Moreover, we discussed best practices and considerations for using popups responsibly and effectively. We emphasized the importance of not overusing popups, considering timing and frequency, making them easy to close, respecting user privacy, and complying with relevant regulations.

To illustrate the potential of popups, we showcased examples of effective implementations on different types of websites, demonstrating how they can be used to prevent cart abandonment, increase newsletter subscriptions, and generate leads.

Finally, we explained how to measure the performance of your popups using Elementor Pro's built-in analytics or Google Analytics. We highlighted key metrics like impressions, views, conversions, and close rate, and discussed how to use this data to optimize your popups for better results.

By understanding these concepts and implementing the strategies outlined in this chapter, you can leverage the power of popups to enhance your website's engagement, drive conversions, and achieve your marketing goals.

Theme Builder: Customize Every Aspect of Your Site

Outline

- What is the Elementor Theme Builder?
- Why Use the Theme Builder?
- Accessing the Theme Builder
- Key Components of the Theme Builder
- Creating Custom Headers
- Creating Custom Footers
- Designing Single Post/Page Templates
- Building Archive Page Templates
- Creating 404 Pages
- Global Widgets and Site Parts
- Tips for Using the Theme Builder
- Chapter Summary

What is the Elementor Theme Builder?

The Theme Builder is a groundbreaking feature exclusive to Elementor Pro that revolutionizes how you design and customize your WordPress website. It empowers you to break free from the constraints of traditional themes and create a truly unique and tailored website that reflects your brand's identity and vision.

In essence, the Theme Builder acts as your website's architect, allowing you to design and control every aspect of its appearance. It enables you to create custom templates for various parts of your site, such as:

- **Header:** The topmost section of your website, often containing your logo, navigation menu, and other essential elements.
- **Footer:** The bottom section of your website, typically housing copyright information, contact details, and social media links.
- **Blog Archive:** The page that displays a list of your blog posts, including options for filtering and sorting.
- **Single Post/Page Layouts:** The design and structure of individual blog posts or pages.
- **Search Results Page:** The page that displays results when users search your website.
- **404 Page (Page Not Found):** The page shown when a user tries to access a non-existent page on your site.

With the Theme Builder, you can create these templates using Elementor's intuitive drag-and-drop interface, incorporating your favorite widgets, sections, and columns to build the exact layouts you envision. You have complete control over the styling, including colors, fonts, backgrounds, and more.

Moreover, the Theme Builder allows you to leverage dynamic content, pulling in relevant information from your WordPress database to populate your templates automatically. This means you can display the latest blog posts, featured products, or user-specific information without having to manually update each page.

By eliminating the limitations of traditional themes, the Theme Builder gives you unprecedented freedom to create a website that is truly your own. It's a powerful tool that can transform your website's design and functionality, elevating your brand and enhancing the user experience.

Why Use the Theme Builder?

The Theme Builder is a game-changer for WordPress users who crave complete control over their website's design and functionality. It offers a multitude of benefits that can elevate your website to new heights:

Full Design Control

Unlike traditional themes that often come with pre-defined layouts and limitations, the Theme Builder empowers you to customize every nook and cranny of your website's design. From the header and footer to archive pages, single posts, and even 404 pages, you have the freedom to create unique templates that align perfectly with your brand identity and vision. This level of control ensures a cohesive and visually stunning website that stands out from the crowd.

Reusability

The Theme Builder promotes efficiency by allowing you to create reusable templates. Once you've designed a template for a specific type of page or section, you can easily apply it to multiple pages or posts. This saves you valuable time and effort, as you don't have to recreate the same design elements repeatedly. You can also update a template once, and the changes will automatically reflect on all pages using that template.

Dynamic Content

Elementor's Theme Builder seamlessly integrates with its dynamic content feature. This means you can incorporate dynamic elements into your templates, such as displaying the latest blog posts, featured products, or personalized user information. This dynamic content automatically updates based on the context, ensuring that your website always displays the most relevant and up-to-date information.

Improved Performance

Traditional WordPress themes often come with a lot of code and features that you might not even use. This can slow down your website's loading speed and impact its overall performance. With the Theme Builder, you can create lean and optimized templates that only include the necessary code and functionality, potentially improving your website's speed and performance.

In summary, the Theme Builder is a versatile and powerful tool that gives you unprecedented control over your website's design and functionality. By creating custom, reusable templates, incorporating dynamic content, and optimizing for performance, you can create a website that is truly unique, engaging, and efficient.

Accessing the Theme Builder

Accessing the Theme Builder in Elementor Pro is a straightforward process that opens up a world of design possibilities for your WordPress website. Here's how to get started:

1. **Log in to Your WordPress Dashboard:** The first step is to log in to your WordPress dashboard using your admin credentials. This is the central hub where you manage your website's content and settings.
2. **Navigate to Templates > Theme Builder:** Once you're logged in, hover over the "Templates" tab in the left-hand menu of your dashboard. A submenu will appear, and you'll see an option called "Theme Builder." Click on it.
3. **Add New Template:** The Theme Builder interface will open, displaying a library of pre-designed templates. To start creating your own custom template, click on the "Add New" button at the top of the screen.

4. **Choose Template Type:** A popup window will appear, asking you to select the type of template you want to create. You'll see several options, including:
    - **Header:** The topmost section of your website.
    - **Footer:** The bottom section of your website.
    - **Single Post:** The layout for individual blog posts.
    - **Single Page:** The layout for individual pages (e.g., About Us, Contact Us).
    - **Archive:** The layout for archive pages, such as blog archives, category archives, or tag archives.
    - **Search Results:** The layout for search results pages.
    - **404 Page:** The page displayed when a user tries to access a non-existent page on your website.
    - **WooCommerce:** Templates for product pages, shop pages, cart pages, and more (if you have WooCommerce installed).
5. Choose the type of template you want to create and click on the "Create Template" button. This will open the Elementor editor where you can start designing your custom template.

Key Components of the Theme Builder

The Theme Builder interface in Elementor Pro is designed to streamline the process of creating and customizing templates. It offers a user-friendly layout with three main components that work seamlessly together:

Preview Area

The Preview Area is the central part of the Theme Builder interface, where you see a live preview of your template as you design it. It acts as a visual representation of your work, allowing you to see how your template will look on the front end of your website. You can interact with the preview by clicking on elements, scrolling through the page, and even testing out different responsive modes to see how your template adapts to various screen sizes.

Editor Panel

The Editor Panel is located on the left side of the screen and is your toolbox for building your template. It contains all the familiar Elementor widgets, sections, and columns that you can drag and drop onto the Preview Area to create your desired layout. You can also access global widgets and site parts from the Editor Panel, making it easy to reuse elements across your website.

Settings Panel

The Settings Panel is situated on the right side of the screen and is where you fine-tune the details of your template. It houses a variety of settings, including:

- **Display Conditions:** Control where and when your template will be displayed on your website. You can set conditions based on post types, categories, tags, author archives, and more.
- **Dynamic Content:** Connect your template to dynamic content sources, such as post titles, featured images, author information, or custom fields.
- **Advanced Settings:** Configure additional settings for your template, such as entrance and exit animations, custom CSS, and more.

By navigating and utilizing these three key components—the Preview Area, Editor Panel, and Settings Panel—you can efficiently create and customize templates for various parts of your website, ensuring a consistent and visually appealing design across your entire site.

Creating Custom Headers

The header is often the first thing visitors see when they land on your website, making it a crucial element for establishing brand identity and providing navigation. Elementor Pro's Theme Builder empowers you to create fully customized headers that perfectly align with your website's design and functionality.

1. Access the Theme Builder:

Navigate to *Templates > Theme Builder* in your WordPress dashboard. Click on "Add New" and select "Header" as the template type. Give your header a name and click "Create Template."

2. Choose a Structure:

You can start with a pre-designed header template from Elementor's library or begin with a blank canvas. If you're new to Elementor, starting with a template can be a helpful way to understand the structure and layout of a typical header.

3. Add Widgets:

Populate your header with essential widgets:

- **Site Logo:** Upload your logo using the Site Logo widget. Customize its size and alignment, and add a link to your homepage.
- **Navigation Menu:** Use the Nav Menu widget to create your website's navigation menu. Choose the menu you want to display and customize its appearance.
- **Search Bar:** (Optional) Add the Search Form widget to allow visitors to search your website's content.
- **Additional Elements:** You can add other elements like contact information, social media icons, or a call-to-action button.

4. Customize Styling:

Use Elementor's styling options to customize the appearance of your header.

- **Background:** Choose a background color, gradient, or image.
- **Typography:** Select fonts and adjust font sizes, weights, and line heights for the text elements in your header.
- **Colors:** Customize the colors of your logo, navigation menu, and other elements to match your brand identity.
- **Spacing:** Adjust the margins and padding of your widgets to create a visually appealing layout.

5. Set Display Conditions:

Use display conditions to control where your header appears on your website. You can choose to display it on all pages, specific pages, or even exclude it from certain pages.

- **Include:** Select the types of pages or posts where you want to display the header (e.g., all pages, all posts, specific categories or tags).
- **Exclude:** Select the types of pages or posts where you don't want to display the header (e.g., the checkout page or specific individual pages).

6. Publish Your Header:

Once you're satisfied with your design and settings, click the "Publish" button to save your header template. It will now be applied to the pages you've specified in the display conditions.

Remember, your header is the first impression visitors have of your website. Invest time in creating a well-designed, user-friendly, and visually appealing header that accurately reflects your brand and guides visitors to explore your content.

Creating Custom Footers

The footer is often the last thing visitors see before leaving your website, and it plays a crucial role in providing important information and navigation options. With Elementor Pro's Theme Builder, you can design custom footers that enhance your website's user experience and reinforce your brand identity.

1. Access the Theme Builder:

Navigate to *Templates* > *Theme Builder* in your WordPress dashboard. Click on "Add New" and select "Footer" as the template type. Give your footer a name and click "Create Template."

2. Choose a Structure:

You can start with a pre-designed footer template from Elementor's library or begin with a blank canvas. If you're starting from scratch, consider dividing your footer into sections and columns to create a more organized layout.

3. Add Widgets:

Populate your footer with relevant widgets:

- **Site Logo:** Consider adding your logo again in the footer for brand reinforcement.
- **Navigation Menu:** Include a navigation menu (possibly a simplified version of your main menu) to help users find important pages.
- **Social Icons:** Use the Social Icons widget to display links to your social media profiles.
- **Text Editor:** Add your copyright information, contact details (address, phone number, email), or a brief "About Us" blurb.
- **Subscribe Form:** Encourage visitors to sign up for your newsletter by adding a subscription form.
- **Recent Posts/Comments:** You can display recent posts or comments to keep your footer dynamic.

4. Customize Styling:

Use Elementor's styling options to customize the appearance of your footer.

- **Background:** Choose a background color, gradient, or image. Consider using a contrasting color to make your footer stand out from the rest of the page.
- **Typography:** Select fonts and adjust font sizes, weights, and line heights for the text elements in your footer. Make sure the text is easily readable.
- **Colors:** Customize the colors of your logo, text, links, and other elements to match your brand identity.

5. Set Display Conditions:

Use display conditions to control where your footer appears on your website. Most likely, you'll want to display it on all pages. However, you can exclude it from specific pages if needed.

6. Publish Your Footer:

Once you're happy with your design, click the "Publish" button to save your footer template. It will now be automatically applied to all the pages you've specified in the display conditions.

Designing Single Post/Page Templates

The Theme Builder allows you to craft unique and engaging templates for individual posts and pages on your website. These templates govern the layout and design of your content, ensuring a consistent look and feel while incorporating dynamic elements that automatically populate with relevant information.

1. Access the Theme Builder:

Navigate to *Templates > Theme Builder* and click "Add New." Select either "Single Post" or "Single Page" as your template type, depending on whether you're designing for blog posts or other pages. Give your template a name and click "Create Template."

2. Choose a Layout:

You can start with a pre-designed template from Elementor's library or begin from scratch. Consider the type of content you'll be displaying and choose a layout that complements it. For instance, a blog post template might feature a large featured image at the top, followed by the post title, author information, and the main content.

3. Add Widgets:

Incorporate relevant widgets to display your content dynamically:

- **Post Title:** Use the "Post Title" widget to display the title of your blog post or page.
- **Post Content:** Use the "Post Content" widget to dynamically display the content of your post or page.
- **Featured Image:** Use the "Featured Image" widget to showcase the main image associated with your post.
- **Post Info:** This widget displays various details about your post, such as the author name, date, categories, and tags.
- **Post Comments:** Enable comments on your blog post with this widget.
- **Post Navigation:** Add links to previous and next posts for easy navigation.
- **Author Box:** Introduce the author of the post with their bio and social links.

You can also add other widgets like headings, text editors, images, and buttons to further customize your template.

4. Utilize Dynamic Content:

Elementor's dynamic content feature is a game-changer for single post/page templates. It allows you to pull in data from your WordPress database and display it dynamically within your template.

For example, you can use dynamic tags to:

- **Display the post/page title:** `{{post_title}}`
- **Display the post/page content:** `{{post_content}}`
- **Show the featured image:** `{{post_featured_image}}`
- **Display the author's name:** `{{author_name}}`
- **Show the post date:** `{{post_date}}`

This ensures that your template will automatically populate with the correct information for each individual post or page.

5. Customize Styling:

Use Elementor's styling options to customize the appearance of your template. Adjust colors, fonts, backgrounds, and other visual elements to match your brand identity and create a visually appealing design.

6. Set Display Conditions:

Define the display conditions for your template. You can choose to apply it to all posts, specific categories of posts, or individual posts.

7. Publish Your Template:

Once you're satisfied with your design and settings, click the "Publish" button to save your template. It will now be applied to all the posts or pages that meet the specified display conditions.

Building Archive Page Templates

Archive pages serve as a collection of your blog posts, categorized by date, category, tag, or author. Elementor Pro's Theme Builder allows you to create custom templates for these archive pages, ensuring they match your website's design and provide a seamless user experience.

1. Access the Theme Builder:

Navigate to *Templates > Theme Builder* and click "Add New." Select the appropriate archive type (e.g., "Archive," "Category," "Tag," or "Author") as your template type. Name your template and click "Create Template."

2. Choose a Layout:

You can start with a pre-designed archive template from Elementor's library or begin with a blank canvas. Consider the type of archive you're creating and choose a layout that complements it. For instance, a blog archive might benefit from a grid or masonry layout, while a category archive might use a list layout.

3. Add Widgets:

Incorporate widgets to display your archive content dynamically:

- **Archive Title:** Use the "Archive Title" widget to display the title of the archive page dynamically (e.g., "Category: Recipes," "Tag: Travel," "Author: John Doe").
- **Archive Posts:** The "Archive Posts" widget is essential for displaying the list of posts in the archive. You can customize the layout, style, and number of posts to display.
- **Pagination:** Add pagination to your archive page if you have a large number of posts. This allows users to navigate through different pages of your archive.
- **Search Bar (Optional):** Consider adding a search bar to make it easier for users to find specific posts within the archive.
- **Additional Elements:** You can add other widgets like headings, text editors, or images to provide additional information or context about the archive.

4. Utilize Dynamic Content:

Elementor's dynamic content functionality is invaluable for archive page templates. It allows you to display content that dynamically changes based on the specific archive being viewed. For instance, the Archive Title widget automatically pulls in the relevant title (category name, tag name, or author name) for each archive page.

You can also use dynamic tags within the Archive Posts widget to display specific post information, such as the post title, featured image, excerpt, date, or author name.

5. Customize Styling:

Use Elementor's styling options to customize the appearance of your archive page template. Adjust colors, fonts, backgrounds, and other design elements to create a visually appealing and cohesive look that aligns with your overall website design.

6. Set Display Conditions:

Define the display conditions for your template. For example, if you're creating a category archive template, you might want to display it only on pages that show posts from that specific category. Elementor Pro allows you to set up complex display conditions based on various criteria, such as post types, categories, tags, authors, and more.

7. Publish Your Template:

Once you're satisfied with your design and settings, click the "Publish" button to save your archive page template. It will now be applied automatically to all the archive pages that match your specified display conditions.

Creating 404 Pages

A 404 page is what visitors encounter when they try to access a page on your website that doesn't exist or has been moved. While a default 404 page might suffice, creating a custom one with Elementor can turn this potentially frustrating experience into an opportunity to engage users and guide them back to your website's main content.

Why Customize Your 404 Page?

A custom 404 page serves several important purposes:

- **User Experience:** A well-designed 404 page can prevent visitors from leaving your site out of frustration. By providing helpful navigation options and a friendly message, you can encourage them to stay and explore further.
- **Branding:** A custom 404 page can reinforce your brand identity by maintaining a consistent look and feel with the rest of your website.
- **SEO:** Search engines prefer websites with user-friendly 404 pages, as they signal that the site is well-maintained and provides a good user experience.

Designing Your 404 Page with Elementor

1. **Access the Theme Builder:**
   Navigate to *Templates > Theme Builder* and click "Add New." Select "404 Page" as your template type. Name your template and click "Create Template."
2. **Choose a Layout:**
   You can start with a pre-designed 404 page template or design your own. Keep in mind that a 404 page should be simple, uncluttered, and easy to navigate.
3. **Add Widgets:**
   Incorporate widgets to guide users back to your website's main content:
   - **Heading:** Use a clear and concise heading like "Page Not Found" or "Oops! Something went wrong."
   - **Text Editor:** Add a friendly message apologizing for the inconvenience and explaining that the requested page couldn't be found.
   - **Search Bar:** Include a search bar to help users find the content they're looking for.
   - **Navigation Menu:** Add a navigation menu to your 404 page, allowing users to easily navigate to other parts of your website.
   - **Image or Video:** You can add a relevant image or video to make your 404 page more visually appealing.
4. **Customize Styling:**
   Style your 404 page to match your website's design. Use the same colors, fonts, and design elements as the rest of your site to maintain consistency.

5. **Publish Your 404 Page:**
   Once you're satisfied with your design, click "Publish" to save your 404 page template. Elementor will automatically display this page whenever a user encounters a 404 error on your website.

By creating a custom 404 page with Elementor, you can turn a potentially frustrating experience into a positive one, guiding lost visitors back to your website's main content and ensuring they continue their journey on your site.

Global Widgets and Site Parts

Elementor Pro introduces the concepts of Global Widgets and Site Parts, powerful tools that streamline your design workflow and enhance consistency across your website.

Global Widgets

Global Widgets are essentially reusable widgets that you can create once and then insert into multiple templates or pages across your website. When you modify a Global Widget, the changes are automatically reflected in every instance where the widget is used, saving you the hassle of manually updating each individual widget.

Think of Global Widgets like a master copy of a widget that you can duplicate and use throughout your site. They are ideal for elements that you want to appear consistently across different pages, such as calls to action, social media icons, or copyright information.

To create a Global Widget:

1. Design your widget in the Elementor editor as you normally would.
2. Right-click on the widget handle and select "Save as Global."
3. Give your Global Widget a name and click "Save."

You can then insert your Global Widget into any page or template by dragging it from the Global tab in the widget panel.

Site Parts

Site Parts are similar to Global Widgets, but they encompass larger sections of your website, such as headers, footers, or navigation menus. By creating Site Parts, you can ensure that these crucial elements remain consistent across your entire site.

To create a Site Part:

1. Design the section you want to save as a Site Part in the Elementor editor.
2. Right-click on the section handle and select "Save as Template."
3. Choose "Site Part" as the template type and give it a name.

Once you've created a Site Part, you can easily insert it into any page or template by dragging it from the Global tab in the widget panel. You can also manage and edit your Site Parts in the Theme Builder.

By utilizing Global Widgets and Site Parts, you can streamline your design process, ensure consistency across your website, and easily make global changes without having to edit each page individually.

Tips for Using the Theme Builder

The Theme Builder is a powerful tool, but like any tool, it's most effective when used strategically and with best practices in mind. Here are some tips to help you get the most out of the Theme Builder:

1. **Start with a Plan:** Before you dive into designing templates, take some time to plan your website's structure and content. Identify the different types of pages and sections you need, such as a homepage, blog archive, single post template, and contact page. Outline the content and elements you want to include in each template. Having a clear plan will streamline your design process and ensure consistency throughout your website.
2. **Use a Consistent Style:** Maintain a cohesive visual language across all your templates. This includes using the same fonts, colors, button styles, and other design elements. Consistency helps reinforce your brand identity and makes your website easier to navigate and use.
3. **Leverage Dynamic Content:** Dynamic content is a key feature of Elementor Pro that allows you to display information that changes based on various factors, such as user data, website settings, or post/page details. Utilize dynamic content to personalize your templates and display relevant information, such as the post title, author, date, or featured image.
4. **Test Your Templates:** Always preview your templates on different devices and screen sizes to ensure they are responsive and look great on all platforms. Use Elementor's responsive mode to test how your templates adapt to different screen widths. You can also use browser developer tools or online simulators to test on various devices.
5. **Back Up Your Website:** Before making any significant changes to your templates, it's crucial to create a backup of your website. This allows you to easily revert to a previous version if something goes wrong or if you're not happy with the changes. You can use a backup plugin like UpdraftPlus to automate this process.
6. **Start Simple:** If you're new to the Theme Builder, start with simple templates for your header and footer. Once you're comfortable with the basics, you can gradually experiment with more complex templates like single post or archive pages.
7. **Explore the Template Library:** Elementor Pro's template library offers a wide variety of pre-designed templates that you can use as inspiration or starting points for your own designs. Explore these templates to get ideas and discover new ways to use the Theme Builder.

By following these tips, you can harness the full power of Elementor Pro's Theme Builder to create a custom, professional, and visually stunning website that reflects your brand and delivers an exceptional user experience.

Chapter Summary

This chapter introduced you to Elementor Pro's Theme Builder, a powerful tool for creating custom templates and taking full control of your WordPress website's design. We discussed the benefits of using the Theme Builder, including full design control, reusability, dynamic content integration, and improved performance. We also provided step-by-step instructions on how to access the Theme Builder, explaining its key components: the Preview Area, Editor Panel, and Settings Panel.

Furthermore, we delved into creating custom headers and footers, showcasing how you can add widgets, customize styling, and set display conditions for each. We then explored designing single post/page templates and building archive page templates, emphasizing the use of dynamic content to display relevant information automatically.

Additionally, we covered creating custom 404 pages using the Theme Builder, transforming a potential negative experience into an opportunity to engage visitors and guide them back to your main content.

We also explained the concepts of Global Widgets and Site Parts, powerful features that enable you to create reusable elements and maintain consistency across your website.

Finally, we offered tips for using the Theme Builder effectively, emphasizing the importance of planning, consistency, dynamic content utilization, testing, and website backups.

WooCommerce Integration: Building an Online Store (Optional)

Outline

- Introduction to WooCommerce
- Installing and Setting Up WooCommerce
- Designing Your Online Store with Elementor
- Key WooCommerce Widgets in Elementor
- Customizing WooCommerce Templates with Elementor
- Additional WooCommerce Features and Extensions
- Chapter Summary

Introduction to WooCommerce

If you're looking to build an online store using WordPress, look no further than WooCommerce. This powerful and versatile plugin has emerged as the leading e-commerce solution for WordPress, powering millions of online stores worldwide.

WooCommerce seamlessly integrates with your WordPress website, transforming it into a fully functional online store. It provides all the essential tools and features you need to sell products or services online, including:

- **Product Management:** Easily add, edit, and organize your products, complete with images, descriptions, prices, and inventory management.
- **Shopping Cart and Checkout:** Provide a secure and user-friendly shopping experience for your customers, with a customizable shopping cart and checkout process.
- **Payment Gateways:** Accept payments through a wide range of payment gateways, including PayPal, Stripe, and many others.
- **Shipping Options:** Configure various shipping methods, such as flat rate, free shipping, and local pickup.
- **Order Management:** Track and manage customer orders, including order status, shipping details, and customer information.
- **Marketing and Promotions:** Create discounts, coupons, and other promotional offers to attract and retain customers.
- **Reporting and Analytics:** Gain insights into your store's performance with detailed reports on sales, revenue, and customer behavior.

WooCommerce's popularity stems from its flexibility, scalability, and extensive customization options. It's suitable for a wide range of businesses, from small startups to large enterprises. Whether you're selling physical products, digital downloads, subscriptions, or services, WooCommerce can be tailored to meet your specific needs.

Furthermore, WooCommerce boasts a vast community of users and developers who contribute to its ongoing development and provide support and resources. This thriving ecosystem ensures that WooCommerce remains a cutting-edge e-commerce solution with regular updates, new features, and a wide array of extensions and themes to enhance your store's functionality and design.

In the following sections, we'll delve deeper into installing and setting up WooCommerce, designing your online store with Elementor, and exploring some of the key features and extensions that make WooCommerce the go-to choice for building online stores on WordPress.

Installing and Setting Up WooCommerce

Getting your WooCommerce store up and running is a breeze, thanks to its user-friendly installation and setup process. Here's a step-by-step guide to get you started:

1. **Install WooCommerce:**
   - **Access Plugins:** From your WordPress dashboard, navigate to the "Plugins" menu and click on "Add New."
   - **Search:** In the search bar, type "WooCommerce" and press enter.
   - **Install:** The WooCommerce plugin should appear at the top of the search results. Click the "Install Now" button next to it.
   - **Activate:** Once the installation is complete, click the "Activate" button to enable WooCommerce on your website.
2. **Run the Setup Wizard:**
   Upon activation, WooCommerce will launch a setup wizard to guide you through the initial configuration of your store. The wizard will prompt you to set up the following essential aspects:
   - **Store Details:** Enter your store's address, country, and currency.
   - **Industry:** Select the industry that best describes your business.
   - **Product Types:** Choose the types of products you'll be selling (physical, digital, or both).
   - **Business Details:** Specify the number of products you plan to sell and whether you're already selling elsewhere.
   - **Theme:** Choose a theme for your store. WooCommerce offers a variety of free and premium themes specifically designed for online stores.
   - **Jetpack (Optional):** You'll be asked if you want to install Jetpack, a plugin that offers various features like security, performance optimization, and marketing tools. You can choose to install it or skip this step for now.
3. **Customize Your Store (Optional):**
   After completing the setup wizard, you'll be directed to the WooCommerce dashboard. From here, you can further customize your store's settings, such as:
   - **Products:** Add and manage your products.
   - **Shipping:** Set up shipping zones and rates.
   - **Payments:** Choose which payment methods you want to accept (e.g., PayPal, Stripe, credit cards).
   - **Taxes:** Configure tax rates based on your location and customer locations.
   - **Marketing:** Set up marketing options like email notifications and discounts.
4. **Start Selling!**
   Once you've configured the essential settings, you're ready to start adding products and promoting your online store.

Congratulations! You've successfully installed and set up WooCommerce. You're now one step closer to launching your online store and selling your products or services to the world.

Designing Your Online Store with Elementor

One of the most significant advantages of using WooCommerce with Elementor is the seamless integration between the two platforms. This integration allows you to leverage Elementor's powerful drag-and-drop editor to design and customize every aspect of your online store, including:

- **Product Pages:** Craft visually stunning product pages that showcase your products in their best light. Use Elementor's widgets to add high-quality images, detailed descriptions, customer reviews, related products, and eye-catching call-to-action buttons.
- **Shop Pages:** Design your main shop page or category pages with custom layouts that highlight your products and make them easy to browse. Use Elementor's grid or carousel layouts to create visually appealing product displays.

- **Cart Pages:** Customize the shopping cart page to provide a seamless experience for your customers. You can add elements like order summaries, coupon codes, and shipping calculators to make the checkout process smooth and intuitive.
- **Checkout Pages:** Design a secure and user-friendly checkout page that guides customers through the payment process. You can customize the form fields, add trust badges, and incorporate your branding elements to build confidence and encourage conversions.
- **Thank You Pages:** Create personalized thank-you pages to acknowledge and appreciate your customers' purchases. You can use dynamic content to display order details, offer discounts on future purchases, or encourage social sharing.

Seamless Integration for Creative Freedom

Elementor's integration with WooCommerce gives you complete creative freedom to design an online store that aligns with your brand identity and vision. You can choose from a wide range of pre-designed templates or create custom layouts from scratch. The drag-and-drop interface makes it easy to add and arrange elements, customize colors and fonts, and create a visually stunning shopping experience for your customers.

No Coding Required

You don't need any coding knowledge to design your WooCommerce store with Elementor. The intuitive interface and pre-built widgets make it easy to build and customize your store without writing a single line of code. This empowers you to take control of your store's design and create a unique online presence that stands out from the competition.

By leveraging the seamless integration between Elementor and WooCommerce, you can create a beautifully designed and highly functional online store that not only showcases your products effectively but also delivers a seamless shopping experience for your customers, ultimately driving sales and boosting your bottom line.

Key WooCommerce Widgets in Elementor

Elementor enhances your WooCommerce store design capabilities by offering a set of specialized widgets that seamlessly integrate with your online shop. These widgets empower you to create engaging and user-friendly product displays, shopping carts, and checkout pages, all without requiring any coding knowledge.

Products Widget

The Products widget is a versatile tool for showcasing your products in various formats. You can choose to display your products in a grid, list, or carousel layout. You can also filter and sort products based on categories, tags, attributes, or price. This widget provides extensive customization options, allowing you to control the appearance of each product card, including the image, title, price, rating, and add to cart button.

Product Images Widget

Visuals play a crucial role in e-commerce, and the Product Images widget lets you showcase your product images in a variety of styles. You can create image carousels, galleries, or simply display a single image with zoom functionality. This widget offers customization options for image size, aspect ratio, lightbox settings, and navigation controls.

Add To Cart Widget

The Add To Cart widget is a must-have for any online store. It enables customers to easily add products to their shopping cart with a single click. You can customize the button's text, style, and placement to match your website's design and encourage clicks.

Cart Widget

The Cart widget displays the contents of the customer's shopping cart, including product names, quantities, prices, and subtotal. It also provides options for updating quantities, removing items, and proceeding to checkout. You can customize the cart's appearance, such as the layout, colors, and fonts.

Checkout Widget

The Checkout widget streamlines the checkout process for your customers. It displays the order summary, shipping and billing information fields, and payment options. You can customize the checkout page's layout, add trust badges, and incorporate your branding elements to create a seamless and secure checkout experience.

By utilizing these WooCommerce widgets in conjunction with Elementor's drag-and-drop interface, you can design a visually appealing and user-friendly online store that drives sales and enhances the customer experience.

Customizing WooCommerce Templates with Elementor

Elementor Pro's Theme Builder takes your WooCommerce store's design to the next level, empowering you to create custom templates for various WooCommerce pages. This allows you to tailor the look and feel of your product pages, shop pages, cart, checkout, and other essential elements, providing a unique and engaging shopping experience for your customers.

Accessing WooCommerce Templates in Theme Builder

1. **Navigate to Theme Builder:** In your WordPress dashboard, go to *Templates > Theme Builder*.
2. **Choose WooCommerce:** In the Theme Builder library, select the "WooCommerce" tab. This will display a list of available WooCommerce templates, including:
   - **Single Product:** The template for individual product pages.
   - **Product Archive:** The template for shop pages, category pages, and tag pages.
   - **Cart:** The template for the shopping cart page.
   - **Checkout:** The template for the checkout page.
   - **Thank You:** The template for the order confirmation page.
   - **My Account:** The template for the customer account dashboard.

Creating Custom Templates

To create a custom template for a specific WooCommerce page:

1. **Select the Template Type:** Click on the "Add New" button next to the desired template type (e.g., Single Product).
2. **Name Your Template:** Give your template a descriptive name (e.g., "Custom Product Page").
3. **Design Your Layout:** Use Elementor's drag-and-drop editor to design your custom layout. You can add sections, columns, and widgets just like you would on any other page.
4. **Incorporate WooCommerce Widgets:** Elementor provides specialized WooCommerce widgets for displaying product information, adding to cart buttons, and creating product galleries. Utilize these widgets to showcase your products and create an intuitive shopping experience.
5. **Customize Styling:** Apply your brand's styling to your templates using Elementor's extensive design options. Ensure consistency with your overall website design to create a cohesive look and feel.

6. **Set Display Conditions:** Define the display conditions for your template. For example, if you're creating a Single Product template, you would typically set the condition to "All Products."
7. **Publish Your Template:** Click the "Publish" button to save your template. It will now be applied to all relevant WooCommerce pages on your website.

Customization Examples

Here are some examples of how you can customize WooCommerce templates with Elementor:

- **Single Product:** Create a unique product page layout with a gallery of images, detailed descriptions, customer reviews, and related products.
- **Shop Page:** Design a visually appealing shop page with a custom grid or list layout, filters for sorting products, and promotional banners.
- **Cart Page:** Customize the cart page to include order summaries, coupon codes, and shipping calculators.
- **Checkout Page:** Create a streamlined checkout process with a clear layout, trust badges, and your branding elements.

By leveraging the power of Elementor Pro's Theme Builder, you can create a truly unique and customized online store that stands out from the crowd and delivers an exceptional shopping experience for your customers.

Additional WooCommerce Features and Extensions

While WooCommerce's core functionality is impressive, its true power lies in its extensibility. The platform boasts a vast ecosystem of extensions and plugins that can be added to enhance your online store's capabilities and tailor it to your specific needs. While a deep dive into all these features is beyond the scope of this book (and chapter, as this is an optional section for readers not interested in e-commerce), let's briefly touch upon some key areas:

Payment Gateways

WooCommerce supports a wide array of payment gateways, allowing you to accept payments from customers worldwide through various methods. Popular options include PayPal, Stripe, Square, Authorize.Net, and many more. Integrating these gateways typically involves installing the respective plugin and configuring your account settings. Once set up, your customers can choose their preferred payment method during checkout.

Shipping Methods

Shipping is a critical aspect of any online store. WooCommerce allows you to configure various shipping methods to cater to your specific requirements. You can set up:

- **Flat Rate Shipping:** Charge a fixed fee for shipping, regardless of the order's weight or destination.
- **Free Shipping:** Offer free shipping on all orders or for orders that meet a minimum purchase amount.
- **Local Pickup:** Allow customers to pick up their orders from your physical store or designated location.
- **Table Rate Shipping:** Create complex shipping rules based on weight, destination, or order value.
- **Live Rates from Carriers:** Get real-time shipping rates from carriers like USPS, UPS, FedEx, or DHL.

Product Variations

If your products come in different sizes, colors, or other variations, you can easily manage them using WooCommerce's product variation feature. This allows you to create multiple versions of a product with different attributes and prices, all within a single product listing. Customers can then choose their desired variation before adding the product to their cart.

Inventory Management

WooCommerce provides robust tools for managing your product inventory. You can track stock levels for each product and variation, set up low stock notifications to alert you when inventory is running low, and even hide out-of-stock products from your store automatically.

Order Management

WooCommerce offers a comprehensive order management system. You can view and manage all customer orders from your WordPress dashboard. You can track order statuses, update shipping details, process refunds, and communicate with customers regarding their orders.

This is just a glimpse into the vast world of WooCommerce features and extensions. Whether you need to add subscriptions, memberships, bookings, or any other specialized functionality to your online store, there's likely a WooCommerce extension available to meet your needs.

Chapter Summary

This chapter provided an overview of WooCommerce, a powerful e-commerce plugin that can transform your WordPress website into a fully functional online store. We explored the key features and benefits of WooCommerce, highlighting its popularity, flexibility, scalability, and extensive customization options.

We also provided step-by-step instructions on how to install and set up WooCommerce, guiding you through the setup wizard and basic configuration settings. We then discussed how Elementor's seamless integration with WooCommerce empowers you to design and customize your online store with ease, creating unique layouts for product pages, shop pages, cart pages, and checkout pages.

Furthermore, we introduced the key WooCommerce widgets available in Elementor, such as Products, Product Images, Add To Cart, Cart, and Checkout, explaining how they can be used to create an engaging and user-friendly shopping experience.

We also touched upon Elementor Pro's Theme Builder, which allows you to create custom templates for various WooCommerce pages, further enhancing your store's design and functionality.

Finally, we briefly discussed some of the additional features and extensions available for WooCommerce, such as payment gateways, shipping methods, product variations, inventory management, and order management. These features can be explored further if you are interested in building a more advanced online store.

While this chapter is optional for those not interested in building an online store, it provides a comprehensive overview of WooCommerce and its integration with Elementor, giving you the foundation to create a successful e-commerce website.

SEO Basics for Elementor: Get Found on Google

Outline

- What is SEO?
- Why SEO Matters for Your Website
- Elementor's Built-in SEO Features
- On-Page SEO with Elementor
- Technical SEO with Elementor
- Using SEO Plugins with Elementor
- Measuring and Improving Your SEO Performance
- Chapter Summary

What is SEO?

Search Engine Optimization (SEO) is the practice of strategically enhancing your website to improve its visibility and ranking in search engine results pages (SERPs). It's the digital equivalent of optimizing your brick-and-mortar store for foot traffic and visibility.

When someone searches for a particular keyword or phrase on Google, Bing, or other search engines, these platforms employ complex algorithms to determine which websites are most relevant and useful to the searcher. SEO involves understanding these algorithms and making necessary adjustments to your website's content, structure, and technical aspects to align with their criteria.

A higher ranking in search results translates to increased organic traffic—visitors who find your website through unpaid search listings. This organic traffic is highly valuable, as it consists of users actively seeking information, products, or services related to your niche. By appearing prominently in search results, you can attract a steady stream of targeted traffic without incurring ongoing advertising costs.

Think of SEO as a long-term investment in your website's visibility and success. By consistently optimizing your site for search engines, you can gradually improve your rankings, attract more qualified visitors, and ultimately achieve your business goals.

Why SEO Matters for Your Website

In the digital age, where competition for online attention is fierce, SEO is not merely an option but a necessity for any website aiming to thrive. Let's delve deeper into why SEO is a critical factor for your website's success:

Increased Visibility

Higher rankings in search results equate to greater visibility for your website. When your site appears on the first page of Google for relevant keywords, it's like having prime real estate in a bustling marketplace. It's the first thing potential visitors see, significantly increasing the likelihood of them clicking on your link and exploring your content.

Organic Traffic

SEO is the key to attracting organic traffic, which refers to visitors who find your website through unpaid search results. Unlike paid advertising, where you pay for clicks, organic traffic is free and sustainable in the long run. When your website ranks well for relevant keywords, you tap into a steady stream of potential customers actively searching for information, products, or services related to your niche.

Credibility and Trust

Users tend to associate higher search rankings with credibility and trustworthiness. A website that appears on the first page of Google is often perceived as more authoritative and reliable than one buried deep in the search results. This can significantly impact user behavior, leading to increased click-through rates, longer visit durations, and higher conversions.

Cost-Effectiveness

While SEO requires an initial investment of time and effort, it's a highly cost-effective strategy in the long run. Unlike paid advertising, where you have to continuously pay for clicks, organic traffic generated through SEO is essentially free. This makes SEO a sustainable and budget-friendly approach to attracting a steady stream of targeted traffic to your website.

Competitive Advantage

In today's competitive online landscape, SEO can give you a significant edge over your rivals. By outranking your competitors in search results, you can capture a larger share of the market and attract more potential customers. Investing in SEO is like leveling up your website's marketing game, giving you a competitive advantage that can translate into increased sales, leads, or brand awareness.

Elementor's Built-in SEO Features

Elementor is not just a powerful page builder; it also comes equipped with several built-in SEO features that can help you optimize your website for search engines. While Elementor isn't a replacement for a dedicated SEO plugin, these features provide a solid foundation for improving your website's visibility and ranking in search results.

Clean Code

Elementor generates clean and semantic HTML code, which is a crucial factor for SEO. Clean code means that your website's code is well-structured, organized, and free of unnecessary elements. Semantic code uses HTML tags that accurately describe the meaning of the content, making it easier for search engines to understand and index your pages. This can lead to better search rankings and increased organic traffic.

Mobile Responsiveness

Mobile responsiveness is a critical aspect of modern SEO. Google and other search engines prioritize mobile-friendly websites in their search results, as they provide a better user experience for the growing number of mobile users. Elementor's responsive design capabilities ensure that your website adapts seamlessly to different screen sizes, including desktops, tablets, and mobile phones. This mobile-friendliness is essential for achieving higher rankings and attracting more mobile traffic.

Image Optimization

Images can significantly impact your website's loading speed, which is a crucial factor for both user experience and SEO. Large, unoptimized images can slow down your pages, leading to higher bounce rates and lower search rankings. Elementor automatically optimizes images for web use by compressing them without sacrificing quality. This means that your images will load faster, improving your website's overall performance and SEO.

Customizable Meta Tags

Meta tags are snippets of text that provide information about a web page to search engines and web browsers. The two most important meta tags for SEO are the title tag and the meta description.

- **Title Tag:** The title tag is the text that appears in the browser tab and in search engine results. It should be concise, descriptive, and include relevant keywords.
- **Meta Description:** The meta description is a brief summary of your page's content that appears below the title tag in search results. It should be engaging and encourage users to click on your link.

Elementor allows you to easily edit the title tag and meta description for each page or post within the editor. This makes it easy to optimize your meta tags for specific keywords and improve your website's visibility in search results.

On-Page SEO with Elementor

On-page SEO refers to the practice of optimizing individual web pages to rank higher in search engine results and attract more relevant organic traffic. It involves various elements on your page, from the content itself to its structure and HTML tags. Elementor, with its intuitive interface and versatile widgets, simplifies the process of on-page SEO optimization.

Keywords

Keywords are the words and phrases that people use to search for information online. To optimize your page for SEO, you need to identify relevant keywords that your target audience is searching for and incorporate them strategically into your content.

Here's how you can use Elementor to optimize keywords:

1. **Keyword Research:** Conduct thorough keyword research using tools like Google Keyword Planner or SEMrush. Identify keywords that have a good search volume and low competition.
2. **Page Titles and Headings:** Incorporate your primary keyword into your page title and main heading (H1 tag). Use secondary keywords in your subheadings (H2, H3, etc.).
3. **Content:** Naturally weave your keywords into your body text. Avoid keyword stuffing, which can negatively impact your SEO.
4. **Image Alt Text:** Add descriptive alt text to your images that include your target keywords.

Meta Descriptions

Meta descriptions are brief summaries of your page's content that appear in search engine results. A well-crafted meta description can entice users to click on your link and improve your click-through rate.

Here's how to optimize your meta descriptions with Elementor:

1. **Edit Page/Post Settings:** In the Elementor editor, click on the gear icon in the bottom-left corner to open the Page Settings panel.
2. **SEO Tab:** Go to the "SEO" tab and locate the "Meta Description" field.
3. **Write Your Description:** Craft a concise and compelling description that accurately summarizes your page's content and includes your target keyword(s).
4. **Keep it Under 160 Characters:** Search engines typically truncate meta descriptions that are longer than 160 characters.

Header Tags

Header tags (H1, H2, H3, etc.) are used to structure your content and create a hierarchy. They also help search engines understand the organization and importance of your content.

Use Elementor's Heading widget to add headings to your pages. Make sure to:

- Use only one H1 tag per page, typically for the main title.

- Use H2 tags for subheadings and H3 tags for further subdivisions.
- Incorporate relevant keywords into your headings.

Internal Linking

Internal linking refers to linking between pages within your website. It helps users navigate your site and discover related content. It also signals to search engines which pages are most important.

In Elementor, you can add internal links using the Text Editor widget or the Button widget. When linking to other pages on your website, use descriptive anchor text that includes relevant keywords.

Content Optimization

The most crucial aspect of on-page SEO is creating high-quality, engaging, and informative content that satisfies the user's search intent. Your content should be well-researched, well-written, and provide value to your readers.

In Elementor, you can use the Text Editor widget to create and format your content. Make sure your content is easy to read, includes relevant keywords, and provides a comprehensive answer to the user's query.

By implementing these on-page SEO techniques in Elementor, you can optimize your web pages to rank higher in search results, attract more organic traffic, and ultimately achieve your website's goals.

Technical SEO with Elementor

While Elementor excels at facilitating the visual design of your website, it's equally important to address the technical aspects of SEO to ensure your site's optimal performance and visibility in search engine rankings. Elementor offers various tools and features to help you tackle these technical elements.

Page Speed

Page speed, or the time it takes for your website to load, is a crucial factor for user experience and SEO. Slow-loading websites frustrate users and lead to higher bounce rates. Search engines also penalize slow-loading sites, affecting your ranking in search results.

Elementor provides several ways to optimize your page speed:

- **Minimize Heavy Elements:** Avoid using too many heavy elements, such as animations, videos, or complex widgets, as they can slow down your page.
- **Optimize Images:** Compress and optimize your images before uploading them to Elementor. You can use Elementor's built-in image optimizer or a dedicated image optimization plugin to reduce file sizes without sacrificing quality.
- **Enable Browser Caching:** Caching stores a copy of your website's files on the visitor's browser, so they don't have to be downloaded again on subsequent visits. This can significantly improve loading times.
- **Minify CSS and JavaScript:** Minification removes unnecessary characters from your code, reducing file size and improving loading speed. Elementor Pro offers built-in CSS and JavaScript minification options.

Mobile Optimization

Mobile optimization is a non-negotiable aspect of modern SEO. With the majority of web traffic coming from mobile devices, search engines like Google prioritize mobile-friendly websites in their rankings. Elementor's responsive design capabilities make it easy to create websites that adapt seamlessly to different screen sizes, ensuring your site looks and functions flawlessly on mobile devices.

Structured Data (Schema Markup)

Structured data, also known as schema markup, is a way of adding additional information to your website's code that helps search engines better understand your content. This can lead to richer search results, such as star ratings, product prices, or event details, which can improve click-through rates.

Elementor Pro allows you to add schema markup to your pages using the Schema Pro plugin integration. You can easily mark up different types of content, such as articles, events, products, or local businesses, to provide search engines with the information they need to display rich results.

XML Sitemaps

An XML sitemap is a file that lists all the pages on your website. It helps search engines crawl and index yoursite more efficiently, ensuring that all your pages are discovered and included in search results.

Elementor Pro can automatically generate an XML sitemap for your website. You can also use dedicated SEO plugins like Yoast SEO or Rank Math to create and manage your sitemaps.

By addressing these technical SEO aspects within Elementor, you can improve your website's performance, visibility, and ranking in search results, driving more organic traffic and achieving your online goals.

Using SEO Plugins with Elementor

While Elementor provides a solid foundation for SEO, using a dedicated SEO plugin like Yoast SEO or Rank Math can significantly enhance your website's search engine optimization efforts. These plugins offer a comprehensive suite of tools and features that help you optimize your website for better visibility, higher rankings, and increased organic traffic.

Yoast SEO

Yoast SEO is one of the most popular and widely used SEO plugins for WordPress. It offers a user-friendly interface and a wide range of features, making it suitable for both beginners and experienced SEO professionals.

Key features of Yoast SEO include:

- **Keyword Optimization:** Analyze your content for relevant keywords, optimize your meta descriptions, and get suggestions for improving your on-page SEO.
- **Readability Analysis:** Assess the readability of your content and get suggestions for making it more user-friendly.
- **XML Sitemaps:** Automatically generate XML sitemaps for your website and submit them to search engines.
- **Breadcrumbs:** Create breadcrumb navigation to help users and search engines understand your website's structure.
- **Social Media Integration:** Optimize your content for social media sharing.
- **Advanced Features:** Access advanced features like canonical URLs, redirect management, and internal linking suggestions.

Rank Math

Rank Math is another popular SEO plugin that offers a similar range of features as Yoast SEO, but with a more streamlined interface and some unique features of its own.

Key features of Rank Math include:

- **Keyword Optimization:** Similar to Yoast SEO, Rank Math provides keyword analysis and optimization suggestions.
- **Content AI:** This unique feature uses artificial intelligence to analyze your content and provide suggestions for improving its SEO and readability.
- **404 Monitor:** Tracks 404 errors on your website and helps you fix them.
- **Local SEO:** Optimize your website for local search results.
- **Advanced Schema Generator:** Create rich snippets for your content to enhance its appearance in search results.

How SEO Plugins Enhance Your SEO Efforts

Both Yoast SEO and Rank Math can help you with the following aspects of SEO:

- **Keyword Research:** Identify relevant keywords with high search volume and low competition.
- **On-Page Optimization:** Optimize your page titles, meta descriptions, header tags, and content for your target keywords.
- **Technical SEO:** Generate XML sitemaps, fix broken links, and improve your website's overall technical health.
- **Content Analysis:** Assess your content's readability and SEO potential and get suggestions for improvement.
- **Local SEO:** Optimize your website for local search results to attract customers in your area.
- **Social Media Optimization:** Integrate with social media platforms to maximize your content's reach.

Choosing the Right SEO Plugin

Both Yoast SEO and Rank Math are excellent choices for enhancing your website's SEO. The best plugin for you depends on your personal preferences and specific needs. Yoast SEO is known for its user-friendly interface and comprehensive feature set, while Rank Math offers a more streamlined interface and some unique features like Content AI.

Whichever plugin you choose, integrating it with Elementor is a straightforward process. Both plugins offer seamless integration with Elementor, allowing you to optimize your pages and posts directly within the Elementor editor.

Measuring and Improving Your SEO Performance

SEO is an ongoing process that requires continuous monitoring and optimization. To gauge the effectiveness of your SEO efforts and identify areas for improvement, it's crucial to track your website's performance using various tools and metrics.

Essential SEO Tools

Two indispensable tools for tracking your website's SEO performance are:

1. **Google Search Console:** This free tool from Google provides valuable insights into how your website appears in Google search results. It shows you which keywords your site ranks for, how often your pages appear in search results, and how many users click on your links. You can also use Search Console to identify and fix technical issues that might be hindering your SEO performance.
2. **Google Analytics:** This powerful analytics platform allows you to track a wide range of website data, including traffic sources, user behavior, conversions, and more. By analyzing your Google Analytics data, you can gain valuable insights into how users interact with your website and identify areas where you can improve the user experience and SEO.

Key Metrics to Track

To measure and improve your SEO performance, focus on tracking these key metrics:

- **Organic Traffic:** This refers to the number of visitors who find your website through unpaid search results. An increase in organic traffic indicates that your SEO efforts are paying off.
- **Keyword Rankings:** Track your website's rankings for your target keywords. Improving your rankings can lead to more organic traffic and better visibility.
- **Click-Through Rate (CTR):** This is the percentage of users who click on your link in search results. A high CTR indicates that your title tag and meta description are compelling and relevant to the search query.
- **Bounce Rate:** This is the percentage of visitors who leave your website after viewing only one page. A high bounce rate could indicate that your content is not relevant or engaging, or that your website has technical issues.
- **Average Session Duration:** This measures the average amount of time users spend on your website. A longer session duration indicates that users find your content valuable and engaging.

Using Data to Optimize Your Website

By analyzing the data from Google Search Console and Google Analytics, you can identify areas where you can improve your website's SEO performance. For example:

- If your organic traffic is low, you might need to focus on keyword research and on-page optimization.
- If your keyword rankings are not improving, you might need to build more backlinks or create more high-quality content.
- If your CTR is low, you might need to rewrite your title tags and meta descriptions to make them more compelling.
- If your bounce rate is high, you might need to improve your website's design, navigation, or content.

By regularly monitoring your SEO performance and making data-driven decisions, you can continually optimize your website for better search engine visibility and attract more targeted traffic.

Chapter Summary

This chapter delved into the fundamentals of SEO and how you can leverage Elementor to optimize your WordPress website for search engines. We began by defining SEO as the practice of improving your website's visibility and ranking in search engine results pages (SERPs), explaining how it can lead to increased organic traffic and visibility.

We then discussed the importance of SEO for your website's success, highlighting its role in increasing visibility, attracting organic traffic, building credibility, ensuring cost-effectiveness, and providing a competitive advantage.

Next, we explored Elementor's built-in SEO features, including clean code generation, mobile responsiveness, automatic image optimization, and customizable meta tags. These features provide a solid foundation for your SEO efforts, even without additional plugins.

We went on to discuss on-page SEO techniques you can implement with Elementor, such as keyword research, meta description optimization, proper header tag usage, internal linking, and content optimization. These practices focus on improving individual pages to rank higher in search results.

Additionally, we covered technical SEO aspects you can address with Elementor, including page speed optimization, mobile optimization, structured data implementation, and XML sitemap generation. These technical elements are crucial for ensuring your website's optimal performance and search engine visibility.

We also recommended using dedicated SEO plugins like Yoast SEO or Rank Math to further enhance your SEO efforts. These plugins provide comprehensive tools for keyword research, on-page optimization, technical SEO, and other essential aspects.

Finally, we emphasized the importance of measuring and improving your SEO performance using tools like Google Search Console and Google Analytics. By tracking key metrics such as organic traffic, keyword rankings, click-through rates, and bounce rates, you can gain valuable insights into your website's performance and identify areas for improvement.

By mastering these SEO basics and utilizing the tools and techniques available in Elementor, you can optimize your website for search engines, attract more targeted traffic, and ultimately achieve your online goals. Remember, SEO is an ongoing process that requires continuous monitoring and optimization, so stay committed to learning and implementing the latest best practices.

Section V:
Tips, Troubleshooting, and Maintenance

Common WordPress Errors and How to Fix Them

Outline

- Introduction
- Error Establishing a Database Connection
- White Screen of Death (WSoD)
- 500 Internal Server Error
- 404 Page Not Found Error
- Memory Exhausted Error
- Maximum Execution Time Exceeded
- Briefly Mention Other Common Errors
- General Troubleshooting Tips
- Chapter Summary

Introduction

WordPress is a powerful and versatile platform, but like any software, it's not immune to errors. Whether you're a seasoned WordPress pro or a beginner just starting, encountering an error message can be frustrating and disruptive. The good news is that most WordPress errors can be resolved with a little troubleshooting and some know-how.

In this chapter, we'll guide you through some of the most common WordPress errors you might encounter while building your website with Elementor. We'll explain the causes of these errors, provide step-by-step instructions on how to diagnose and fix them, and offer general troubleshooting tips to help you resolve any unexpected issues.

Don't be discouraged if you run into an error. By understanding the common causes and following the troubleshooting steps outlined in this chapter, you can quickly get your website back up and running smoothly.

Let's dive in and tackle those pesky WordPress errors head-on!

Error Establishing a Database Connection

The "Error Establishing a Database Connection" is a common WordPress error that can be alarming, as it essentially means your website has lost communication with its brain—the database. This error prevents your site from loading and displaying any content.

Common Causes

This error usually stems from one of the following issues:

1. **Incorrect Database Credentials:** The most frequent cause is incorrect information (database name, username, password) in your `wp-config.php` file. This file is crucial for connecting WordPress to your database.
2. **Database Server Issues:** Sometimes, the issue lies with your hosting provider's database server. It could be temporarily down for maintenance or experiencing technical difficulties.
3. **Corrupted Database Tables:** Your database tables can get corrupted due to various reasons, such as failed updates, plugin conflicts, or server errors.

Troubleshooting and Fixing the Error

Follow these steps to troubleshoot and potentially resolve this error:

1. **Check Database Credentials:**
   - **Access wp-config.php:** Use an FTP client (like FileZilla) or your hosting provider's file manager to access the root directory of your WordPress installation and open the `wp-config.php` file.
   - **Verify Information:** Carefully check that the database name, username, and password match the ones provided by your hosting provider. Correct any errors if found.
   - **Save and Upload:** Save the changes to the `wp-config.php` file and upload it back to your server, replacing the old file.
2. **Contact Your Hosting Provider:**
   If the credentials are correct, the issue might be with your hosting provider's database server. Contact their support and inquire about any ongoing maintenance or issues with the database server. They should be able to diagnose and resolve any server-side problems.
3. **Repair Corrupted Database Tables:**
   If the above steps don't solve the issue, your database tables might be corrupted. You can try repairing them using the following methods:
   - **phpMyAdmin:** If your hosting provider offers phpMyAdmin access, you can use it to repair database tables. Look for the "Repair table" option in phpMyAdmin's interface.
   - **WordPress Repair Feature:** WordPress has a built-in database repair feature. Add the following line to your `wp-config.php` file:

     ```
     define( 'WP_ALLOW_REPAIR', true );
     ```

     Then, visit the URL `http://www.yourdomain.com/wp-admin/maint/repair.php` in your browser to access the repair tool. Once the repair is complete, remove the line you added to the `wp-config.php` file.

   - **Plugins:** Several WordPress plugins like WP-DBManager can help you repair and optimize your database tables.

Additional Tips

- **Backups:** Always maintain regular backups of your website's files and database. In case of any errors, you can easily restore your site to a previous working state.
- **Update WordPress:** Keep your WordPress core, themes, and plugins updated to the latest versions. Updates often include bug fixes and security patches that can prevent errors.

By following these troubleshooting steps, you can resolve the "Error Establishing a Database Connection" and get your WordPress website back online. If the problem persists, don't hesitate to seek further assistance from your hosting provider or the WordPress community forums.

White Screen of Death (WSoD)

The White Screen of Death (WSoD) is a dreaded sight for any WordPress user. It's characterized by a blank white screen that appears instead of your website's content, offering no error messages or clues about the cause.

Common Causes

The WSoD can be triggered by a variety of factors, making it a bit of a puzzle to solve. Here are some common culprits:

1. **Plugin or Theme Conflicts:** Newly installed or updated plugins or themes can sometimes conflict with each other or with your WordPress core files, leading to the WSoD.
2. **Exhausted Memory Limit:** Your website might be trying to use more memory than your hosting plan allows. This can cause the PHP process to crash, resulting in the WSoD.
3. **PHP Errors:** Errors in your website's PHP code, often caused by poorly coded plugins or themes, can trigger the WSoD.

Troubleshooting the WSoD

Don't panic if you encounter the WSoD. It's often fixable with some basic troubleshooting steps:

1. **Deactivate Plugins:**
    - The first step is to deactivate all your plugins. You can do this by going to "Plugins" > "Installed Plugins" in your WordPress dashboard and selecting "Deactivate" from the bulk actions dropdown menu.
    - If your website starts working after deactivating all plugins, then the issue is likely caused by a plugin conflict. Reactivate your plugins one by one, checking your website after each activation to identify the culprit plugin.
2. **Switch to a Default Theme:**
    - If deactivating plugins doesn't solve the issue, try switching to a default WordPress theme like Twenty Twenty-Three. This will help you determine if the problem is related to your current theme.
    - If your website loads properly with the default theme, then the issue is likely caused by your active theme. You can then try updating your theme to the latest version or contact the theme developer for support.
3. **Increase PHP Memory Limit:**
    - If you suspect that the WSoD is caused by exhausted memory, you can try increasing the PHP memory limit. You can do this by editing your `wp-config.php` file and adding the following line:

    ```php
    define( 'WP_MEMORY_LIMIT', '256M' );
    ```

    (Replace '256M' with the desired memory limit.)

    - Alternatively, you can try increasing the memory limit through your hosting provider's control panel.
4. **Check Error Logs:**
    - Your website's error logs can provide valuable clues about the cause of the WSoD. You can usually find the error logs in your hosting account's file manager or by contacting your hosting provider.
    - Look for any PHP errors or warnings that might be related to the WSoD. If you find any errors, try searching online for solutions or contact a developer for assistance.

By systematically following these troubleshooting steps, you can often identify and resolve the cause of the White Screen of Death and restore your WordPress website to its former glory. Remember, patience and persistence are key when tackling this error, and don't hesitate to seek help from your hosting provider or the WordPress community if needed.

500 Internal Server Error

The 500 Internal Server Error is a generic error message that indicates something has gone wrong on your website's server, but the server can't be more specific about the exact problem. This can be a frustrating error to encounter, as it doesn't provide a clear indication of the cause.

Common Causes

While the 500 Internal Server Error can stem from various server-related issues, some of the most common culprits include:

1. **Incorrect File Permissions:** File permissions control who can read, write, and execute files on your server. Incorrect file permissions can prevent your website's scripts from running properly, triggering the 500 error.
2. **Corrupted .htaccess File:** The `.htaccess` file is a configuration file that controls various aspects of your website's server behavior, including redirects, security, and caching. If this file becomes corrupted, it can cause a 500 Internal Server Error.
3. **PHP Errors:** Errors in your website's PHP code, often caused by poorly coded plugins or themes, can also trigger this error.

Troubleshooting the 500 Internal Server Error

Here are some troubleshooting steps you can take to try and resolve the 500 Internal Server Error:

1. **Check File Permissions:**
    - Use an FTP client or your hosting provider's file manager to access your website's files.
    - Ensure that the file permissions for your WordPress files and folders are set correctly. Generally, files should have a permission of 644, and folders should have a permission of 755.
2. **Test the .htaccess File:**
    - Locate the `.htaccess` file in the root directory of your WordPress installation (usually the `public_html` folder).
    - Rename the file to something like `.htaccess_old`.
    - Go to your WordPress dashboard and navigate to *Settings > Permalinks*. Click "Save Changes" to generate a new `.htaccess` file.
    - Check if your website loads properly. If it does, the issue was likely caused by a corrupted `.htaccess` file.
3. **Check Error Logs:**
    - Your website's error logs can provide valuable clues about the cause of the 500 error. You can usually find the error logs in your hosting account's cPanel or by contacting your hosting provider.
    - Look for any PHP errors or warnings that occurred around the time the error started. If you find any errors, try searching online for solutions or contact the developer of the plugin or theme causing the error.
4. **Contact Your Hosting Provider:**
    - If you've tried the above steps and are still seeing the 500 Internal Server Error, it's time to contact your hosting provider. They have access to more detailed server logs and can diagnose and fix the issue for you.

By following these steps, you can often resolve the 500 Internal Server Error and get your WordPress website back online. Remember to remain patient and methodical in your troubleshooting approach, and don't hesitate to seek help from your hosting provider if needed.

404 Page Not Found Error

The 404 Page Not Found error is a common issue that occurs when a visitor tries to access a page on your website that doesn't exist or can't be found. This can happen for several reasons, and while it might not seem like a critical error, it can negatively impact user experience and even your SEO.

Common Causes

The most common reasons for encountering a 404 error include:

1. **Broken Links:** Links on your website or from external sources might be pointing to a page that has been deleted, renamed, or moved to a different URL.
2. **Incorrect Permalinks:** Permalinks are the permanent URLs of your pages and posts. If your permalinks are set up incorrectly, it can lead to 404 errors when users try to access those URLs.
3. **Missing Files:** If a file associated with a particular page is missing or deleted from your server, it will trigger a 404 error.

Troubleshooting the 404 Page Not Found Error

Fortunately, resolving the 404 error is often straightforward. Here are some troubleshooting steps you can take:

1. **Check for Broken Links:**
   - Utilize a plugin like **Broken Link Checker** to scan your website for broken links. This plugin will identify any links that point to non-existent pages and provide options to fix them.
   - If you find broken links, update them with the correct URLs or remove them altogether.
2. **Reset Permalinks:**
   - In your WordPress dashboard, go to *Settings > Permalinks*.
   - Without making any changes, simply click the "Save Changes" button. This will often resolve permalink-related 404 errors.
3. **Check if the Requested File Exists:**
   - Use an FTP client or your hosting provider's file manager to check if the requested file actually exists on your server.
   - If the file is missing, you can either restore it from a backup or recreate it if necessary.
4. **Create a Custom 404 Error Page:**
   - A custom 404 error page can help improve user experience and reduce bounce rates. Instead of a plain "404 Page Not Found" message, you can create a more visually appealing and helpful page that:
     - Apologizes for the inconvenience.
     - Provides a search bar to help users find the content they're looking for.
     - Suggests alternative pages or sections on your website.
     - Includes a link to your homepage or contact page.

You can easily create a custom 404 page using Elementor by going to *Templates > Theme Builder* and selecting the "404 Page" template type.

By addressing these common causes and implementing the troubleshooting steps, you can effectively resolve 404 Page Not Found errors and ensure a smooth browsing experience for your visitors.

Memory Exhausted Error

The "Memory Exhausted Error" in WordPress typically manifests as a blank white screen or an error message stating "Fatal error: Allowed memory size of xxxxxx bytes exhausted." This error occurs when your website's scripts or processes attempt to use more memory than your hosting plan permits.

Why Does This Error Occur?

WordPress, along with its themes and plugins, relies on PHP (a scripting language) to function. Each hosting plan allocates a specific amount of memory that PHP can utilize. When your website's operations, such as image processing, plugin execution, or complex queries, exceed this limit, the memory exhausted error is triggered.

Increasing the PHP Memory Limit

Fortunately, increasing the PHP memory limit is often a straightforward solution to resolve this error. You have two primary methods to achieve this:

1. **Editing wp-config.php:**
   - Locate the `wp-config.php` file in your WordPress root directory (usually the "public_html" folder) using an FTP client or your hosting provider's file manager.
   - Open the file and add the following line of code:

   ```
   define( 'WP_MEMORY_LIMIT', '256M' );
   ```

   - Replace '256M' with the desired memory limit. Common values are 128M, 256M, or 512M. Choose a value that is higher than the current limit but within your hosting plan's restrictions.
   - Save the file and re-upload it to your server.
2. **Through Hosting Provider's Control Panel:**
   - Many hosting providers offer an option to adjust the PHP memory limit directly through their control panel (e.g., cPanel).
   - Log in to your hosting account and navigate to the PHP settings or configuration section.
   - Look for an option to increase the `memory_limit` value.
   - Set the desired memory limit and save the changes.

Important Considerations

- **Hosting Plan Limits:** Be aware of the memory limit imposed by your hosting plan. Exceeding this limit might not be possible without upgrading your plan.
- **Optimal Values:** The ideal memory limit depends on your website's complexity and the plugins you use. If you're unsure, start with 256M and increase it if necessary.
- **Performance Impact:** While increasing the memory limit can resolve the error, it might also slightly impact your website's performance. Monitor your site's speed after making changes.
- **Alternative Solutions:** If increasing the memory limit doesn't solve the problem, investigate other potential causes, such as plugin conflicts or inefficient code.

Maximum Execution Time Exceeded

The "Maximum Execution Time Exceeded" error in WordPress signifies that a PHP script on your website has surpassed the time limit allocated by your server for execution. This limit is a safeguard to prevent scripts from running indefinitely and consuming excessive server resources.

Why Does This Error Occur?

Several factors can trigger this error, including:

1. **Complex Scripts:** Scripts that perform resource-intensive tasks, such as importing large amounts of data, processing images, or executing complex calculations, can exceed the default time limit.
2. **Poorly Coded Plugins or Themes:** Inefficiently written code within plugins or themes can lead to scripts taking longer to execute.
3. **Low Server Resources:** If your hosting plan has limited resources, the server might not be able to handle the demands of your scripts within the default time frame.

Increasing the Maximum Execution Time

You can resolve this error by increasing the maximum execution time allowed for PHP scripts. Here are the primary methods:

1. **Editing php.ini:**
   - **Locate php.ini:** The `php.ini` file is the main configuration file for PHP. It's typically located in your server's root directory, but the exact location can vary depending on your hosting setup. You might need to contact your hosting provider for assistance if you can't find it.
   - **Modify max_execution_time:** Open the `php.ini` file and locate the line that says `max_execution_time`. Change the value (in seconds) to a higher number, such as 300 (5 minutes).
   - **Save and Restart:** Save the changes to the `php.ini` file and restart your web server for the changes to take effect.
2. **Through Hosting Provider's Control Panel:**
   - Many hosting providers offer a user-friendly interface for managing PHP settings within their control panel.
   - Log in to your hosting account and navigate to the PHP configuration section.
   - Look for the `max_execution_time` setting and increase its value to a higher number.
   - Save the changes.
3. **Editing .htaccess (Alternative):**

As an alternative, you can try adding the following line to your `.htaccess` file, which is located in your WordPress root directory:
php_value max_execution_time 300

   -
   - Replace '300' with your desired value in seconds. However, this method might not work on all servers, and it's generally recommended to modify the `php.ini` file if possible.

Important Note

It's crucial to increase the maximum execution time cautiously. While it can resolve the error, setting it too high could potentially lead to performance issues or even security risks if a malicious script is running for an extended period. Start with a reasonable value and gradually increase it if needed. If the error persists, investigate the root cause, such as inefficient code or plugins, rather than simply increasing the time limit indefinitely.

Other Common Errors

In addition to the errors we've covered in detail, here are a few other common WordPress errors you might encounter:

1. **"Parse error: syntax error"**: This error indicates a problem with the PHP code on your website. It's usually caused by a missing semicolon, unclosed bracket, or other syntax error. To fix it, carefully review the code in the specified file and line number mentioned in the error message, and correct the syntax error.

2. **"The link you followed has expired"**: This error typically occurs when trying to upload a file that exceeds the maximum upload size limit set by your server. To resolve it, you can increase the upload size limit in your `php.ini` file or `.htaccess` file, or try uploading the file in smaller chunks.
3. **"Are you sure you want to do this?"**: This is not technically an error but a security prompt that appears when you try to perform a sensitive action in WordPress, such as deleting a post or changing your password. It's a reminder to confirm your intention before proceeding. Double-check that you want to perform the action and click "OK" to continue.

General Troubleshooting Tips

When faced with a WordPress error, it's easy to feel overwhelmed. But don't worry! Many errors can be resolved with some basic troubleshooting steps. Here are some general tips to help you diagnose and fix common WordPress issues:

1. **Clear Browser Cache and Cookies:**
   Sometimes, outdated cached files or cookies in your browser can cause conflicts and display errors. Clear your browser's cache and cookies, then try reloading your website to see if the error persists.
2. **Deactivate All Plugins:**
   Plugin conflicts are a frequent source of WordPress errors. To determine if a plugin is the culprit, deactivate all your plugins by going to "Plugins" > "Installed Plugins" in your dashboard and selecting "Deactivate" from the bulk actions dropdown menu. If the error disappears, reactivate your plugins one by one, testing your website after each activation to pinpoint the problematic plugin.
3. **Switch to a Default Theme:**
   If the error persists even after deactivating all plugins, try switching to a default WordPress theme like Twenty Twenty-Three. If this resolves the issue, it indicates that the error is likely caused by your current theme. You can then try updating your theme or contacting the theme developer for support.
4. **Check Error Logs:**
   Your website's error logs can provide valuable clues about the cause of the error. Most hosting providers offer access to error logs through their control panel (e.g., cPanel). Look for error messages related to the time the issue occurred, and then try searching online for solutions or consult with a developer.
5. **Contact Your Hosting Provider:**
   If you've tried all the above steps and the error still persists, don't hesitate to reach out to your hosting provider's support team. They have access to server logs and can often diagnose and resolve server-related issues that might be causing the error.

Additional Tips:

- **Update WordPress Core, Themes, and Plugins:** Regularly updating your WordPress core, themes, and plugins to the latest versions can prevent many errors from occurring in the first place. Updates often include bug fixes and security patches.
- **Check File Permissions:** Ensure that the file permissions for your WordPress files and folders are set correctly. Incorrect permissions can prevent your website from functioning properly.
- **Increase PHP Memory Limit:** If you encounter memory-related errors, try increasing the PHP memory limit in your `wp-config.php` file or through your hosting provider's control panel.
- **Debug Mode:** Enable WordPress's debug mode to display more detailed error messages, which can help you pinpoint the cause of the issue. However, remember to disable debug mode after troubleshooting, as it can reveal sensitive information to visitors.
- **Consult Online Resources:** The WordPress community is vast and supportive. Numerous online forums, blogs, and tutorials offer solutions to common WordPress errors. Don't hesitate to seek help from these resources if you get stuck.

By following these troubleshooting tips and utilizing the resources available, you can confidently tackle most WordPress errors and keep your website running smoothly.

Chapter Summary

This chapter has equipped you with the knowledge and tools to troubleshoot common WordPress errors that you may encounter while building your website with Elementor. We started by reassuring you that most errors are solvable with simple troubleshooting steps.

We then covered several common errors, including the "Error Establishing a Database Connection," the dreaded "White Screen of Death," the "500 Internal Server Error," and the "404 Page Not Found Error." For each error, we explained the potential causes and provided step-by-step instructions on how to diagnose and fix them.

Additionally, we touched on other frequent errors like "Memory Exhausted" and "Maximum Execution Time Exceeded," offering solutions for each. We also briefly mentioned some less common but still important errors and suggested solutions.

Finally, we provided a list of general troubleshooting tips to help you resolve any WordPress errors you might encounter. These tips include clearing your browser cache, deactivating plugins, switching to a default theme, checking error logs, and contacting your hosting provider for assistance. We also emphasized the importance of keeping your WordPress core, themes, and plugins updated, checking file permissions, increasing the PHP memory limit when needed, and enabling debug mode for more detailed error messages.

By understanding the causes of common WordPress errors and following the troubleshooting steps outlined in this chapter, you can confidently address these issues and keep your website running smoothly. Remember, the WordPress community is always there to offer support and guidance if you need further assistance.

Speeding Up Your Website: Optimization Tips

Outline

- Why Website Speed Matters
- Factors Affecting Website Speed
- How to Measure Your Website Speed
- Essential Tips to Speed Up Your WordPress Website
- Additional Optimization Tips
- Chapter Summary

Why Website Speed Matters

In the fast-paced digital world, website speed is a critical factor that can make or break your online success. It significantly impacts user experience, search engine rankings, and ultimately, your website's ability to achieve its goals.

User Experience

Website speed is a cornerstone of a positive user experience. In today's instant-gratification era, users expect websites to load quickly. A delay of even a few seconds can lead to frustration and cause visitors to abandon your site in favor of a faster alternative.

Studies have shown that website speed directly correlates with user engagement. Fast-loading websites tend to have:

- **Lower Bounce Rates:** Users are less likely to leave a page quickly if it loads fast.
- **Higher Conversion Rates:** A seamless user experience encourages users to complete desired actions, such as making a purchase or filling out a form.
- **Increased Page Views:** Visitors are more likely to explore multiple pages on a fast-loading website.
- **Improved User Satisfaction:** A positive experience leads to greater satisfaction and a higher likelihood of users returning to your website in the future.

On the other hand, slow-loading websites have the opposite effect:

- **High Bounce Rates:** Users are more likely to leave a page if it takes too long to load.
- **Lower Conversion Rates:** Frustrated users are less likely to convert into customers or clients.
- **Decreased Page Views:** Users are less likely to explore other pages on a slow website.
- **Poor User Satisfaction:** A negative experience can leave a lasting impression, making users less likely to return.

Search Engine Rankings

Website speed is also a significant factor in search engine optimization (SEO). Google and other search engines prioritize fast-loading websites in their rankings because they want to provide the best possible experience for their users. A slow website can negatively impact your SEO ranking, making it harder for potential visitors to find you.

Overall Website Performance

Website speed affects not only user experience and SEO but also your website's overall performance. A slow website can:

- **Increase Server Load:** Slow-loading pages put a strain on your server, potentially leading to downtime or crashes.
- **Impact Revenue:** For e-commerce websites, slow loading times can lead to lost sales, as frustrated customers abandon their shopping carts.
- **Damage Brand Reputation:** A slow and unresponsive website can make your brand appear unprofessional and unreliable.

Investing in website speed optimization is essential for delivering a positive user experience, improving your SEO, and ensuring the overall success of your website. By prioritizing speed, you can attract and retain more visitors, increase conversions, and ultimately achieve your online goals.

Factors Affecting Website Speed

Understanding the factors that contribute to a slow-loading website is crucial for identifying and addressing bottlenecks in your site's performance. Numerous elements can influence how fast your website loads, some of which include:

Large Image Sizes

Images are often the primary culprits behind slow-loading websites. High-resolution images, while visually appealing, can significantly increase file sizes, leading to longer download times. Unoptimized images can easily consume valuable bandwidth and delay page loading, especially for users with slower internet connections.

Too Many HTTP Requests

Every time a browser loads your website, it needs to request various resources from your server, including HTML, CSS, JavaScript files, and images. Each request takes time to process, and having too many of them can significantly slow down your website. Minimizing the number of HTTP requests by combining files, optimizing images, and leveraging browser caching can make a noticeable difference in loading speed.

Unoptimized Code

Poorly written or bloated code in your website's themes, plugins, or custom scripts can hinder performance. Inefficient code can take longer to execute, leading to slower page rendering and increased loading times. Cleaning up your code, removing unnecessary elements, and minifying CSS and JavaScript files can optimize your website's code and improve its speed.

Slow Server Response Time

The speed at which your server responds to requests plays a vital role in website performance. A slow server can significantly delay the delivery of your website's content to visitors. Several factors can influence server response time, including server hardware, software configuration, and the amount of traffic your website receives. Choosing a reliable web host with fast servers and optimized configurations is essential for achieving optimal website speed.

Lack of Caching

Caching involves storing frequently accessed data, such as web pages or images, in a temporary storage location (cache) to reduce the need to fetch the data from the original source repeatedly. This can significantly improve website speed, as subsequent requests for the same data can be served from the cache, which is much faster than retrieving it from the server. Implementing caching using plugins like WP Super Cache or W3 Total Cache can drastically enhance your website's performance.

External Scripts

Integrating external scripts from third-party sources, such as social media widgets, analytics tools, or advertising networks, can add overhead to your website's loading time. Each external script requires an additional HTTP request and may introduce additional code and resources, slowing down your website. Carefully consider which external scripts are essential for your website's functionality and weigh their impact on performance.

Render-Blocking Resources

Certain CSS and JavaScript files can block the rendering of your website's content. This means that the browser cannot display the content until these files are downloaded and processed, leading to a delay in the time it takes for users to see your page. Optimizing your CSS and JavaScript files by minifying them, deferring non-essential scripts, and eliminating render-blocking resources can significantly improve your website's perceived loading speed.

How to Measure Your Website Speed

Before you embark on the journey of optimizing your website's speed, it's crucial to first understand how fast (or slow) it currently loads. Luckily, several reliable online tools can help you measure your website's speed and identify areas that need improvement. Here are three popular options:

Google PageSpeed Insights

Google PageSpeed Insights is a free tool developed by Google that analyzes your website's performance on both mobile and desktop devices. It provides a score ranging from 0 to 100, with a higher score indicating better performance.

The tool also provides detailed insights into your website's loading time, including:

- **First Contentful Paint (FCP):** The time it takes for the first text or image to appear on the screen.
- **Largest Contentful Paint (LCP):** The time it takes for the largest content element (usually an image or video) to become visible.
- **Speed Index:** How quickly the page's content is visually displayed.
- **Total Blocking Time (TBT):** The time during which the main thread is blocked, preventing user interaction.
- **Cumulative Layout Shift (CLS):** A measure of the visual stability of the page.

In addition to these metrics, PageSpeed Insights also offers actionable recommendations on how to improve your website's performance, such as optimizing images, reducing server response times, and eliminating render-blocking resources.

GTmetrix

GTmetrix is another comprehensive website speed test tool that provides detailed performance reports and optimization recommendations. It analyzes your website from multiple locations worldwide and provides a waterfall chart that visually depicts how your page loads over time. GTmetrix also grades your website's performance on various metrics, such as PageSpeed and YSlow scores, making it easier to identify areas for improvement.

Pingdom Website Speed Test

Pingdom Website Speed Test is a user-friendly tool that analyzes your website's speed from different geographical locations. It provides a detailed breakdown of your website's performance, including loading time, page size, requests, and performance grade. Pingdom also offers recommendations for improving your website's speed, such as optimizing images, minifying code, and leveraging browser caching.

Which Tool Should You Use?

All three tools offer valuable insights into your website's speed, and it's often recommended to use a combination of them to get a comprehensive understanding of your website's performance.

- **Google PageSpeed Insights:** Ideal for beginners and those who want actionable recommendations directly from Google.
- **GTmetrix:** Offers more in-depth analysis and is suitable for users who want a detailed understanding of their website's performance.
- **Pingdom:** Provides a user-friendly interface and tests your website from multiple locations worldwide.

No matter which tool you choose, regularly testing your website's speed is crucial for identifying and addressing performance bottlenecks, ensuring a fast and smooth user experience, and improving your website's overall success.

Essential Tips to Speed Up Your WordPress Website

Optimizing your WordPress website's speed is a crucial aspect of providing a positive user experience and improving your search engine rankings. Here are some actionable tips to help you achieve a faster website:

Image Optimization

Images are often the largest files on a website, and unoptimized images can significantly slow down your pages. Compressing and resizing images reduces their file size without sacrificing quality.

Actionable Steps:

1. Use image optimization plugins like **Smush** or **ShortPixel** to automatically compress and resize your images upon upload.
2. Manually compress images using online tools like TinyPNG or Kraken.io before uploading them.
3. Consider using WebP image format, which offers smaller file sizes than JPEG or PNG.

Caching

Caching stores static versions of your website's pages, reducing the need to generate them dynamically for each visitor. This significantly improves loading times, especially for returning visitors.

Actionable Steps:

1. Install and configure a caching plugin like **WP Super Cache** or **W3 Total Cache**.
2. Enable page caching, browser caching, and object caching in your plugin settings.

Content Delivery Networks (CDNs)

A CDN is a network of servers distributed across the globe. When a user visits your website, the CDN serves your website's static assets (images, CSS, JavaScript) from the server closest to them, reducing latency and improving loading times.

Actionable Steps:

1. Sign up for a CDN service like **Cloudflare** or **StackPath**.
2. Configure your WordPress website to use the CDN.

Minification of CSS and JavaScript

Minification removes unnecessary characters (like whitespace and comments) from your CSS and JavaScript files, reducing their size and making them faster to download.

Actionable Steps:

1. Use a plugin like **Autoptimize** or **WP Rocket** to minify your CSS and JavaScript files automatically.
2. If you're comfortable with code, you can manually minify your files using online tools or code editors.

Code Optimization

Clean and efficient code is essential for fast-loading websites. Avoid using bloated or poorly written code in your themes and plugins.

Actionable Steps:

1. Choose well-coded and lightweight themes and plugins.
2. Remove any unused or unnecessary code from your website.
3. Consider hiring a developer to optimize your website's code if needed.

Lazy Loading

Lazy loading defers the loading of images and videos until they are about to enter the user's viewport. This means that only the images and videos that are visible on the screen are loaded initially, significantly improving initial page load times.

Actionable Steps:

1. Enable lazy loading for images and videos in your theme or plugin settings.
2. If your theme or plugin doesn't support lazy loading, you can use a dedicated lazy loading plugin.

Using a Lightweight Theme

The theme you choose can significantly impact your website's speed. Lightweight themes with minimal code and features tend to load faster than bulky themes with lots of bells and whistles.

Actionable Steps:

1. Choose a fast and well-coded theme that is optimized for performance.
2. Avoid themes with excessive animations, sliders, or other heavy elements.

Managing Plugins

Plugins can add valuable functionality to your website, but they can also slow it down if not managed properly.

Actionable Steps:

1. Use only essential plugins.
2. Regularly review your installed plugins and deactivate or delete any that you're not using.
3. Keep your plugins updated to the latest versions for optimal performance and security.

Choosing a Fast Web Host

Your web hosting provider plays a crucial role in your website's speed. Choose a reliable host with fast servers, ample bandwidth, and good performance optimization features like caching and CDNs.

Actionable Steps:

1. Research different hosting providers and compare their features and pricing.
2. Read reviews and testimonials to gauge their reputation for speed and reliability.
3. Choose a hosting plan that matches your website's traffic and resource needs.

Additional Optimization Tips

While the essential tips covered in the previous section will significantly boost your website's speed, here are some additional optimization techniques you can implement to squeeze out even more performance:

- **Limit the Use of External Scripts:** External scripts from third-party sources, such as social media widgets, analytics tools, or advertising networks, can add considerable overhead to your website's loading time. Each script requires an additional HTTP request and may introduce extra code and resources. Evaluate the necessity of each external script and consider removing or replacing those that significantly impact performance.
- **Optimize Your Database:** Over time, your WordPress database can accumulateunnecessary data, such as post revisions, spam comments, or trashed items. This can bloat your database and slow down your website. Regularly clean up your database using plugins like WP-Optimize or WP-Sweep to remove unnecessary data and improve performance.
- **Use a Lightweight Slider Plugin or Static Images:** Sliders can be visually appealing, but they often come with a lot of JavaScript and CSS code that can slow down your website. If you must use a slider, choose a lightweight plugin that is optimized for performance. Alternatively, consider using static images instead, especially on mobile devices.
- **Enable GZIP Compression:** GZIP compression is a technique that reduces the size of files sent from your server to the visitor's browser. This can significantly improve loading times, especially for text-based files like HTML, CSS, and JavaScript. Most web hosting providers offer GZIP compression as a standard feature.
- **Prioritize Above-the-Fold Content:** Above-the-fold content refers to the content that is immediately visible to the user when they land on your page, without having to scroll. Prioritize the loading of this content by optimizing images, deferring non-essential scripts, and minimizing the use of render-blocking resources. This will give visitors a faster initial impression of your website and improve their overall experience.

By following these tips and consistently monitoring your website's speed, you can ensure that your site is optimized for performance and delivers a seamless user experience. Remember, a fast-loading website not only benefits your visitors but also boosts your SEO and contributes to your online success.

Chapter Summary

This chapter delved into the crucial topic of website speed optimization, a key factor in user experience, SEO, and overall website performance. We explored why website speed matters, highlighting its impact on bounce rates, conversion rates, and search engine rankings. We then identified the various factors that can contribute to a slow-loading website, such as large image sizes, excessive HTTP requests, unoptimized code, slow server response times, lack of caching, external scripts, and render-blocking resources.

To assess your website's speed, we introduced you to online tools like Google PageSpeed Insights, GTmetrix, and Pingdom Website Speed Test, which can provide valuable insights and recommendations for improvement.

The chapter also provided actionable tips to speed up your WordPress website. We covered essential strategies like image optimization, caching, utilizing content delivery networks (CDNs), minifying CSS and JavaScript, code optimization, lazy loading, choosing a lightweight theme, managing plugins, and selecting a fast web host.

Additionally, we offered further optimization tips, including limiting external scripts, optimizing your database, using lightweight slider plugins or static images, enabling GZIP compression, and prioritizing above-the-fold content.

By implementing these optimization techniques and regularly monitoring your website's speed, you can significantly enhance its performance, provide a better user experience, and improve your search engine rankings. Remember, a fast-loading website is essential for success in the digital landscape.

Security Essentials: Protecting Your Site

Outline

- The Importance of Website Security
- Common Security Threats to WordPress Websites
- Essential Security Measures for WordPress
- Additional Security Tips
- Chapter Summary

The Importance of Website Security

In the digital age, where we conduct a significant portion of our lives online, website security is of paramount importance. Your WordPress website, whether it's a personal blog or an e-commerce store, can be a treasure trove of sensitive information, including customer data, financial information, and intellectual property.

A security breach can have devastating consequences, including:

- **Data Theft:** Hackers can steal sensitive information, such as credit card numbers, addresses, and login credentials, putting your customers and your business at risk.
- **Malware Infection:** Malicious software can infect your website, causing it to malfunction, display unwanted content, or even spread to other websites and devices.
- **Reputation Damage:** A security breach can erode trust in your brand and damage your reputation. Customers may be hesitant to do business with you if they fear their information is not secure.
- **Financial Losses:** A security breach can lead to significant financial losses, including lost revenue, legal fees, and the cost of remediation.
- **Legal Liabilities:** You may be held liable for damages if a security breach results in the theft of customer data or other sensitive information.

Proactive Security Measures are Essential

Given the potential consequences of a security breach, it's crucial to take proactive measures to safeguard your WordPress website. This involves implementing a multi-layered security approach that includes:

- **Choosing a Secure Web Host:** Your web hosting provider plays a significant role in your website's security. Choose a reputable host that offers robust security features, such as firewalls, malware scanning, and regular backups.
- **Using Strong Passwords and User Management:** Employ strong passwords for all user accounts, especially the admin account. Regularly update passwords and limit user access based on roles and responsibilities.
- **Installing Security Plugins:** Security plugins like Wordfence or iThemes Security can add an extra layer of protection to your website by monitoring for threats, scanning for malware, and blocking malicious traffic.
- **Keeping Your Website Updated:** Regularly update your WordPress core, themes, and plugins to the latest versions to patch security vulnerabilities.
- **Implementing Two-Factor Authentication:** Two-factor authentication (2FA) adds an extra layer of security by requiring a second verification code, typically sent to your phone, in addition to your password.
- **Monitoring and Logging:** Keep a close eye on your website's activity logs and security alerts to detect any suspicious activity.

- **Installing a Website Firewall:** A web application firewall (WAF) filters out malicious traffic and protects your website from common attacks.
- **Using an SSL Certificate:** An SSL certificate encrypts data transmitted between your website and visitors, preventing hackers from intercepting sensitive information.
- **Educating Yourself and Your Team:** Stay informed about the latest security threats and best practices. Train your team members on how to identify and respond to potential security risks.

By taking these proactive security measures, you can significantly reduce the risk of a security breach and protect your website, your customers, and your business. Remember, website security is not a one-time task; it's an ongoing effort that requires vigilance and regular maintenance.

Common Security Threats to WordPress Websites

WordPress is the most popular content management system in the world, but its popularity also makes it a prime target for hackers and malicious actors. Understanding the common security threats that WordPress websites face is crucial for implementing effective protection measures.

Brute Force Attacks

Brute force attacks are one of the most common ways hackers try to gain access to WordPress websites. In a brute force attack, hackers use automated tools to systematically guess usernames and passwords until they find the right combination. Once they have access to your WordPress dashboard, they can wreak havoc on your website, from stealing data to injecting malware.

Malware

Malware, short for malicious software, is a broad term that encompasses various types of harmful software, including viruses, trojans, worms, ransomware, and spyware. Hackers can inject malware into your website through vulnerabilities in plugins, themes, or the WordPress core. Once installed, malware can steal sensitive data, redirect traffic to malicious websites, or even render your website unusable.

Here are some common types of malware that target WordPress websites:

- **Backdoors:** Hidden entry points that allow hackers to bypass your website's security and gain unauthorized access.
- **Pharma Hacks:** Redirect visitors to pharmaceutical websites or display unwanted pharmaceutical ads.
- **Japanese Keyword Hacks:** Inject Japanese keywords into your website's content to manipulate search engine results.

SQL Injection

SQL injection is a type of attack where hackers exploit vulnerabilities in your website's code to inject malicious SQL (Structured Query Language) queries into your database. These queries can be used to steal data, modify your website's content, or even delete your entire database.

Cross-Site Scripting (XSS)

Cross-site scripting (XSS) attacks occur when hackers inject malicious scripts into your website that can be executed by other users' browsers. These scripts can steal sensitive information, such as cookies or login credentials, or redirect users to malicious websites.

Denial of Service (DoS) Attacks

Denial of Service (DoS) attacks aim to overwhelm your website with traffic, making it unavailable to legitimate visitors. This can be achieved by flooding your website with requests from multiple sources or by exploiting vulnerabilities in your website's software. DoS attacks can disrupt your business operations, damage your reputation, and result in financial losses.

Protecting Your WordPress Website

To protect your WordPress website from these security threats, it's essential to take proactive measures such as:

- Choosing a secure web host
- Using strong passwords and managing user permissions
- Installing security plugins
- Keeping your WordPress core, themes, and plugins updated
- Implementing two-factor authentication
- Monitoring and logging website activity
- Using a website firewall
- Installing an SSL certificate

By implementing these security measures, you can significantly reduce the risk of your WordPress website being compromised and protect your valuable data and reputation.

Essential Security Measures for WordPress

Securing your WordPress website should be a top priority to protect your data, your visitors' information, and your online reputation. A multi-layered approach is crucial for establishing a robust defense against potential threats. Let's delve into the essential security measures you should implement:

Choose a Secure Web Host

Your web hosting provider plays a significant role in your website's security. Opt for a reputable provider that prioritizes security and offers features like:

- **Firewalls:** Network security systems that monitor and control incoming and outgoing traffic, blocking unauthorized access.
- **Malware Scanning:** Regular scans of your website to detect and remove malicious software.
- **Regular Backups:** Automated backups of your website's files and database, allowing you to restore your site in case of data loss or corruption.

Strong Passwords and User Management

Weak passwords are a major vulnerability. Enforce strong password policies for all user accounts, especially the administrator account. Encourage the use of complex passwords with a combination of uppercase and lowercase letters, numbers, and symbols.

Limit user access based on their roles and responsibilities. Not every user needs administrative privileges. Assign appropriate roles like editor, author, or contributor to restrict access to sensitive areas of your website.

Security Plugins

Security plugins are valuable tools for enhancing your website's protection. They offer a range of features like:

- **Wordfence:** Comprehensive security with a firewall, malware scanner, login security, and security scans.

- **iThemes Security:** Offers features like brute force protection, file change detection, and strong password enforcement.
- **Sucuri Security:** Provides website security hardening, malware detection and removal, and a web application firewall.

Choose a security plugin that aligns with your needs and budget, and keep it regularly updated.

Regular Updates and Backups

WordPress, themes, and plugins are regularly updated to fix bugs and security vulnerabilities. Always keep your WordPress installation, themes, and plugins up to date to ensure you have the latest security patches.

Regularly back up your website's files and database. This allows you to quickly restore your site to a previous working state in case of a security breach, data corruption, or accidental deletion.

Two-Factor Authentication

Two-factor authentication (2FA) adds an extra layer of security by requiring users to enter a second verification code, usually sent to their phone or email, in addition to their password. This makes it significantly more difficult for hackers to gain access to your website, even if they have your password.

Monitoring and Logging

Regularly monitor your website for suspicious activity using security plugins or other monitoring tools. These tools can alert you to unusual login attempts, file changes, or other potential threats.

Maintain logs of user activity and access attempts. This can help you identify patterns of suspicious behavior and take corrective action if needed.

Website Firewall

A web application firewall (WAF) acts as a shield between your website and the internet, filtering out malicious traffic and blocking known attack patterns. A WAF can prevent SQL injection attacks, cross-site scripting attacks, and other common web-based threats.

Secure Socket Layer (SSL) Certificate

An SSL certificate encrypts the data transmitted between your website and visitors, making it difficult for hackers to intercept sensitive information like passwords or credit card numbers. An SSL certificate also adds a padlock icon to your website's address bar, signifying to users that your site is secure.

Additional Security Tips

While the essential security measures we've discussed form a strong foundation for protecting your WordPress website, there are additional steps you can take to further fortify your site's defenses:

- **Limit Login Attempts:** Brute force attacks often involve numerous failed login attempts. You can thwart these attacks by limiting the number of allowed login attempts before locking out the user temporarily. Plugins like Limit Login Attempts Reloaded can help you implement this feature.
- **Use Unique Usernames:** Avoid using common usernames like "admin" or "administrator," as these are often targeted by hackers. Choose unique usernames that are difficult to guess.
- **Disable File Editing:** By default, WordPress allows users with administrative privileges to edit theme and plugin files directly from the dashboard. This can be a security risk if an attacker gains access to your admin account. Disable file editing from the WordPress dashboard to prevent

unauthorized modifications. You can do this by adding the following line to your `wp-config.php` file:

```
define( 'DISALLOW_FILE_EDIT', true );
```

- **Install Plugins and Themes from Trusted Sources:** Only install plugins and themes from reputable sources like the official WordPress repository or trusted third-party developers. Avoid downloading plugins or themes from unknown or suspicious websites, as they might contain malicious code.
- **Regularly Scan for Malware:** Even with proactive security measures, it's still possible for malware to infect your website. Regularly scan your website for malware using a security plugin or an online scanner.
- **Use Strong Passwords for FTP and Database:** If you use FTP to access your website files or phpMyAdmin to manage your database, make sure to use strong and unique passwords for these accounts as well.
- **Enable Web Application Firewall (WAF) Rules:** If your web hosting provider offers a web application firewall (WAF), enable the recommended rules for WordPress. This can help filter out malicious traffic and protect your website from common web-based attacks.
- **Educate Yourself and Your Team:** Stay informed about the latest security threats and best practices by following security blogs, forums, and newsletters. If you have a team managing your website, ensure they are also educated about security risks and trained on how to identify and respond to potential threats.

By implementing these additional security tips, you can further strengthen your WordPress website's defenses and minimize the risk of security breaches. Remember, website security is an ongoing process that requires vigilance and regular attention. By staying proactive and informed, you can protect your valuable data and maintain the trust of your website visitors.

Chapter Summary

This chapter has emphasized the crucial importance of website security for safeguarding sensitive information, maintaining user trust, and preventing financial and reputational damage. We explored common security threats that WordPress websites face, including brute force attacks, malware, SQL injection, cross-site scripting (XSS), and denial-of-service (DoS) attacks. Understanding these threats is the first step towards protecting your website.

We then outlined essential security measures for WordPress, providing a comprehensive overview of best practices. These include choosing a secure web host, using strong passwords and user management, installing security plugins, regularly updating and backing up your website, enabling two-factor authentication, monitoring and logging activity, using a website firewall, and installing an SSL certificate.

We also provided additional security tips to further fortify your website, such as limiting login attempts, using unique usernames, disabling file editing, and being cautious about installing plugins and themes from untrusted sources.

By implementing these security measures and remaining vigilant, you can significantly reduce the risk of your WordPress website being compromised. Remember, website security is an ongoing process that requires continuous attention and adaptation to new threats. By prioritizing security, you not only protect your website and data but also build trust with your visitors and safeguard your online reputation.

Regular Maintenance Tasks: Keep Your Site Healthy

Outline

- Introduction
- Why Website Maintenance is Important
- Core Updates
- Theme and Plugin Updates
- Content Updates
- Security Scans and Checks
- Performance Optimization
- Backups
- Broken Link Checks
- Database Optimization
- Spam Comment Management
- Monitoring Uptime and Downtime
- User Management
- Chapter Summary

Introduction

Think of your WordPress website as a finely tuned machine, like a car. Just as a car requires regular maintenance to run smoothly and efficiently, your website also needs ongoing care to ensure optimal performance, security, and functionality. Neglecting website maintenance can lead to various problems, such as slow loading times, security vulnerabilities, broken links, and outdated content.

In this chapter, we'll provide you with a comprehensive checklist of regular maintenance tasks that will help you keep your WordPress website in top shape. By following these recommendations and establishing a routine maintenance schedule, you can prevent potential issues, enhance your website's performance, and ensure a smooth and enjoyable experience for your visitors.

Let's dive in and explore the essential maintenance tasks that will keep your WordPress website running like a well-oiled machine.

Why Website Maintenance is Important

Regular website maintenance is not just a chore; it's an investment in the long-term health and success of your online presence. Neglecting maintenance can lead to a host of issues that can negatively impact your website's security, performance, user experience, and search engine optimization (SEO). Let's explore the importance of website maintenance in detail:

Security

The internet is rife with security threats, from hackers and malware to brute force attacks and data breaches. Regular maintenance helps you identify and address vulnerabilities in your WordPress website before they can be exploited by malicious actors. By keeping your software updated, installing security patches, and monitoring for suspicious activity, you can significantly reduce the risk of your website being compromised.

Performance

A slow-loading website can frustrate visitors and drive them away. Regular maintenance tasks like updating plugins and themes, cleaning up databases, and removing unused files can significantly improve your website's speed and performance. Faster loading times not only enhance user experience but also contribute to better search engine rankings.

User Experience

Outdated content, broken links, and technical glitches can create a negative user experience, leading to higher bounce rates and lower engagement. By regularly updating your content, fixing broken links, and ensuring that all features are working properly, you can create a seamless and enjoyable experience for your visitors, encouraging them to return to your site.

SEO

Search engines like Google favor websites that are well-maintained, secure, and up-to-date. Regular maintenance tasks like updating content, fixing broken links, and optimizing for speed can positively impact your search engine rankings. A higher ranking in search results translates to increased visibility and organic traffic, driving more potential customers to your website.

In essence, website maintenance is not just about fixing problems; it's about proactively ensuring that your website remains secure, fast, user-friendly, and optimized for search engines. By dedicating time and resources to regular maintenance, you can safeguard your website's health, enhance its performance, and ultimately achieve your online goals.

Core Updates

WordPress is constantly evolving, with developers releasing updates regularly to enhance its functionality, security, and performance. These core updates often include bug fixes, security patches, and new features that can benefit your website.

The Importance of Keeping WordPress Updated

It's crucial to keep your WordPress core up-to-date for several reasons:

- **Security:** WordPress updates often include patches for security vulnerabilities that hackers could exploit. By updating your WordPress core, you ensure that your website is protected against the latest security threats.
- **Performance:** Updates may introduce performance improvements, making your website faster and more efficient.
- **Features:** New versions of WordPress often include new features and enhancements that can improve your website's functionality and user experience.
- **Compatibility:** Updates ensure that your website remains compatible with the latest plugins and themes, preventing potential conflicts and errors.

How to Update WordPress Through the Dashboard

Updating your WordPress core is a simple process that can be done directly from your WordPress dashboard. Here's how:

1. **Check for Updates:**
   - Log in to your WordPress dashboard.
   - You'll usually see a notification badge on the "Dashboard" or "Updates" icon in the left-hand menu if updates are available.
   - Click on the "Updates" icon to see a list of available updates.
2. **Update WordPress:**

- If a new version of WordPress is available, you'll see an option to "Update Now." Click on this button to start the update process.
- WordPress will automatically download and install the update. This process may take a few minutes.
- Once the update is complete, you'll see a success message.

Best Practices for Updating WordPress

- **Backup Before Updating:** Before updating WordPress, it's always a good practice to create a backup of your website's files and database. This will allow you to restore your site to its previous state if anything goes wrong during the update process.
- **Update Regularly:** Make it a habit to check for updates regularly and install them promptly. This will ensure that your website is always running on the latest and most secure version of WordPress.
- **Update Themes and Plugins:** In addition to updating WordPress core, make sure to also keep your themes and plugins updated to their latest versions.

By following these simple steps and best practices, you can keep your WordPress website secure, up-to-date, and running smoothly.

Theme and Plugin Updates

Just like the WordPress core, themes and plugins are constantly being updated by their developers. These updates often bring new features, bug fixes, security patches, and performance improvements. Keeping your themes and plugins up-to-date is just as important as updating the core software itself.

Risks of Outdated Themes and Plugins

Running outdated themes and plugins can pose significant risks to your website:

- **Security Vulnerabilities:** Outdated software often contains security flaws that hackers can exploit to gain unauthorized access to your website, steal data, or inject malicious code.
- **Compatibility Issues:** Newer versions of WordPress may introduce changes that are not compatible with older themes or plugins. This can lead to errors, broken functionality, or even the dreaded "white screen of death."
- **Performance Issues:** Outdated plugins and themes might not be optimized for the latest WordPress version, resulting in slower loading times and subpar performance.
- **Missed Features and Improvements:** By not updating, you miss out on new features, enhancements, and bug fixes that could improve your website's functionality and user experience.

Updating Themes and Plugins Through the Dashboard

Updating your themes and plugins is a simple process that can be done directly from your WordPress dashboard. Here's how:

1. **Check for Updates:**
   - Log in to your WordPress dashboard.
   - Look for the Updates icon in the left-hand menu. If there are updates available, you'll see a notification badge indicating the number of updates.
   - Click on the Updates icon to see a list of available updates for your themes and plugins.
2. **Update Themes and Plugins:**
   - Select the themes or plugins you want to update.
   - Click the "Update" button next to each item.
   - WordPress will automatically download and install the updates.
   - Once the updates are complete, you'll see a success message.

Best Practices for Updating Themes and Plugins

- **Backup Before Updating:** Before updating any theme or plugin, it's crucial to create a backup of your website. This allows you to revert to a previous version if the update causes any issues.
- **Test Updates on a Staging Site:** If you have a staging environment (a copy of your website that's not live), it's a good idea to test updates there first before applying them to your live site. This can help you identify any potential conflicts or errors before they affect your visitors.
- **Check Compatibility:** Ensure that the themes and plugins you use are compatible with the latest version of WordPress. You can check the plugin or theme's documentation or the WordPress Plugin Directory for compatibility information.
- **Monitor for Issues:** After updating a theme or plugin, monitor your website for any errors or unexpected behavior. If you encounter any problems, you can try deactivating the recently updated theme or plugin to see if it resolves the issue.

By following these guidelines and staying on top of your updates, you can ensure that your WordPress website remains secure, functional, and up-to-date with the latest features and improvements.

Content Updates

While a visually appealing and functional website is crucial, the content you present is equally important. Keeping your website's content fresh and up-to-date is vital for engaging visitors, maintaining relevance, and improving your search engine rankings.

The Importance of Fresh Content

Regularly updating your content offers several benefits:

- **Retaining Visitors:** Fresh content keeps visitors coming back to your site for new information, insights, or products.
- **Attracting New Visitors:** Search engines favor websites that are regularly updated with relevant content, potentially leading to higher rankings and increased organic traffic.
- **Building Credibility:** Up-to-date content demonstrates that you are actively engaged in your field and that your information is reliable and trustworthy.
- **Improving Conversions:** Fresh content can lead to increased conversions by keeping visitors interested and engaged.
- **Staying Relevant:** In a constantly changing digital landscape, keeping your content updated helps you stay relevant and competitive.

Creating an Editorial Calendar

An editorial calendar is a valuable tool for planning and scheduling your content updates. It helps you stay organized, maintain consistency, and ensure that you're publishing content that aligns with your goals and target audience. You can create an editorial calendar using a spreadsheet, project management tool, or dedicated editorial calendar software.

Reviewing and Updating Existing Content

In addition to creating new content, it's essential to review and update your existing content regularly. This ensures that your information remains accurate and relevant. Here's how to review and update existing content:

1. **Check for Accuracy:** Review your content for any outdated or inaccurate information. Update statistics, facts, and figures to ensure they are current.
2. **Update Broken Links:** Broken links can frustrate users and negatively impact your SEO. Use a plugin like Broken Link Checker to scan your website for broken links and fix them.

3. **Refresh Images and Media:** If your content includes images or videos, make sure they are still relevant and visually appealing. Replace outdated or low-quality visuals with fresh, high-resolution images.
4. **Improve Readability:** Review your content's readability and make it more engaging. Break down long paragraphs into shorter ones, add headings and subheadings, and use bullet points or numbered lists for easier scanning.
5. **Add Internal Links:** Link to other relevant pages or posts on your website to improve navigation and encourage visitors to explore your site further.

Additional Tips for Content Updates

- **Repurpose Content:** Turn your existing content into different formats, such as social media posts, infographics, or videos, to reach a wider audience.
- **Solicit Feedback:** Ask your readers for feedback on your content to identify areas where you can improve.
- **Use Analytics:** Track your content's performance using Google Analytics to see which posts are most popular and which ones need improvement.

By regularly updating your content and following these best practices, you can keep your website fresh, engaging, and relevant, attracting and retaining more visitors and ultimately achieving your online goals.

Security Scans and Checks

Regular security scans and checks are essential for identifying and addressing vulnerabilities in your WordPress website before they can be exploited by malicious actors. This proactive approach can save you from the headaches and potential damage caused by security breaches.

Security Plugins

Leveraging security plugins is a convenient and effective way to perform regular scans and enhance your website's protection. Two popular and reliable options are:

- **Wordfence Security:** This comprehensive plugin offers a web application firewall, malware scanner, login security features, and regular security scans to detect and block potential threats. It provides detailed reports on scan results, blocked attacks, and other security-related information.
- **Sucuri Security:** This plugin focuses on website hardening, malware detection and removal, and a web application firewall. It also offers a monitoring service that alerts you of any security issues and provides professional cleanup services if your website gets hacked.

Reviewing Security Reports

After running a security scan, carefully review the report generated by your security plugin. The report will typically highlight any vulnerabilities, malware infections, or suspicious activities detected on your website. Pay close attention to the following:

- **Vulnerabilities:** These are weaknesses in your website's code or configuration that hackers could exploit. Address vulnerabilities promptly by updating your WordPress core, themes, plugins, and server software.
- **Malware:** If malware is detected, immediately take action to remove it. This might involve using a malware removal tool or seeking professional help from a security expert.
- **Suspicious Activity:** Monitor your website's logs for any unusual activity, such as failed login attempts, file changes, or unexpected traffic spikes. Investigate these activities to determine if they are legitimate or malicious.

Taking Action to Address Issues

If you find any vulnerabilities or security issues during your scans, it's crucial to address them promptly. Here are some steps you can take:

- **Update Software:** Ensure your WordPress core, themes, and plugins are updated to the latest versions. Updates often include security patches that fix vulnerabilities.
- **Change Passwords:** If there are signs of unauthorized access, change the passwords for all user accounts, especially the administrator account.
- **Scan and Remove Malware:** Use a malware removal tool or seek professional help to remove any detected malware from your website.
- **Hardening Security:** Implement additional security measures, such as two-factor authentication, limiting login attempts, and using a web application firewall.

By regularly performing security scans and checks, reviewing reports, and taking prompt action to address any issues, you can significantly enhance your WordPress website's security and protect it from potential threats.

Performance Optimization

Website performance is not a one-time task but an ongoing effort. Regularly optimizing your website's speed is crucial for maintaining a positive user experience, improving search engine rankings, and ultimately, achieving your online goals.

Why Performance Optimization Matters

A slow-loading website can have a significant impact on your website's success:

- **User Experience:** Slow loading times frustrate users and lead to higher bounce rates. Studies have shown that even a one-second delay in page load time can result in a 7% reduction in conversions.
- **SEO:** Search engines like Google consider website speed as a ranking factor. Faster websites tend to rank higher in search results, leading to increased organic traffic.
- **Conversions:** A fast and responsive website provides a better user experience, which can lead to higher engagement, more conversions, and increased sales.

Optimizing Images

Images are often the largest files on a website and can significantly impact loading times. Optimizing your images can drastically improve your website's speed.

Tips for image optimization:

- **Compress images:** Reduce the file size of your images without sacrificing quality using tools like TinyPNG or Kraken.io.
- **Resize images:** Use appropriate image dimensions for different screen sizes to avoid loading unnecessarily large images on smaller devices.
- **Use the correct file format:** Choose the right image format for different types of images. JPEG is generally best for photographs, while PNG is better for images with transparency or graphics with sharp lines.
- **Consider WebP:** WebP is a modern image format that offers smaller file sizes than JPEG or PNG for the same quality.
- **Lazy Loading:** Implement lazy loading to defer the loading of images until they are about to enter the viewport, improving initial page load times.

Caching Plugins

Caching plugins store static versions of your website's pages, reducing the need to generate them dynamically for each visitor. This significantly improves loading times, especially for returning visitors.

Recommended caching plugins:

- **WP Super Cache:** A free and popular caching plugin that is easy to set up and use.
- **W3 Total Cache:** A more advanced caching plugin with various features and customization options.
- **WP Rocket:** A premium caching plugin that offers a wide range of optimization features and excellent performance.

Minimizing HTTP Requests

Each resource (image, stylesheet, script) on your website requires a separate HTTP request to be downloaded from the server. The more requests your website makes, the longer it will take to load.

Tips for minimizing HTTP requests:

- **Combine CSS and JavaScript files:** Reduce the number of requests by combining multiple CSS and JavaScript files into one.
- **Use CSS sprites:** Combine multiple small images into a single image and use CSS to display the desired portion of the image.
- **Limit the use of web fonts:** Each web font you use requires an additional request. Choose a limited number of web fonts or consider using system fonts.

By implementing these optimization techniques, you can significantly improve your WordPress website's speed and performance, providing a better user experience and boosting your SEO. Remember, website speed optimization is an ongoing process that requires regular attention and fine-tuning.

Backups

In the world of website management, the adage "better safe than sorry" holds true. Regular backups are your insurance policy against unforeseen disasters that can strike your WordPress website. Whether it's a server crash, a hacking attempt, a data corruption, or accidental deletion, a backup can be your lifeline to restore your website to a previous working state.

Why Backups are Essential

Backups serve as a safety net, protecting your website from:

- **Data Loss:** Hardware failures, software glitches, or human errors can lead to data loss. A backup ensures that you can recover your website's data quickly and easily.
- **Hacking Attempts:** Even with the best security measures in place, your website can still be vulnerable to hacking. A backup allows you to restore your website to a clean state before the attack.
- **Malware Infection:** Malware can corrupt your website's files or database. A backup can help you remove the malware and restore your site to its original condition.
- **Accidental Deletions:** Mistakes happen. If you accidentally delete files or make changes that break your website, a backup can save the day.

Backup Plugins for WordPress

WordPress offers a variety of backup plugins that simplify the process of creating and managing backups. Two popular and reliable options are:

- **UpdraftPlus:** This free plugin is easy to use and allows you to create backups of your website's files and database. You can store your backups in the cloud (e.g., Dropbox, Google Drive, Amazon S3) or download them to your computer. UpdraftPlus also offers features like scheduled backups, incremental backups, and one-click restores.
- **BackupBuddy:** This premium plugin offers more advanced features than UpdraftPlus, such as the ability to migrate your website to a new server, store backups off-site, and schedule differential backups (which only backup files that have changed since the last full backup).

Best Practices for Backups

- **Frequency:** Back up your website regularly, at least once a week or more often if you update your site frequently.
- **Storage:** Store your backups in multiple locations, such as on your computer and in the cloud, to ensure redundancy.
- **Testing:** Regularly test your backups to ensure that you can restore your website successfully.
- **Automation:** Use a backup plugin to automate the backup process so you don't have to remember to do it manually.

By implementing a robust backup strategy, you can rest assured that your WordPress website is protected against data loss and other unforeseen events.

Broken Link Checks

Broken links are like potholes on the road of your website's user experience. They can frustrate visitors, increase bounce rates, and even harm your SEO efforts. It's essential to regularly check for and fix broken links to maintain a smooth and seamless browsing experience.

Why Broken Links are Detrimental

- **Frustration and Disappointment:** When visitors click on a link and encounter a 404 error page, they feel frustrated and might leave your website altogether. This can lead to a loss of potential customers or readers.
- **Negative Impact on SEO:** Search engines consider broken links as a sign of a poorly maintained website. This can negatively impact your search rankings, making it harder for potential visitors to find your site.
- **Loss of Credibility:** Broken links make your website appear unprofessional and outdated, which can erode trust and damage your reputation.

Using Broken Link Checker

Broken Link Checker is a popular and reliable WordPress plugin that can help you identify and fix broken links on your website. It scans your website's content, including posts, pages, comments, and custom fields, for broken links and notifies you of any issues it finds.

The plugin provides a list of all broken links, along with their location on your website and the HTTP status code of the error. You can then easily edit the links to point to the correct URLs or remove them if necessary.

How to Use Broken Link Checker

1. **Install and Activate:** Go to *Plugins > Add New* in your WordPress dashboard and search for "Broken Link Checker." Install and activate the plugin.
2. **Configure Settings:** Go to *Settings > Link Checker* to configure the plugin's settings. You can choose how often the plugin should scan your website, which types of links to check, and how you want to be notified of broken links.

3. **Review and Fix Broken Links:** Once the plugin has completed a scan, you'll see a list of broken links in the *Tools > Broken Links* section of your dashboard. Click on each link to edit or remove it.

Additional Tips

- **Regularly Scan Your Website:** Set up Broken Link Checker to scan your website regularly (e.g., weekly or monthly) to catch any new broken links that might appear.
- **Monitor External Links:** Remember that broken links can also occur on external websites that you link to. Monitor your external links periodically to ensure they are still working.
- **Use 301 Redirects:** If you've moved a page or post to a new URL, set up a 301 redirect from the old URL to the new one. This will prevent visitors from encountering a 404 error and will also pass on the SEO value of the old page to the new one.

By regularly checking for and fixing broken links, you can enhance your website's user experience, improve its SEO, and maintain a professional and credible online presence.

Database Optimization

Your WordPress website's database is like its filing cabinet, storing everything from post and page content to comments, settings, and user data. Over time, this database can accumulate unnecessary clutter, such as post revisions, trashed items, spam comments, and unused tables from deactivated plugins. This digital clutter can slow down your website, as it takes longer for the database to process requests and retrieve information.

Why Optimize Your Database?

Database optimization is a crucial aspect of website maintenance. A lean and efficient database can significantly improve your website's performance in several ways:

- **Faster Loading Times:** A smaller database requires less processing time, leading to faster page loading speeds and a smoother user experience.
- **Reduced Server Load:** A streamlined database puts less strain on your server, ensuring optimal performance and reliability.
- **Improved Backup Efficiency:** Smaller database files are faster and easier to back up and restore.
- **Enhanced Security:** Removing unnecessary data can reduce the risk of data breaches and vulnerabilities.

Using Plugins for Database Optimization

WordPress offers several plugins that can help you optimize your database effortlessly:

- **WP-Optimize:** This popular plugin allows you to clean up your database by removing post revisions, drafts, spam comments, trashed items, and other unnecessary data. It also optimizes database tables to improve performance and reduce storage space.
- **WP-Sweep:** Similar to WP-Optimize, WP-Sweep cleans up your database by removing unused, orphaned, and duplicated data. It also offers additional features like scheduling automatic cleanups and optimizing database tables.

How to Optimize Your Database

1. **Install and Activate a Plugin:** Choose a database optimization plugin like WP-Optimize or WP-Sweep and install it on your WordPress website.
2. **Review and Select Options:** Explore the plugin's settings and select the types of data you want to clean up. You can usually choose to remove revisions, trashed posts, spam comments, transient options, and other unnecessary data.

3. **Run the Optimization:** Click the "Optimize" or "Sweep" button to initiate the optimization process. The plugin will then analyze your database and remove the selected data.
4. **Monitor Performance:** After optimizing your database, monitor your website's speed and performance to see if there are any improvements. You can use online speed test tools like GTmetrix or Google PageSpeed Insights to measure your website's loading time.

Additional Optimization Tips

- **Disable or Delete Unused Plugins:** Deactivated plugins can still leave behind database tables. If you're not using a plugin, delete it to remove its associated data from your database.
- **Regularly Schedule Cleanups:** Set up scheduled cleanups using your chosen plugin to automate the optimization process and keep your database lean and efficient.
- **Consider Professional Help:** If you have a large or complex database, you might want to consider hiring a WordPress expert to help you optimize it.

By regularly optimizing your database, you can ensure that your WordPress website runs smoothly, loads quickly, and provides a positive experience for your visitors.

Spam Comment Management

Spam comments are an unfortunate reality for many websites, especially those with active blogs or forums. These unsolicited comments often promote irrelevant products or services, contain malicious links, or simply aim to disrupt discussions. They can clutter your website, annoy your genuine readers, and even damage your reputation if they contain offensive or inappropriate content.

The Impact of Spam Comments

Spam comments can negatively affect your website in several ways:

- **User Experience:** Spam comments clutter your comment sections, making it difficult for legitimate users to find and engage with genuine comments. This can lead to a poor user experience and deter visitors from returning to your site.
- **Reputation:** If your website is filled with spam comments, it can reflect poorly on your brand and make you appear unprofessional or negligent. This can damage your reputation and credibility.
- **SEO:** Some spam comments contain links to malicious websites. If search engines detect these links on your site, it could negatively impact your search rankings.

Moderating Comments

WordPress allows you to moderate comments before they are published on your website. This means you can review each comment and decide whether to approve, reply, edit, trash, or mark it as spam. While manual moderation can be effective, it can also be time-consuming, especially if you receive a large volume of comments.

To moderate comments in WordPress:

1. Go to the "Comments" section in your WordPress dashboard.
2. Review each comment and choose the appropriate action (Approve, Reply, Edit, Trash, or Spam).
3. If you approve a comment, it will be published on your website. If you trash or mark it as spam, it will be removed.

Anti-Spam Plugins

Anti-spam plugins can automate the process of filtering out spam comments, saving you time and effort. One of the most popular and effective anti-spam plugins is Akismet.

Akismet analyzes comments and compares them to a global database of known spam. It can then automatically filter out spam comments before they are published on your website. Akismet also learns from your actions, becoming more effective over time at identifying and blocking spam.

Using Akismet

1. **Install and Activate:** Go to *Plugins > Add New* in your WordPress dashboard and search for "Akismet." Install and activate the plugin.
2. **Get an API Key:** You'll need an Akismet API key to use the plugin. You can get a free key for personal use or a paid key for commercial use.
3. **Configure Settings:** Go to *Settings > Akismet* to configure the plugin's settings. You can choose how you want Akismet to handle spam comments (e.g., automatically trash them, mark them as spam, or put them in moderation).

Additional Tips

- **Disable Comments on Certain Pages:** If you don't want to allow comments on certain pages (e.g., your homepage or contact page), you can disable comments for those specific pages.
- **Use a Captcha:** A captcha is a test that helps distinguish between human users and bots. Adding a captcha to your comment form can help reduce spam.
- **Monitor Your Comments Regularly:** Even with anti-spam measures in place, some spam comments might still slip through. Regularly monitor your comments and manually remove any spam that you find.

By effectively managing spam comments, you can keep your website clean, protect your reputation, and ensure a positive experience for your visitors.

Monitoring Uptime and Downtime

Your website's uptime, which is the percentage of time it's accessible online, is critical for user experience, business continuity, and SEO. Even brief periods of downtime can lead to frustrated visitors, lost revenue, and negative impacts on your search engine rankings. Therefore, actively monitoring your website's uptime is crucial to ensure it's always available to your audience.

Why Monitor Uptime?

- **User Experience:** Website downtime can be frustrating for visitors who are unable to access your content or services. This can lead to a negative perception of your brand and discourage them from returning.
- **Business Continuity:** For businesses that rely on their website for sales or lead generation, downtime can directly translate to lost revenue and missed opportunities.
- **SEO:** Search engines like Google may penalize websites with frequent or prolonged downtime, impacting your visibility in search results.

Uptime Monitoring Services

Uptime monitoring services offer a convenient and reliable way to track your website's uptime. These services continuously ping your website from different locations around the world, checking if it's responding. If your website goes down, you'll receive an instant alert via email, SMS, or other notification channels.

Some popular uptime monitoring services include:

- **UptimeRobot:** Offers a free plan with 5-minute monitoring intervals and paid plans with more frequent checks and additional features.

- **Pingdom:** Provides comprehensive uptime monitoring, real user monitoring (RUM), and website speed tests. It offers various paid plans with different features and monitoring intervals.
- **StatusCake:** Offers uptime monitoring, server monitoring, SSL monitoring, and domain monitoring. It has a free plan with 30-minute checks and paid plans with more frequent checks and additional features.
- **Better Uptime:** Better Uptime also provides incident management, status pages, and on-call scheduling so you can get a team alerted in case of an outage.

How to Choose an Uptime Monitoring Service

When selecting an uptime monitoring service, consider the following factors:

- **Monitoring Intervals:** Choose a service that offers frequent checks, ideally every minute or less.
- **Alert Notifications:** Ensure the service provides various alert options, such as email, SMS, or push notifications, so you can be notified immediately if your website goes down.
- **Reporting:** Look for a service that offers detailed reports on uptime, downtime, and response times.
- **Additional Features:** Some services offer additional features like root cause analysis, website speed tests, and server monitoring.
- **Pricing:** Compare the pricing of different services and choose one that fits your budget.

Best Practices for Uptime Monitoring

- **Choose Multiple Monitoring Locations:** Monitor your website from multiple locations worldwide to get a more accurate picture of its availability.
- **Set up Alert Notifications:** Configure alerts to be notified immediately if your website experiences downtime.
- **Regularly Review Reports:** Analyze uptime reports to identify trends and potential issues.
- **Have a Plan for Downtime:** Develop a plan for how to respond to downtime to minimize its impact on your business.

By actively monitoring your website's uptime, you can quickly identify and resolve issues, ensuring that your website is always available to your visitors. This not only improves the user experience but also protects your brand reputation and helps you maintain high search engine rankings.

User Management

As your WordPress website grows, so does the number of users who have access to it. Regular user management is crucial for maintaining security, optimizing performance, and ensuring that only authorized individuals have the appropriate level of access.

Why User Management Matters

- **Security:** Inactive or unused user accounts can be vulnerable to hacking attempts. By removing these accounts, you reduce the potential entry points for unauthorized access.
- **Performance:** A large number of user accounts can slow down your website's performance. Removing unnecessary accounts can help optimize your site's speed.
- **Data Protection:** GDPR and other data protection regulations require you to manage user data responsibly. Regularly reviewing and updating user information ensures compliance with these regulations.

Removing Inactive Users

Inactive users are those who haven't logged in to your website for an extended period. These accounts are potential security risks, as they could be compromised by hackers.

To remove inactive users:

1. Go to *Users > All Users* in your WordPress dashboard.
2. Filter the list of users by "Inactive" to see users who haven't logged in recently.
3. Select the users you want to remove and choose "Delete" from the bulk actions dropdown menu.
4. Confirm the deletion.

Updating User Roles and Permissions

As your team or website's needs change, it's important to review and update user roles and permissions. Ensure that each user has the appropriate level of access to perform their tasks without jeopardizing your website's security.

To update user roles and permissions:

1. Go to *Users > All Users* in your WordPress dashboard.
2. Click on the username of the user you want to edit.
3. In the user's profile, change their role to the appropriate level (e.g., Administrator, Editor, Author, Contributor, Subscriber).
4. Click "Update User" to save your changes.

Monitoring User Activity

Regularly monitor user activity to detect any unusual behavior or potential security breaches. You can use security plugins like Wordfence or iThemes Security to track user logins, failed login attempts, file changes, and other activities.

If you notice any suspicious activity, take immediate action to investigate and address the issue. This might involve changing passwords, restricting user access, or even blocking IP addresses.

Best Practices for User Management

- **Regularly Review User Accounts:** Set a schedule for reviewing user accounts, such as quarterly or annually.
- **Remove Unnecessary Accounts:** Delete any inactive or unused user accounts.
- **Assign Roles Carefully:** Only give users the permissions they need to perform their tasks.
- **Use Strong Passwords:** Encourage all users to create strong passwords and change them regularly.
- **Limit Administrator Accounts:** Avoid having too many administrators, as this increases the risk of unauthorized access.

By following these user management practices, you can enhance your website's security, optimize its performance, and ensure that only authorized individuals have access to sensitive areas.

Chapter Summary

This chapter has highlighted the significance of regular maintenance tasks in keeping your WordPress website healthy and secure. We compared website maintenance to car maintenance, stressing that neglect can lead to significant issues down the line.

The importance of website maintenance was detailed, emphasizing its role in bolstering security, enhancing performance, improving user experience, and positively impacting SEO.

We discussed the need for regular core updates, theme and plugin updates, and content updates to maintain functionality, security, and relevance. Additionally, we provided step-by-step instructions on how to perform these updates through your WordPress dashboard.

We also stressed the significance of routine security scans and checks using plugins like Wordfence or Sucuri Security to identify vulnerabilities and malware.

To ensure your website runs smoothly, we recommended regular performance optimizations such as image optimization, using caching plugins, and minimizing HTTP requests.

Regular backups were emphasized as crucial for safeguarding your website data against unforeseen events. Plugins like UpdraftPlus or BackupBuddy were suggested to automate this process.

Broken link checks, database optimization, and spam comment management were highlighted as essential tasks for maintaining a user-friendly and high-performing website. We recommended using plugins like Broken Link Checker and Akismet to automate these tasks.

Finally, we discussed the importance of monitoring your website's uptime and regularly reviewing and managing user accounts to ensure optimal performance and security.

By diligently performing these maintenance tasks, you can ensure that your WordPress website remains secure, up-to-date, fast, and user-friendly, leading to improved user satisfaction and higher search engine rankings. Remember, regular maintenance is key to a healthy and thriving website.

Appendices

Appendix A: Elementor Shortcuts and Tips

Elementor is a powerful page builder, and like any powerful tool, it has a multitude of shortcuts and tips that can significantly enhance your workflow and productivity. This appendix provides a handy reference for some of the most useful shortcuts and tips to help you master Elementor and create stunning websites with ease.

Keyboard Shortcuts

Keyboard shortcuts are a great way to speed up your workflow and perform actions quickly without having to navigate through menus or click on icons. Here are some essential keyboard shortcuts for Elementor:

- **Save:** Cmd/Ctrl + S
- **Undo:** Cmd/Ctrl + Z
- **Redo:** Cmd/Ctrl + Shift + Z
- **Copy:** Cmd/Ctrl + C
- **Paste:** Cmd/Ctrl + V
- **Duplicate:** Cmd/Ctrl + D
- **Delete:** Delete
- **Navigator:** Cmd/Ctrl + Shift + N
- **Finder:** Cmd/Ctrl + Shift + F
- **Responsive Mode:** Cmd/Ctrl + Shift + M
- **Show/Hide Panel:** Cmd/Ctrl + P

Right-Click Menu

Elementor's right-click menu provides quick access to various actions and settings for the selected widget or section. Here are some useful options you can find in the right-click menu:

- **Edit:** Opens the settings panel for the selected widget or section.
- **Duplicate:** Creates a copy of the selected widget or section.
- **Copy/Paste Style:** Copies or pastes the styling of the selected widget or section.
- **Navigate To:** Quickly jumps to a specific section or widget on your page.
- **Save as Template:** Saves the selected section or widget as a reusable template.

Finder Tool

The Finder tool allows you to quickly locate and select any widget or section on your page. To use the Finder tool:

1. Press Cmd/Ctrl + Shift + F.
2. Start typing the name of the widget or section you're looking for.
3. Click on the desired item in the search results to select it.

Navigator Panel Tips

- **Expand/Collapse:** Click on the arrow icons next to sections or columns to expand or collapse them. This helps you focus on specific areas of your page.
- **Rearrange:** Drag and drop elements within the Navigator Panel to change their order on the page.
- **Hide/Show:** Right-click on an element in the Navigator Panel and select "Hide" to temporarily hide it from view. This can be useful for focusing on specific sections or widgets.

Reusable Templates and Blocks

Create reusable templates for sections, pages, or entire layouts that you use frequently. This saves you time and ensures consistency across your website. You can also save individual widgets as global widgets to reuse them on different pages.

Keyboard Navigation

Use the arrow keys to navigate between widgets and sections in the Elementor editor. Hold down the Shift key while pressing the arrow keys to move elements faster.

Hotkeys for Widgets

Some widgets have hotkeys that allow you to quickly add them to your page. For example, you can press "H" to add a Heading widget or "T" to add a Text Editor widget.

By mastering these shortcuts and tips, you can significantly enhance your efficiency and productivity when working with Elementor.

Appendix B: Resources for Further Learning

Your journey to mastering WordPress and Elementor doesn't end with this book. The world of web design and development is constantly evolving, and there are always new things to learn and discover. This appendix provides a curated list of resources to help you continue your learning journey and stay up-to-date with the latest trends and techniques.

Official Resources

- **WordPress.org:** The official WordPress website is a treasure trove of information, tutorials, and documentation. You can find comprehensive guides on everything from installation and setup to theme and plugin development.
- **Elementor Website:** The official Elementor website offers a wealth of resources, including documentation, tutorials, webinars, and a community forum.
- **WooCommerce Website:** If you're interested in building an online store, the official WooCommerce website provides detailed documentation, tutorials, and extensions.

Blogs and Online Communities

- **Elementor Blog:** The Elementor blog features articles, tutorials, and case studies on various aspects of web design and development with Elementor.
- **WPBeginner:** This popular WordPress blog offers tutorials, guides, and reviews on various WordPress topics, including Elementor.
- **Elegant Themes Blog:** This blog (by the creators of Divi) provides insights into web design, WordPress, and Elementor.
- **WordPress.org Support Forums:** The official WordPress support forums are a great place to ask questions and get help from the WordPress community.
- **Elementor Facebook Group:** The official Elementor Facebook group is a vibrant community where you can connect with other Elementor users, ask questions, and share your work.

Online Courses and Tutorials

- **Udemy:** Udemy offers a wide range of WordPress and Elementor courses, from beginner to advanced levels.
- **Skillshare:** Skillshare provides a variety of creative courses, including web design and development with Elementor.
- **YouTube:** You can find countless tutorials and walkthroughs on WordPress and Elementor on YouTube.

Additional Resources

- **Envato Elements:** A subscription service that offers unlimited downloads of WordPress themes, plugins, graphics, and other creative assets.
- **ThemeForest:** A marketplace for purchasing premium WordPress themes, including many Elementor-compatible themes.
- **CodeCanyon:** A marketplace for purchasing premium WordPress plugins, including many Elementor add-ons and extensions.

This appendix is just a starting point. There are many other valuable resources available online and offline. Explore, experiment, and never stop learning to continue growing your WordPress and Elementor skills.

Conclusion

Congratulations! You've reached the end of "WordPress Made Easy: Build Your Dream Website with Elementor." Throughout this comprehensive guide, we've embarked on a journey together, exploring the vast landscape of WordPress and the revolutionary Elementor page builder.

We started by understanding the foundations of WordPress, from its humble origins as a blogging platform to its evolution into a robust content management system (CMS) that powers a significant portion of the internet. We delved into the technical aspects of choosing a domain name, selecting a web hosting provider, and installing WordPress. We then explored the WordPress dashboard, your command center for managing your website's content, appearance, and functionality.

We also dove deep into the world of themes and plugins, the essential building blocks of your WordPress website. You learned how to choose the right theme for your website's purpose and style, and how to leverage plugins to add new features and functionalities.

Next, we embarked on an exciting journey into the realm of Elementor. We started with an introduction to Elementor's drag-and-drop interface, exploring its user-friendly tools and extensive customization options. We then took a tour of the Elementor interface, familiarizing ourselves with its various components, including the widget panel, content area, navigator, and settings panel.

We learned how to build pages efficiently using Elementor templates and blocks, harnessing the power of pre-designed elements to save time and achieve professional-looking results. We then explored the vast array of widgets available in Elementor, from basic elements like headings and text to more advanced widgets like sliders, forms, and dynamic content.

We also covered essential aspects of web design, such as styling with colors and fonts, organizing content with sections and columns, and creating responsive designs that adapt to different screen sizes. These techniques empower you to create visually appealing and user-friendly websites that leave a lasting impression on your visitors.

In the latter part of the book, we delved into advanced Elementor techniques like dynamic content, popups, and the Theme Builder, giving you the tools to create truly personalized and engaging websites. We also explored WooCommerce integration, allowing you to build and customize your own online store, and discussed essential SEO strategies to improve your website's visibility in search engine results.

Finally, we provided valuable tips for troubleshooting common WordPress errors, speeding up your website, ensuring its security, and performing regular maintenance tasks to keep it healthy.

By now, you should have a solid understanding of how to use WordPress and Elementor to build your dream website. However, remember that web design is a continuous learning process. The resources provided in Appendix B can guide you further on your journey to WordPress mastery.

As you embark on your own web design projects, embrace creativity, experiment with different approaches, and never stop learning. The possibilities with WordPress and Elementor are endless, and with dedication and passion, you can create a website that truly reflects your vision and achieves your goals.

Printed in Great Britain
by Amazon